Philosophical Foundations of Language in the Law

Editors

PROFESSOR ANDREI MARMOR

*Professor of Philosophy and Maurice Jones Jr Professor of Law,
University of Southern California*

PROFESSOR SCOTT SOAMES

Director, School of Philosophy, University of Southern California

OXFORD
UNIVERSITY PRESS

OXFORD
UNIVERSITY PRESS

Great Clarendon Street, Oxford, OX2 6DP
United Kingdom

Oxford University Press is a department of the University of Oxford.
It furthers the University's objective of excellence in research, scholarship,
and education by publishing worldwide. Oxford is a registered trade mark of
Oxford University Press in the UK and in certain other countries

British Library Cataloguing in Publication Data
Data available

Library of Congress Cataloging in Publication Data
Library of Congress number: 2011017234

ISBN 978–0–19–957238–0 (hbk.)
ISBN 978–0–19–967370–4 (pbk.)

Printed in Great Britain
on acid-free paper by
CPI Group (UK) Ltd. Croydon CR0 4YY

Contents

List of Contributors

Timothy Endicott is Professor of Legal Philosophy and Dean of the Faculty of Law in the University of Oxford. He has been a Fellow of Balliol College since 1999. He is the author of *Vagueness in Law* (OUP 2000), and *Administrative Law* (OUP 2009).

Mark Greenberg is Associate Professor of Philosophy and Professor of Law at UCLA. He works primarily in the areas of philosophy of mind and language and philosophy of law. Before coming to UCLA, he taught philosophy at Princeton University.

Richard Holton is Professor of Philosophy at MIT. He works mainly on issues surrounding moral psychology and the philosophy of action. His book *Willing, Wanting, Waiting* was published by OUP in 2009.

Andrei Marmor was Professor at Tel Aviv University from 1990 to 2000 and has been professor of philosophy and professor of law at the University of Southern California since 2003. He is the Director of the USC Center for Law and Philosophy and Editor in chief of the *Journal of Ethics & Social Philosophy*. His most recent book is *Philosophy of Law* (Princeton 2011).

John Perry is professor emeritus at Stanford University and distinguished professor of philosophy at the University of California, Riverside. He has written many articles on the philosophy of language and the philosophy of mind, and several books, including *Knowledge, Possibility, and Consciousness*, *Reference and Reflexivity*, and *Identity, Personal Identity, and the Self*.

Gideon Rosen is Stuart Professor of Philosophy and Chair of the Council of the Humanities at Princeton University.

Scott Soames is the Director of the School of Philosophy at the University of Southern California, and was formerly Professor of Philosophy at Princeton University for 24 years. He is the Editor-in-Chief of *The Princeton Series in the Foundations of Contemporary Philosophy* and serves on the advisory boards of *Analytica* and *Philosophical Perspectives*.

Jeremy Waldron is University Professor and Professor of Law at New York University and Chichele Professor of Social and political theory at the University of Oxford. His most recent book is *Torture, Terror, and Trade-Offs: Philosophy for the White House* (OUP 2010).

Gideon Yaffe is Professor of Philosophy and Law at the University of Southern California. He is the author of various books and articles on action, freedom, and legal and moral responsibility, as well as the history of thought about those topics, including, most recently, *Attempts* with OUP in 2010.

1

Introduction

The close connection between philosophy of language and philosophy of law was emphasized by H.L.A. Hart, and has been recognized for decades. As early as in his inaugural lecture, Hart argued that many central issues in jurisprudence depend on an adequate conception of language. Later, in his seminal work, *The Concept of Law*, he made it clear that he saw philosophy of language as playing a foundational role in his theory of law.[1] In the preface to that work, he says:

[T]he book may also be regarded as an essay in descriptive sociology; for the suggestion that inquiries into the meaning of words merely throws light on words is false. Many important distinctions, which are not immediately obvious, between types of social situation or relationships may best be brought to light by an examination of the standard uses of the relevant expressions and of the way in which these depend on social context, itself often left unstated. In this field of study it is particularly true that we may use, as Professor J.L. Austin said, 'a sharpened awareness of words to sharpen our perception of the phenomena'.[2]

A few pages later, however, Hart warns us that the purpose of his book 'is not to provide a definition of law, in the sense of a rule by reference to which the correctness of the use of the word can be tested'.[3] Though a methodology of focusing on meaning while eschewing definition may initially seem strange, Hart's approach conformed to that of the leading figures—Wittgenstein, Ryle, and Austin—of the Ordinary Language School of philosophy of his day. The analyses sought by these philosophers were nearly always attempts to trace the intricate web of conceptual connections among different members of a family of related terms, rather than analytic statements of necessary and sufficient conditions for a term to apply to an object.[4] Also in keeping with the philosophy of day was Hart's suggestion that understanding the ordinary use of words in specific contexts is both a form of descriptive sociology and

---

[1] Hart (1961). (All references here are to the first edition.)   [2] ibid at p v.
[3] ibid at p 17.
[4] For discussion see, eg Soames (2003a, ch 3).

an important key to understanding the social institutions (like the law) in which such usage occurs.

In spite of Hart's linguistic characterization of his methodology, questions about the relationship between language and law did not become central for some decades after the publication of *The Concept of Law*. Partly because of the important substantive issues raised in the book, and partly because it does not contain much that is specific to philosophy of language (apart from the then ubiquitous metaphilosophical conviction that all conceptual connections are ultimately linguistic), commentators have largely ignored Hart's remarks about the role of language in understanding law. This persisted until the mid-1980s, when R. M. Dworkin raised the issue in his critique of what he took to be Hart's method. In *Law's Empire*, Dworkin argued that, in spite of Hart's explicit denial, the only way to understand his theory of law is to assume that it actually does aim to provide a definition of law, in the sense of criteria by reference to which the correctness of the use of the word can be tested. Dworkin dubbed theories of law that adopt this methodology 'semantic theories of law', and argued that such approaches cannot provide adequate interpretations of legal practice.[5]

Dworkin's characterization of Hart's 'semantic' methodology engendered much debate. Many commentators (including Marmor) argued that *The Concept of Law* does not attempt to define or elucidate ordinary uses of the term 'law' or 'legal validity', nor does it presuppose that such a definition of 'law' is possible.[6] Although Hart was influenced by prominent ordinary language philosophers of his time, and to some extent shared their deference to ordinary use in philosophical analysis, this seldom, if ever, led either him, or them, to search for philosophically illuminating definitions. Thus, it is not surprising *The Concept of Law* contains no attempt to define 'law'.

More notable, perhaps, is the paucity of explicitly linguistic, let alone ordinary-language style, analyses in that work. The main foray into philosophy of language in *The Concept of Law* is in chapter 7, where Hart strives to refute a kind of 'rule skepticism' proffered by the American Legal Realists. As he understood them, these theorists claimed that legal rules, by themselves, rarely determine particular legal outcomes. On the contrary, they maintained, such rules can be understood almost any way one likes; hence the outcomes reached by judges and other officials are rarely determined by the rules they cite. Of equal, if not more, importance, the Realists argued, are judges' instinctive reactions to the cases they adjudicate, shaped by their psychological makeup and social circumstances. Hart argued that this 'Realist' picture is an exaggeration, involving a serious misunderstanding of

[5] Dworkin (1986), ch 1.   [6] Marmor (2005) at pp 4–8.

language. Although it is true that language is 'irreducibly open textured', it is also true that '[g]eneral terms would be useless to us as a medium of communication' unless they were associated with some core of 'generally unchallenged' cases.[7]

An example Hart gives elsewhere,[8] which has become a jurisprudential classic, involves a legal ordinance prohibiting the use of vehicles in public parks. Since the word 'vehicle' is vague, it has many borderline cases. Does the rule prohibit, for example, the use of bicycles, roller skates, or electric wheelchairs, in the park? These questions cannot be answered by a closer look at what 'vehicle' *means* in English. But it is equally true, Hart argued, that the word has a 'core' extension consisting of things to which it clearly does apply. An ordinary automobile, in working order, is clearly a vehicle, if anything is. Indeterminacies notwithstanding, there must be considerable information one can convey by linguistic communication in general, and legal communication in particular.

Legal rules and directives are, of course, expressed in a natural language. Some of that language may be technical, further specified by other legal rules. But understanding what the law prescribes is bound to depend on general features of linguistic communication. The main mistake of Legal Realists, Hart contended, was in looking only at cases in which the meanings of the sentences used leave unanswered questions about what is asserted or stipulated. In such cases, our use of the sentences determines a vague, incomplete, or partially indeterminate content that fails to provide definite verdicts for some of the circumstances in which we are interested. There are, of course, many cases of this kind. However, a glass half empty is also half full. Language could not be the useful tool that it is for conveying information and guiding action if this were the norm. On the contrary, the meanings of the words we use, together with obvious features of contexts of use, typically determine information contents the evaluation of which are determinate enough to provide the guidance we need in most communicative purposes.

Hart's discussion, in chapter 7 of *The Concept of Law*, of instances of both determinacy and indeterminacy in linguistic communication in legal contexts is our starting point, opening the door to a larger question about the role of language in determining the content of law. How much content is determined by linguistic features of legal communication, and how much is left indeterminate or unspecified? It is a central contention of this collection that advances in the philosophy of language in recent decades enable us to provide a more accurate and nuanced answer to this question than the ones provided by Hart and his contemporaries. Though Hart's general conclusion—that the linguistic

[7] Hart (1961) at p 123.
[8] 'Positivism and the Separation of Law and Morals', *Harvard Law Review*, 71, 1958, 593–629.

aspects of legal texts determine much content, while leaving some legal issues indeterminate and open to interpretation—is commonsensical and correct, the philosophical payoff is in the details, and the details are complex.

As Hart recognized, vague predicates give rise to borderline cases. These are cases in which there is, in some sense, no definite answer to the question of whether a predicate is, or is not, true of a given object. In such cases, we are often pulled in both directions—being inclined to resist definitive verdicts in favor of equivocal remarks like 'It sort of is and sort of isn't', 'It's not clearly one or the other', or 'It's up to you. You can call it either one, but neither is definitely correct'. In Hart's example, there is 'no saying' whether a bicycle is a 'vehicle' or not. In some contexts it is fine to say that it is, while in others it is fine to say that it is not. No investigation into the facts in virtue of which the word 'vehicle' means what it does could ever settle that just one of these uses is correct, while the other is incorrect.

In recent decades, philosophers of language have developed sophisticated theories that attempt to explain this and related observations. According to one such theory, vague predicates are both partially defined and context sensitive. To say that a predicate P is partially defined is to say that it is governed by linguistic rules that provide sufficient conditions for P to apply to an object, and sufficient conditions for P not to apply, but no conditions that are both individually sufficient and disjunctively necessary for P to apply, or not to apply. Because the conditions are mutually exclusive, but not exhaustive, there are objects not covered by the rules, for which P is *undefined*. This, in turn, gives rise to context sensitivity. Since the rules of the common language, plus all relevant nonlinguistic facts, do not determine P-verdicts for every object, speakers using P in particular contexts have the discretion of extending its range of application to include some initially undefined cases, depending on their conversational purposes. Often they do so by endorsing or denying a proposition predicating P of an object o. When they do, and other conversational participants go along, the class of things to which the P does, or does not, apply is contextually adjusted to include o, plus objects similar to o (in certain respects). In such cases, P is (partly) 'precisified' by narrowing the range of cases for which it is undefined.[9]

This conception of vague language applies both to the enactment and the interpretation of laws. When law-makers employ a vague term in a legal text, they may use it either with its default interpretation (provided by the rules governing its use in the common language) or with a (partially) precisified

---

[9] For details, see Soames (1999), ch 7; Soames (2003b), (2010b), both reprinted in Soames (2009c); Shapiro and Stewart (2006). Endicott adopts a version of the view that vague predicates are partially defined (2000).

interpretation. In the former case, the application of the law to items for which the term is undefined is left indeterminate, and subject to future interpretation by judicial and other authorities. In the latter case, law-makers wish, and are able, to narrow the range of interpretation by stipulating how the law is to be applied to certain borderline cases. For example, law-makers adopting Hart's ordinance banning vehicles from parks might respond to lobbying on behalf of the disabled by adding a clause 'for the purpose of this ordinance, wheelchairs for the disabled, whether motorized or not, shall *not* count as vehicles'. In such cases, what counts as 'legally P' differs somewhat from what counts as 'P' in ordinary language.

The role of vagueness in interpretation is more interesting and complicated. What should be done when it emerges that the verdict in a case crucially depends on whether or not a vague predicate applies to a given item for which the predicate, as used by the law-makers, is undefined? In principle, several outcomes are possible. In some special cases (though rarely in common law systems), it may be possible to send the matter back to the law-makers for clarification and precisification. In certain other cases, a rule of lenity may dictate favorable verdicts for defendants in situations in which no clear violation is established—where one form of exonerating unclarity involves (linguistic) indeterminacy in the law. However, in many cases neither of these exceptions apply, with the result that judges, and other authorities, are expected to fill gaps by precisifying the governing legal provision in a manner not determined and sometimes not even envisioned by the law-making body. When the relevant judicial decision is such that it sets a legal precedent for similar cases, the result of judicial interpretation is not just an explication, clarification, or application of existing law, but also an (authorized) modification of that law.

Although we have used one particular philosophical theory of vagueness to illustrate these points, analogous points may hold for other theories of vagueness. For example, according to the epistemic theory, vague predicates are always totally defined, with sharp boundaries separating items to which the predicate applies from those to which it does not—eg a single second separating moments when one is young from those when one is not, and a single penny separating one who is rich from one who is not. However, although, for each vague predicate P and item o, P is either true of o or not true of o, there are borderline cases o* for which it is impossible for us ever to *know* whether P is true, or untrue, of o*. So, whereas the previous theory takes borderline cases to be those for which P is undefined, the epistemic theory takes them to be cases for which one can never know how, in fact, P is defined.[10] Although the standard version of this theory does not take vague

[10] The *locus classicus* of the epistemic theory is Williamson (1994).

terms to be context sensitive, the epistemic framework is compatible with that idea, which has been advocated by some epistemicist authors.[11]

How should a proponent of the epistemicist view conceptualize the problem confronting a judge in a case that turns on the application, or non-application, of a vague predicate to a borderline case? One plausible line available to the epistemicist is to reason as follows. If the case is not one that can be returned to the original law-making body for further consideration, and also not one in which a rule of lenity applies, the judge will be faced with the task of reaching a decision that cannot be *known to conform*, or *known not to conform*, to the existing content of the law. Moreover, the values of consistency, of treating similar cases similarly, of rendering the actions of legal authorities predictable, and of making the effective content of legal rules known, or at least knowable, to all concerned will normally conspire to give whatever decision is reached precedential weight. If, over time, the precedent is followed, or if the original court is itself the court of last resort, the effect will be an authorized judicial change in the content of the original legal provision. What was before at best unknowable will come to be known to be legal, or illegal. Although the vague predicate P at the center of this change will not have changed its ordinary meaning, what counts as 'legally P' will have changed, with a resulting change in the law. If this is right, then many of the issues raised by vagueness for theories of legal interpretation will remain more or less constant across different philosophical theories of what vagueness is.[12]

The importance of understanding the consequences of vague language for legal interpretation is consistent with the fact that some issues involving vagueness in the law are normative. Consider, again, the use of the vague term 'vehicle' in Hart's ordinance. Could the law-makers have formulated the prohibition more precisely? If they could, was it a failure of legislative drafting not to? More generally, is avoidable vagueness *always* a defect in the law, or can it sometimes be a useful legislative tool? The essays by Endicott, Soames, and Waldron in this volume argue that vagueness can have value (of various sorts), and discuss the consequences of vagueness for theories of interpretation.

Another area in philosophy of language in which substantial progress has been made concerns the pragmatic aspects of linguistic communication. Philosophers of language and linguists have come to realize that a great deal of successful communication is determined by contextual and normative aspects

---

[11] See Fara (2000).

[12] This is not to say that the need to make good sense of legal interpretation of vague terms has *no* consequences for determining which philosophical theory of vagueness is correct, nor that there are *no* differences between the lessons for legal interpretation that can be drawn from one theory of vagueness and those that can be drawn from another. There may well be. However, these involve matters of nuance and detail that are beyond the scope of this volume.

of conversational situations, over and above the strictly semantic properties of the words used. As a consequence, the study of these factors—'pragmatics' broadly conceived—has taken on a larger role in theories of linguistic communication and language use than it once had.[13] Marmor's chapter in this volume draws on this extensive literature in pragmatics to elucidate ways in which the contents of legal texts depend on, and are partly determined by, pragmatic features of communication. This philosophical exploration of the pragmatic aspects of legal communication goes in both directions: on the one hand, it enables us to form a more complete and nuanced picture of how much legal content is determined by pragmatic elements of communication. On the other hand, it allows us to contrast certain assumptions commonly made about pragmatic aspects of ordinary conversation with those required to understand the use of language in legal contexts. Whereas communicative interactions in ordinary conversations are often regulated by the goal of engaging in a cooperative exchange of information, linguistic interactions in legal settings are often at least partially strategic rather than cooperative. As a result, the use of language in the law may provide limiting cases of familiar pragmatic assumptions about linguistic communication, allowing us to explore ways in which pragmatic aspects of communication are sensitive to different kinds of interactions, with different normative goals in different contexts.

The general question of how much of the content of a legal text is determined by the semantic features of the text has become acute for a relatively new theory of statutory interpretation, *textualism*. Advocates of this theory are morally and politically opposed to the expansive role often assumed by judges in interpreting statutory and constitutional law. According to textualists, the first rule of interpretation is fidelity to the ordinary meaning of statutory or constitutional language. It is taken to be a corollary of this rule that judges interpreting a legal text should not speculate about what the lawmakers intended to say, or achieve, in enacting the text. As the foremost textualist, Justice Scalia, puts it:

The text is the law, and it is the text that must be observed. I agree with Justice Holmes's remark, quoted approvingly by Justice Frankfurter in his article on the construction of statutes: 'Only a day or two ago—when counsel talked of the intention of a legislature, I was indiscreet enough to say I do not care what their intention was. I only want to know what the words mean.' And I agree with Holmes's other remark, quoted approvingly by Justice Jackson: 'We do not inquire what the legislature meant; we ask only what the statute means.'[14]

---

[13] For a brief overview of the relationship between semantics and pragmatics, see Soames (2010a), ch 7.

[14] Scalia (1997) at pp 22–3.

I thought we had adopted a regular method for interpreting the meaning of language in a statute: first, find the ordinary meaning of the language in its textual context; and second, using established canons of construction, ask whether there is any clear indication that some permissible meaning other than the ordinary one applies. If not—and especially if a good reason for the ordinary meaning appears plain—we apply that ordinary meaning.[15]

As these quotations attest, the plausibility of textualism depends, in part, on how much legal content is determined by 'the ordinary meaning of the language in its textual context'. In order to make progress, we need to know what ordinary meaning is and how it interacts with context to generate communicated content.

The first step is to distinguish different types of linguistic content—including the *semantic* content of the words and sentences used by a speaker (linguistic meaning), the *assertive* content of the speaker's utterance (what the speaker says, asserts, or stipulates by using those words in the context of utterance), plus further *implicated* content (which, though not asserted, is suggested or implied by the speaker's saying what he or she does in the context). The semantic content is determined by the literal meanings of the words and the syntactic structure of the sentence. The assertive content is the truth-evaluable proposition asserted by the speaker in the context. It is determined by a variety of factors, including the semantic content of the sentence uttered, the communicative intentions of the speaker, the shared presuppositions of speaker-hearers, and obvious features of the context of utterance. Although assertive content is normally of primary importance in linguistic communication, sometimes the communicative content of a remark includes implicated content that goes beyond this. Such content is a function of semantic and asserted content, shared presuppositions of participants in the speech exchange, and recognized norms for acceptable linguistic moves governing the type of linguistic interaction involved (cooperative exchange of information, strategic bargaining, etc).

Thus, one difficulty for textualism is to articulate what 'the text' is supposed to be. Since it is words and sentences that have 'ordinary meanings,' textualists' reliance on this phrase suggests they are thinking of texts not as what legal authorities assert or stipulate, but rather as purely linguistic entities made up of the words used by such authorities. Since the content of a legal provision is most plausibly identified with the assertive content of the relevant legal document, this is unfortunate and has led to confusion.[16] As some of the

---

[15] *Chisom v Roemer* 501 US 380, 404 (1991) (Scalia J., dissenting).

[16] Prominent textualists like Scalia routinely run together the ideas of (i) fidelity to the meaning of the legislature's statutory language (illustrated by the quotes above) with (ii) fidelity to what the legislature asserted or stipulated in using that language (illustrated by the following):

essays (by Soames and Rosen) in this volume point out, this confusion affects the blanket attack by textualists on appeal to legislative intentions in legal interpretation. Since assertive content cannot be extrapolated without regard to speakers' intentions—both to assert a particular content, and to succeed in so doing by enabling reasonable and attentive hearers to grasp that intention—any defensible form of textualism must distinguish different types of intention, while recognizing the importance for the contents of laws or legal obligations of at least some of them.

Suppose, for example, that a speaker says to a friend she meets late in the evening, 'I haven't eaten anything.' Clearly, the assertive content of this utterance is not identical to the literal meaning of the sentence uttered. No reasonable hearer would take the speaker to have claimed that she has never engaged in the activity of eating. On the contrary, in most contexts the speaker would correctly be understood to have said that she has not yet had dinner (or something similar). In grasping this assertive content, the hearer discerns the content the speaker intends to convey. The role of contextual knowledge is to help the hearer identify the speaker's communicative intention. Though the example is simple, the point it illustrates is important and applies to judicial interpretation of the content of legal texts, where an understanding of the gap that sometimes exists between the linguistic meaning of a legal document and the legal content it is used to assert can be crucial to arriving at correct results.[17]

This is one example of the challenges textualists face in articulating their method of statutory interpretation. These challenges are extensively discussed in the essays by Soames, Perry, and Rosen in this volume. Perry attempts to reinforce what he calls 'meaning-textualism' (as opposed to 'conception-textualism') by explaining how it can accommodate interpretations of constitutional or statutory provisions resulting in legal outcomes that

---

"You will find it frequently said...that the judge's objective in interpreting a statute is to give effect to 'the intent of the legislature'.... Unfortunately, it [this principle] does not square with some of the (few) generally accepted concrete rules of statutory construction. One is the rule that when the text of the statute is clear, that is the end of the matter. Why should that be so, if what the legislature *intended*, rather than what it *said*, is the object of our inquiry?" (*A Matter of Interpretation,* p 16)

"When you are told to decide, not on the basis of what the legislature said, but on the basis of what it *meant* your best shot at figuring out what the legislature meant is to ask yourself what a wise and intelligent person *should* have meant; and that will surely bring you to the conclusion that the law means what you think it *ought* to mean." (*A Matter of Interpretation,* p 18)

It is an open question whether, once (i) and (ii) are properly distinguished, textualists like Scalia might opt for (ii) rather than (i). In one of the cases cited (by him) as best exemplifying his version of textualism—namely *Smith v United States*—Scalia's result is implicitly premised on (ii), even though he wrongly defends that result by appealing to (i). For discussion, see Neale (2007) and Soames, in (2009a).

[17] See also Marmor (2008) at p 423.

accord with their original textual meaning, even though those outcomes would have been repudiated by the framers of those provisions (for violating the framer's conceptions of what they were talking about). Though framed as a defense of textualism, Perry's careful application of this point to the prohibition, in the US Constitution, against 'cruel and unusual punishment' is available to proponents of (some) other theories of legal interpretation as well, thus illustrating the utility of the philosophy of language for various interpretive points of view.

Soames' discussion of textualism takes a different tack. While taking it for granted that the content of the law is what law-makers assert (or stipulate) in adopting a legal text, he highlights cases in which what is so asserted has gaps, or is inconsistent (when applied to new facts of an unforeseen case) either with other asserted (or stipulated) legal content or with the clear legislative purpose of the law. In such cases, pre-existing legal content is insufficient to determine feasible legal outcomes. Thus, he argues, if we take 'interpretation' to cover all that judges are called upon to do in deciding 'hard cases', then we need a theory of interpretation that shares textualists' deference to legislative authorities, while transcending the narrow bounds they place on 'interpretation'.

Rosen's essay explores different versions of textualism vs intentionalism in contract law, bringing to light fascinating cases the factual backgrounds of which put maximum strain on textualist ideas, while causing difficulties for both interpretive approaches. One of these cases illustrates another way in which issues in the philosophy of language bear on questions of legal interpretation. The issue is how the referents of uses of definite descriptions are determined. It is common in contracts and other legal documents to target certain objects or individuals designated by such descriptions for specific legal results. Although this may sound unproblematic, difficulties can arise when an object or an individual the parties have in mind as the one to whom a certain legal result is to apply does not satisfy the description they formulated to designate her. These difficulties multiply when someone else, whom the parties do not take to be in the picture at all, does satisfy it. One of Rosen's examples is a real adjudicated case of this kind. Though the facts in the case are complex, and its proper legal resolution is perplexing, an understanding of the relationship between meaning and assertion in situations in which descriptions are used in this way is a prerequisite for disentangling the issues.

In ordinary conversation, we often indicate the individual about whom we wish to make an assertion by using a description like 'John's wife'. At a party at which everyone assumes that the woman, Mary, accompanying John is his wife, I might say 'John's wife just suggested that we go for a swim before dinner'—thereby conveying Mary's suggestion. Unbeknownst to us, however, John's divorce to someone else is not final, so Mary is not his wife. Although I have made a mistake, misdescribing Mary as being married to John, this does not negate the fact that I asserted that she suggested we go swimming. I may, in virtue of my mistake, also be counted as having asserted the proposition semantically expressed by the sentence I uttered—namely that John's wife suggested that we go for a swim before dinner. So, it could be argued, I have both said something true (about Mary) and something false (about John's wife). Although in the context imagined, the former is surely the most relevant to the conversation, in different circumstances the priorities might be reversed. When this sort of thing occurs in a contract (or other legal document), we face a potential assertive (as opposed to semantic) ambiguity. What are the different potential assertive contents of the clauses containing the relevant descriptions, and which (if any) among them should be taken as incorporated into the content of the contract as a whole? These, and related, questions are discussed in Rosen's essay.

Gideon Yaffe argues that a proper understanding of the use of descriptions is also important to the definition of certain criminal offenses. His topic is *criminal attempts*—crimes defined as attempts to commit other crimes. The question at issue is whether one can be guilty of attempting to commit an offense in cases in which a material condition for committing the offense is not present. For example, can one be guilty of attempted murder by virtue of having attempted to kill someone who was, in fact, already dead? Yaffe draws on recent discussions in the philosophy of language illuminating the distinction between attributive (*de dicto*) and referential (*de re*) uses of descriptions to clarify the problem, and develop a solution.

Though the strengths and weaknesses of (versions of) textualism are discussed in several essays in this volume, Dworkin's theory of interpretation—which is one of textualism's main rivals—is also represented. According to it, understanding the law and determining legal content are normative 'all the way down'. Otherwise put, judges can determine *what the content of the law is* in a given context only on the basis of a normative conception of *what the content of the law should (politically and morally) be*. Legal interpretation, Dworkin claims, can never be detached from its putative moral and political aims, which must be part of any understanding of what the law requires in specific cases. This theory of legal interpretation is deeply suspicious of the idea that non-normative linguistic considerations are capable of playing central roles in determining legal content, and guiding judicial interpretation.

This approach is represented here in Greenberg's essay, which raises a wide range of skeptical points about the constructive role of philosophy of language in elucidating legal interpretation. Like Dworkin, Greenberg believes that there is always a gap between the content communicated by an act of legislation and the legal impact it has on the normative legal landscape, such as an obligation imposed or a right granted. The initial plausibility of such a gap derives from some familiar aspects of speech act theories. It has been long recognized that there are many contexts in which, by saying something, the speaker has also performed a certain action (in addition to saying whatever it is that the speech asserts), like undertaking an obligation, or appointing a person to a certain official position, or adjourning a meeting. In some cases, the relevant expression counts as the performance of an act of a particular sort only because there are certain rules or conventions in the background that confer this performative aspect on the expression used. In other cases, the performative aspect of an expression is achieved by a successful recognition on the part of the hearer of the speaker's relevant intentions. Speech act theorists are divided about the scope of these two kinds of explanation of performatives, some arguing that the rule-based explanation is central, while others claim the intention-based explanation provides an adequate account of most cases.[18] Greenberg, however, seems to assume special factors at work in legal speech. His discussion suggests, first, that every legal speech, such as the enactment of a law, is a type of performative, and, second, that the only way to account for its performative aspect is to recognize the moral considerations that grant it the particular legal impact it has. Though he does not explicitly articulate this moral intermediary between communicated content and legal impact, he does raise many skeptical points about the assumption that what an act of legislation says or asserts is what the law, at least partly, is. In fact, he comes to doubt that an act of legislation is a *speech* act at all. Though as authors we have bones to pick with his arguments, as editors we value the fact that he calls into question some of the main assumptions that we and other contributors rely on. We look forward to continuing elsewhere the debate begun here.

Although there is considerable disagreement among the authors of this volume about important matters of judicial interpretation, most recognize at least some cases in which the existing corpus of law available to a judge is insufficient, due to the special and perhaps unforeseen nature of the facts of a new case, to reach a correct result. In such cases, the judge may be called upon to formulate a previously unarticulated legal rule that distinguishes the case at hand from previously adjudicated cases, and justifies a verdict that would not

---

[18] The rule/convention-based explanation of performatives is advocated by Searle (see, eg his (1969) and (1989) at p 535). The intention-based account was first argued by Strawson (1971) at p 170, and is defended by such pragmatists as Bach and Harnish (see, eg their 1979). See also Marmor (2009) at pp 118–130.

otherwise be forthcoming. Such cases raise a number of conceptual problems, including an interesting puzzle about the logic of legal decisions, and the logical form of legal rules.

Suppose that a particular action of type A is involved, which falls under an existing legal rule stipulating that acts of type A are to be accorded legal status X. Suppose further that the factual background of the case includes information about this particular act—namely that it was performed in certain unusual circumstances C—which (for whatever reason) both undermine according it legal status X and have not previously been encountered as potential exceptions to the existing rule. In this situation the judge articulates a new, more complex, rule that stipulates that acts of type A performed in circumstances C are not to be accorded legal status X. How shall we understand this? Suppose (i) we take a legal rule to be a universal generalization declaring an action to have a certain legal status whenever certain factual conditions are met, and (ii) we take a justified verdict in a case to be one that is the conclusion of a logically valid argument from true factual premises plus a legal rule made true by the fact that it is legally valid. Then, if we take the new rule to justify the verdict 'Not X' in the case at hand, it would appear that we must judge the old rule to be false, *and all the previous verdicts in cases governed by it to be unjustified*. In short, it would appear that what was intended to be a rule creating an exception has the effect of falsifying the previous rule, and undermining all previous uses of it, rather than simply limiting its scope. Worse, since any rule, including the new one, can be expected to require similar future adjustments when presently unforeseen cases bring different novel circumstances into play, it would appear that even the new rule must be false. Surely, this cannot be correct. Richard Holton, in his essay for this volume, explains why it is not, offering a conception of the logical form of legal rules, and the logic of legal arguments, that avoids this troubling result.

There is, of course, much that remains to be resolved concerning the relative importance of, and precise relationship between, broadly linguistic and broadly normative aspects of legal interpretation. However, it is fair to conclude that both have roles to play. As authors as well as editors of this volume, we believe that distinctions drawn from the philosophy of language can help clarify the roles of each by providing a framework within which questions about the contents of legal provisions can be made more precise, and competing conceptions of what interpreting the law is, and should be, can be made more philosophically coherent. We offer these essays as contributions to that enterprise.

2

The Value of Vagueness

Timothy Endicott*

1. Introduction

How can it be valuable to use vagueness in a normative text? The effect is to make a vague norm, and vagueness seems repugnant to the very idea of making a norm. It leaves conduct (to some extent) unregulated, when the very idea of making a norm is to regulate conduct. A vague norm leaves the persons for whom the norm is valid with no guide to their conduct in some cases—and the point of a norm is to guide conduct. A vague norm in a system of norms does not control the officers or officials responsible for applying the norms or resolving disputes—and part of the value of a system of norms is to control the conduct of the persons to whom the system gives normative power.

In this chapter I will seek to resolve these puzzles, and to show that vagueness can be valuable to law-makers (because their use of it is valuable to the people to whom the law is addressed). If I am successful in doing that, it may seem that it is an evaluative conclusion that tells us nothing of the nature of vagueness in normative texts: I will simply have shown that it sometimes happens to be a good thing, and that some vague legal rules happen to be good rules. But in fact, I will argue, the value of vagueness does more than that to explain the role of vagueness in normative texts, and to explain the compatibility of vagueness with the ideal of the rule of law (an ideal that has analogues in all uses of texts to create or to communicate norms). Far from being repugnant to the idea of making a norm, vagueness is of central importance to law-makers (and other persons who craft normative texts). It is a central technique of normative texts: it is needed to pursue the purposes of formulating

* This essay was first published as 'The Value of Vagueness', in Vijay K. Bhatia, Jan Engberg, Maurizio Gotti, and Dorothee Heller (eds), *Vagueness in Normative Texts* (Bern, Peter Lang 2005), Ch 1, 27–48.

such texts. Not all norms are vague. But vagueness is of central importance to the very idea of guiding conduct by norms.

I will start by explaining some important features of the normative texts I am considering, and explaining what it means for such a text to be vague (section 2). Then I will point out some varieties of vagueness commonly used in such texts (section 3). Precision in such texts is valuable in two ways: it has *guidance value* in offering a precise proposal for action to persons subject to a standard, and it has *process value* in controlling the system's techniques for applying the standard (section 4). Those values of precision raise the question I have mentioned already: how can it be valuable to use vagueness in normative texts? The crucial underpinning for an answer to that question is a view of the nature of arbitrariness in norms, and an associated principle that I call the 'normative principle' (section 5). Vagueness brings with it forms of arbitrariness, but there are ways in which vagueness averts other forms of arbitrariness that come with precision (sections 6, 7), and vagueness can be a useful, non-arbitrary technique for allocating power to officials (section 8), or for leaving decisions to private actors (section 9). A summary (section 10) recapitulates the value of vagueness in law, and a conclusion (section 11) points out reasons why the conclusions about the central importance of vagueness in law are important to an understanding of the significance and the role of normative texts in general. The normative principle I assert in section 5 is linked to the ideal of the rule of law and to the nature of law, for reasons which also have implications for understanding other, non-legal normative texts.

2. Legal instruments and legal standards

I will be concerned with a particular kind of normative text, which I will call a 'legal instrument', and a particular kind of norm, which I will call a 'legal standard'. A legal instrument is a normative text with a technical effect. By 'technical' I simply mean that the law itself has techniques for determining the effect of the normative text. The meaning and normative force of *all* normative texts depend in a variety of ways on the context in which they are communicated: if you are a teenager and your mother puts a note on the door of the refrigerator saying 'leave some pizza for your sister!', the effect of the normative text will be determined in subtle ways by a complex variety of understandings and expectations that arise from your relationship with your mother and your sister (and anyone else involved), and from the circumstances in which those relationships are situated (including everything from the role of pizza in the culture of your community to the economics of your family and your society that determine the abundance or scarcity of food in your household). I say that a legal instrument has technical effect because in law the complex contextual factors that contribute to the meaning of any normative text are to some extent regulated by the law itself. The term 'legal instrument' is meant as a reminder of that potential for self-regulation.

A legal instrument is vague if its language is imprecise, so that there are cases in which its application is unclear. I will speak of legal *standards* as vague in the same sense. Because of the technical effect of legal instruments, there is no straightforward, general relation between the language used in a legal instrument to make law, and the law that is made. Law is systematic in the sense (among other senses) that the law itself gives legal effect to statutes (and contracts, wills, and other normative texts). Legal rules of interpretation may give a vague effect to a precise term in a legal instrument. For example, a doctrine excusing minor departures from notice requirements in civil proceedings gives a vague effect to precisely stated deadlines.[1] In general, the use of vague language in legal instruments makes vague legal standards.

So a vague legal standard clearly applies in some cases, and clearly does not apply in others, and there are borderline cases in which the linguistic formulation of the standard leaves its application unclear. We can take examples of both precision and vagueness from the English law concerning the care of children. By statute, it is an offense to cause a child or young person to be 'neglected, abandoned, or exposed, in a manner likely to cause him unnecessary suffering or injury to health' (Children and Young Persons Act 1933, s 1(1)). The statute defines 'child or young person' *precisely*, as referring to a person under the age of 16 years. But when is it lawful to leave a child at home, without supervision? Or when is it lawful to leave a child with a babysitter? And how old does the babysitter have to be? The statute states no ages. The act subjected all these questions to the vagueness of the terms 'neglected' and 'abandoned', and of the qualifying phrase, 'in a manner likely to cause him unnecessary suffering or injury'.

The result is 'communicative under-determinacy': if you are a parent, you may well wish to know when it is lawful to leave your child unattended, or with a babysitter (and how old the babysitter must be). The law offers itself as a guide to your conduct, but if you do turn to it for guidance, you will find less information than you might expect in the situation. It is not that the law is unintelligible: you can see quite clearly that leaving a newborn baby alone all day would count as neglect (and if you told a 5-year-old to babysit, it would still be neglect). Leaving a 15-year-old at home alone for a few hours

---

[1] I suppose that it is conceivable that such rules could give a precise effect to vague instruments, but it is hard to think of examples.

(or leaving an infant with a competent 17-year-old) is not neglect. But there will be cases in between, for which the text of the statute gives no determinate guidance.[2]

A voting age, by contrast, is precise: it determines, without borderline cases,[3] whether it is lawful[4] for you to vote.

3. Varieties of vagueness in legal instruments

Law-makers typically either avoid words like *child*, or give them stipulative, precise definitions like the definition in the Children and Young Persons Act. They define such terms, when they can, by reference to precise criteria, such as an age of majority. Speed limits and blood-alcohol limits are similar examples of the search for precision: if it is possible to measure speed, or blood-alcohol content, law-makers use speed limits and blood-alcohol limits rather than merely using vague rules such as the nineteenth century prohibition on driving a vehicle 'in a wanton or furious manner'.[5] But the search for precision is limited. Vague descriptive terms like *trade* are often used in tax statutes and other forms of regulation of classes of activity such as licensing regimes controlling hunting and fishing, or restricting activities in a park, or controlling uses of land. And a similar form of vagueness is unavoidable in the description of actions that constitute criminal offenses.[6]

Such forms of vagueness in descriptive terms are very important. However, the really extravagant (and very common) instances of vagueness in law are the general evaluative terms used to regulate diverse activities in a broad class. The requirements of reasonableness in various areas of tort law, contract law,

---

[2] Another complication of the legal effect of normative texts is that authoritative decisions as to the effect of the statute in disputed cases may well make the law precise where the text of the statute was vague, eg by holding that in some set of circumstances it was (or was not) neglectful to leave a 12-year-old at home. The effect of precedent itself is very commonly vague, in part for the same reasons that explain the linguistic vagueness of legal instruments. It is important to remember that vagueness is a feature of customary norms, and not only of norms formulated in language. But here I will focus on the linguistic vagueness of normative texts.

[3] Aside from generally inconsequential borderline cases arising from, eg (i) the uncertainties of proof arising from techniques for establishing a person's age, and (ii) any indeterminacies in the legal definition of a year, or a day, etc. Perhaps there are such indeterminacies in all normative texts, but I will not be concerned with them because they will often be trivial. The communicative indeterminacies arising from vagueness are typically very significant, as I will argue in section 3.

[4] At least, in respect of a person's maturity; there may of course be other rules determining the right to vote.

[5] UK Offences Against the Person Act 1861, s 35. The provision is still in force.

[6] For this reason, among others, legal systems necessarily include vague laws. It is necessary because no scheme of regulation that did not control such aspects of the life of a community would count as a legal system (Endicott (2001) at pp 377–83).

and administrative law are important examples of the very widespread use of extremely vague standards in legislation and the common law.

I hope it will be clear from this brief consideration of varieties of vague laws that vagueness in the sense of imprecision is not necessarily trivial. Indeed, law-makers generally avoid trivial vagueness; they never use trivially vague standards (such as 'about 18 years and 3 months old'). Legal instruments lack the hedging terms that we use in many contexts to give a fuzzy edge to asser-tions ('approximately', 'more or less', etc). Probably every legal system has what we might call hedging *techniques* that give a fuzzy edge to legal stand-ards; one example is the variety of *de minimis* rules in common law systems, by which the law refuses to count trivial departures from some standards as breaches. Those are not interpretive techniques, but ways of controlling the effect of a text as described in section 2, above. But in the fashioning of legal instruments, precision is typically used when it is feasible, without any express hedging, and without any mention of such techniques.

Vagueness in legal instruments is generally far from trivial. When law-makers use vague language in framing standards, they typically use extrava-gantly vague language such as 'neglected' or 'abandoned' or 'reasonable'. The resulting vagueness in the law can generate serious and deep disputes over the principles of the standard in question. Because it may allow different, incompatible views as to the nature of the standard and the principles of its application (even among sincere and competent interpreters), it leads to the danger that its application will be incoherent. By that I mean that decisions made in purported application of the norm will not be intelligible as the application of a single norm—a standard that can regulate behaviour.

For these reasons, legal theorists sometimes deny that the law is vague at all when it uses such standards; they claim that the disputes are over *how to con-ceive* the standard, and are not affected by imprecision.[7] To see the mistake in that approach, consider more or less pure evaluative standards in law, such as a rule of tort damages that a successful plaintiff is to receive damages sufficient to make him or her as *well off* as if the tort had not been committed. Suppose that a successful plaintiff has suffered a moderately serious back injury. One dollar in compensation would not make him as well off as if the injury had not been caused (it would be an insult). A billion dollars would be excessive: it would exceed what is required to make the plaintiff as well off as if the injury had not happened. So how much does the legal standard require? It is quite true that disputes about the quantum of damages will be formulated

---

[7] The most striking proponent of this approach is Ronald Dworkin; he discusses 'concepts that admit of different conceptions' in *Taking Rights Seriously* (1977) at p 103, and denies that such concepts are vague in ibid at pp 135–6 and *Law's Empire* (1986) at p 17.

as competing conceptions of welfare. But the problem for understanding the law is not only that the appropriate principles of compensation in such cases are open to controversy, but also that there is no precise sum that the vague legal standard (on any conception) demands. And the two problems are linked. If one dollar is inadequate to do justice, adding another dollar will not (in any conception of welfare) meet the standard either. The result is the operation of the 'sorites' reasoning that fascinates philosophers of vagueness.[8] The vagueness of abstract evaluative terms such as 'neglect' and 'well off' is inextricable from their 'contestability'.

4. The guidance value and the process value of precision

To understand the value of vagueness, it may help to start with something easier: the value of precision. It is important to see that a precise legal standard is *not* necessarily better than a vague one. But precision can undoubtedly be valuable in two related ways. First, is what I will call the '*guidance value*' of precision for persons subject to the rule: a precise standard may let people know their legal rights and obligations. Second, a variety of '*process values*' arise out of the fact that a precise standard can also guide officials.

The guidance value of precision can be more important than the process value of precision, or vice versa, depending on the context. The precision of an age of majority gives guidance both to potential voters and to election officials in the same way. A red traffic light (along with a white line painted on the road to mark the intersection), by contrast, gives valuable guidance to a driver (and gives considerable guidance to officials too—but officials are typically not in as good a position as the driver to assess the precise guidance it offers). A precise blood-alcohol level, on the other hand, is not very useful to a driver as a guide to his or her conduct. But the precision of the standard (as opposed, for example, to a vague rule against driving while intoxicated) has an important process value: a police officer with a breathalyzer can use the precise standard as a guide in deciding whether to restrain a driver and whether to prosecute. And the precision of the standard reduces potential litigation to trivial borderline issues (such as whether the breathalyzer reading is within a margin of error), or to collateral issues (such as fraud, or the reliability of the breathalyzer, or the compatibility of the rule with constitutional rights).

---

[8] And, incidentally, the sorites paradox, ie a 'proof' that no amount of compensation is adequate, and alternative proofs that no amount of compensation is inadequate—either of which would be absurd (Endicott (2000) at ch 5).

Both the guidance and the process values of precision are evident in the law concerning childcare. A parent deciding whether to hire a 13-year-old as a babysitter would be able to use a statute with an age limit to decide whether it is lawful to do so; under the Children and Young Persons Act, the parent needs to decide whether it would be 'neglect' (and may need to guess whether officials would count it as neglect). Officials considering prosecutions for neglect need to make similarly open-ended judgments that will lead to disputes and potentially to litigation—whereas a more precisely defined offense (eg an offense of leaving a child under 10 alone or in the care of a child under 14) would settle matters.

Note that many norms are addressed *to officials or institutions*. Procedural standards requiring that criminal proceedings be commenced within a reasonable time of a charge provide an example. Then the guidance value of precision in such a norm is the norm's value in guiding the official, and the process value is the norm's value in regulating a process (if there is one) for the control of the official's or the institution's action. And then a precise rule requiring, for example, that criminal proceedings be commenced within seven months of a charge, holds out a complex array of benefits at three levels: guidance benefit to the court in deciding when the proceedings may commence, a resulting guidance benefit both to prosecution and to defence in planning and preparation for the proceedings, and a process benefit to any reviewing court in deciding whether the criminal court complied with the law. All three benefits would be lacking in a vague rule that proceedings must commence 'within a reasonable time'.

Yet even in criminal procedure, law-makers very commonly make vague rules of just such a kind. If precision would offer the benefits we have seen, how can a vague standard be better than a precise standard? We may frame the general answer in terms of what I will call the 'normative principle', and the nature of arbitrariness in normative systems.

5. Arbitrariness and the normative principle

Arbitrariness is resistance to or absence of reason. There are as many varieties of arbitrariness as there are varieties of reason. By 'arbitrariness' in a norm, I mean that to some extent it lacks a reasoned justification, because it may be applied in a way that does not achieve the purpose of the norm. A norm is arbitrary in its application if its application is without a reason. The normative principle is opposed to arbitrariness. It is simply the principle that a norm is a reason for action: the point of a norm is to guide conduct for a purpose.

The reason for making the norm is to promote or to achieve the purpose; the norm itself is treated as a reason, or it is not treated as a norm at all. It is a consequence of this understanding of a norm that a normative text is a text formulated and communicated to express a reason for action. Normative texts have the general purpose (whatever other purposes they may have in particular instances) of guiding conduct.

To understand arbitrariness and normativity, it is important to see that a norm may be arbitrary in a variety of senses. Not all such senses are or even can be opposed to the normative principle. Consider the arbitrariness of linguistic rules. The rule that the word for tadpole in English is 'tadpole' is arbitrary (ie lacking in reason) in one sense, as linguists have often remarked: there *is no reason* a language ought to use those phonemes arranged in that order to refer to a tadpole ('renacuajo' or 'rumpetroll' would do as well). Yet at the same time, the rule and actions guided by it are *not* arbitrary in other senses. First, as with all norms of language, there is a good reason to have such norms for the use of words in such ways. That good reason is that it is actually necessary to do so to achieve the coordination that enables communication, self-expression, and all the other priceless benefits of having a language. Second, conduct guided by the norm is far from arbitrary because there is good reason for a particular speaker in a particular situation to go along with the customary norm for the sake of the same coordination that gives purpose to the rule itself. So in a sense it is arbitrary to call a tadpole a 'tadpole', and in another sense it is anything but arbitrary.

The 'arbitrariness' of linguistic rules, then, is no defect in them. But there are forms of arbitrariness that can be very defective features of rules. All badly crafted rules are arbitrary in one sense, because in one way or another they fail to pursue a purpose that justifies the imposition of a standard. Vague standards are not necessarily badly crafted. But they are arbitrary in the special sense that, in some cases, they give a decision-maker no reason for one decision rather than another. As a result, they leave scope to a decision-maker to apply them capriciously, in a way that diverges from their justification. For the same reason, they allow divergent decisions by different decision-makers, which means that part of the purpose of a standard (to achieve general regulation) is to some extent not achieved. It is important to remember in what follows that there are these (and other) various forms of arbitrariness, and that different forms of arbitrariness may be more important and more damaging in different circumstances.

The starting point for understanding the potential value of vague standards is to see that both vagueness *and* precision bring with them forms of arbitrariness.

6. The arbitrariness of precision

The Children and Young Persons Act could have specified a precise age below which a child may not be left unsupervised. But doing so would have incurred quite substantial forms of arbitrariness (for various reasons, and particularly because of the different capacities of children of the same age). A voting age is an example of a rule that incurs such a form of arbitrariness. Assume that the predominant purpose of a voting age is to ensure that people do not vote until they are mature enough to be competent to do so, and mature enough to be reasonably free from the danger of undue influence. Because some people reach the relevant forms of maturity earlier than others, the precise rule is bound to allow some people to vote before they are ready, or to prohibit some from voting after they are ready, or (much more likely) to do both. And the sharp dividing line between lawful and unlawful conduct means that the law will ascribe a very material difference (between having a vote and not having a vote) to an immaterial difference in age (some will be able to vote just because they are a day older than some who cannot vote). A trivial difference in age will make all the difference to the right to vote in a particular election.

So just because of its precision, the application of the standard is arbitrary in the sense that, to some extent, it runs contrary to its own rationale, and draws distinctions that are not justified by its rationale. However, relying upon a vague standard to achieve the same purpose, such as a rule allowing persons to vote when they are 'adult' or 'mature', would incur a different form of arbitrariness: such a standard would leave the question of whether a person may vote to the judgment of election officials (and perhaps to courts asked to resolve disputes), on grounds that are to some extent left to them, and not ruled by law. In the context of elections, of course, that discretion would bring with it a serious danger of abuse or corruption. Moreover, even if we could trust officials to make unbiased judgments of maturity, it is still much better for the law not to authorize the making of such judgments in controlling voting. While it would be quite appropriate for public officials to make judgments of maturity in hiring police officers, democracy requires an official indifference to the capacities of different voters, which means that it is better for public officials not to make such discriminations in controlling voting. The arbitrariness of the precise standard may itself have an important expressive function, signifying the community's refusal to draw invidious distinctions among persons.

So the use of a voting age, you might say, gives rise to far less arbitrariness than would the use of a vague entitlement to vote when mature. Legal control of voting is essential, but there is no precise way of allowing all and only the capable voters to vote.

But now consider the law on time limits for criminal process. There would be advantages in, say, a precise limit of seven months on commencement of proceedings. But here the arbitrariness of precision would be quite a serious defect because of the variations among types of prosecution. Seven months may be more than enough time (it may even be much too long) to allow for prosecution on a shoplifting charge. But it may be hopelessly too little time for the prosecution to prepare for a trial on charges of a major stock market fraud. And different precise time limits for different offenses would not eliminate the arbitrariness of precision, because a precise time limit would not recognize the important variations in the time that it is reasonable (because of the factual background) to spend preparing for trial on different instances of the same charge.

The challenge for law-makers is to determine whether, in a given scheme of regulation, the arbitrariness resulting from precision is worse than the arbitrariness resulting from the application of a vague standard. In some cases, such as the voting age situation, the answer is easy and the arbitrariness of vagueness would be a grave defect in the law. In others, such as the timing of criminal proceedings, the arbitrariness of precision may justify a vague standard.

To summarize the respective forms of arbitrariness that come with precision and with vagueness, consider the difference between the law of taxation and the law of spousal support after a breakdown in a relationship. Tax law generally uses precise rules requiring, for example, the payment of a precise proportion of income. That regime brings with it an important form of arbitrariness, because some people on a higher income are less easily able to carry the tax burden than some people on a lower income (who have a lower cost of living, or have more non-income resources). Assuming that the purpose of the tax is to share the burden of revenue in the community in a way that relates the burden to the ability of people to contribute, the arbitrariness of precision means that, to some extent, the tax cannot achieve its purpose. Tax codes often try to cope with that form of arbitrariness by detailed rules allowing deductions for persons with dependent children etc. Those techniques are quite justifiable, and in most current legal systems they are sophisticated. But while complex rules on deductions can reduce the arbitrariness of precision, they cannot eliminate it. Moreover, their complexity itself runs contrary to the normative principle, to some extent. That is, the complexity of the standards makes it difficult, to some extent, to use the standards as guides. It may necessitate paying a professional tax advisor, and in an extreme case it might become impracticable or quite impossible to use the tax code as a guide.

So why not use a vague tax: 'the taxpayer must pay a proportion of income that is reasonable in the light of the revenue needs of the government and the taxpayer's circumstances'? Such a law would have what I will call the 'fidelity value' of vagueness: it would allow the officials applying the rule to act in a way that is faithful to the purpose of the law, by relating the burden of taxation to the individual conditions of individual taxpayers.

Such a law would, of course, be absurd and intolerable. First, tax assessment requires a huge bureaucracy as it is; one process value of precision is that it simplifies the assessment of tax. A vague tax would require a massive (and massively expensive) investment of official resources—which would run contrary to the revenue-raising purpose of the tax. Much more importantly, though, because of the way in which a vague tax would allocate decision-making power to the tax collectors (and to judges), it would leave taxpayers at the mercy of the officials. Taxation gives the best possible example of the value of precision in constraining the discretion of officials. The arbitrariness of precision is trifling compared to the arbitrariness that vague tax laws would subject us to.

Contrast the law of spousal support. A vague standard (such as that the wealthier spouse must pay a proportion of income that is reasonable in the light of the needs of the recipient spouse and the circumstances of the supporting spouse) would not be radically defective in the way that a similarly vague tax would be. The reason is partly that the danger of abuse by officials is less, and partly that justice between the spouses is consistent with a much more particular approach to their obligations.

7. Precision can be impossible

Precise standards are impossible when the law needs to regulate widely varying conduct with a general standard. The variety of ways in which children may be left more or less alone led to the vague standard of 'neglect' in the Children and Young Persons Act. While it would certainly be possible to set a minimum legal age for babysitters, it would not be possible to define precisely what it means to babysit. Does it include playing with the children while their dad is working upstairs? Or while he has gone to the shop on the corner, or is sleeping? The variety of ways in which a parent may be more or less in charge of the child and more or less absent make precise regulation impossible. And suppose that the parent is always uncontroversially present, but does not feed the child very well, or very frequently, or keep it very clean, or keeps it shut in its room or in a crib all the time, or much of the time. The daunting variety of things that a child needs from its parents corresponds to a wide variety of ways in which a parent may more or less neglect a child. The result is that no legal regulation can provide a precise guide to the responsibilities and liabilities that the law imposes on parents. While the law could be made more precise (eg with age requirements for babysitters), there is no alternative to the vagueness of the terms 'neglected or abandoned' in the Children and Young Persons Act. For these reasons, the 'neglect' standard is similar to H.L.A. Hart's[9] prime example of what he called the 'open texture' of law: the standard of due care in negligence. The law uses a vague standard not merely because a precise alternative would involve greater arbitrariness, but because there *is no* precise alternative. No precise standard of care could generally prescribe the degree of care that is to be taken, both because of the variety of ways in which lack of care can cause risks to others, and because of the variety of interests that would be damaged by requiring excessive care.

Generally, we can say that precision is not even possible, let alone desirable, except in circumstances that allow a quantitative standard (such as, for example, a standard defining the thickness of a particular form of insulation required on a particular calibre of electrical wiring). In formulating building regulations, law-makers face an important set of decisions whether to impose detailed, precise standards, or broad, vague standards. In making or elaborating standards of negligence liability, precise standards are not even an option for law-makers because of the sheer, mind-boggling variety of ways in which people can create more or less unreasonable risks to other people.

In the childcare situation, it is very clear—in a sense—what a good legal regime needs to do: it cannot protect children from all harm, but it should aim to protect them from certain specially damaging harms that social welfare agencies and legal institutions are capable of identifying. The law must not interfere where the parents' methods are only eccentric; and even bad parenting is not in itself enough to justify interference—the law needs to interfere only with specially damaging harms. One reason is that the institutions of the law may not be effective at deciding what counts as bad parenting, and another is that interference will make things worse if it damages the relation between children and parents (there are probably other reasons too). I said that the criteria for a good legal regime are clear *in a sense*, because there is no precise way of setting precise standards that will meet the criteria for a good legal regime. So the purpose of the regulation itself requires vague standards.

The necessity of vague standards for general regulation of varied conduct explains why a decent scheme of regulation of parenting needs vague rules against neglect *as well as* precise rules determining the age at which a parent can no longer be held liable for neglecting a child. We could have a more or less complicated and detailed tax code or code of building regulations, but it

---

[9] Hart (1994) at p 132.

would not even be possible to create a code to list precise descriptions of ways of behaving toward children that are to be unlawful. So vagueness is sometimes necessary.

8. Vague standards delegate power in ways that may comport with the purpose of the law

The vagueness of the law of child neglect leaves wide discretion to social services officials to decide whether to take steps to protect a child. And the vagueness of the law also gives discretion to the courts, which have the final authority to decide any dispute between the officials and parents. It is not instantly apparent, in the law of child neglect, whether these allocations of power are good in themselves or are an unfortunate by-product of the need for vague standards.

A vague standard *may* be a useful way of imposing legal control without fully working out the rationale for the standard. Doing so allocates power to the decision-maker who has the responsibility to resolve disputes over the application of the standard. It may be worthwhile to do so for a variety of reasons, one of which is that common law judicial law-making may be a more effective way of developing just and convenient standards than legislation would be. So the Unfair Contract Terms Act 1977 used very vague standards ('reasonableness', defined as a requirement 'that it should be fair and reasonable...having regard to all the circumstances'[10]). The effect was to delegate to courts the power to determine the reasons for which limitation of liability clauses were to be permitted or not. Vagueness always has this power-allocation function, even when it is not the purpose for which a vague standard was adopted. So the allocation of power should itself be principled. The allocation of power by the vague standards in the Unfair Contract Terms Act is justifiable because of (i) the special expertise of the judges in developing norms of contract law; (ii) the common law doctrine of precedent, which gives them the capacity both to do so incrementally and to revise general rules that turn out to be damaging in particular unforeseen cases; and (iii) the process of the courts that allows the decision-maker to hear argument on behalf of both sides to a dispute. In developing the law of childcare, by contrast, those features of the courts are not so valuable. And there would be no justification at all for allocating power to courts to determine how old a person must be to vote.

---

[10] Section 11(3) and the 'Guidelines' in Sch 2.

Ironically, the potentially valuable power-delegation function of vagueness is a negative correlative to the process value of precision. That is, the process value of precision consists in *reducing* decision-makers' discretion, and yet there may be circumstances, as argued above, in which it is valuable to leave just such a discretion to decision-makers.

9. Vague standards can encourage desirable forms of private ordering that achieve the law's purposes

There is also a negative correlative to the *guidance* value of precision. It may be valuable (for a variety of reasons) to leave the persons affected by a rule uncertain as to its application. The Unfair Contract Terms Act reflects this aspect of the value of vagueness, too. Its vague standards not only delegate power to courts; they also affect a service provider who wants to protect himself from liability, by leaving him uncertain as to how far he can do so. The old law gave the service provider an incentive to construct the most complete exclusion of liability that he could persuade the customer to sign up to. The effect of the new, vague rule against unreasonable clauses is that the service provider has an incentive to seek creative alternatives to excluding liability (eg by advertising that he accepts liability and taking out insurance), or to find ways of making reasonable exclusions of liability that could not have occurred to the drafters of legislation. The uncertainty that arises from the vagueness of negligence law also gives private parties an incentive to avoid the creation of risks, or to contract out of liabilities in a way that will allocate the cost of the risk to the least-cost avoider of the risk.

Precise standards, by contrast, may chill that sort of creativity. A precise standard makes it possible to avoid liability by doing just exactly what is required and no more. If the private parties subject to the duty are in a better position than the law-maker to devise ways of avoiding harm to the persons to whom the duty of care is owed, a vague standard is to that extent preferable. In the law of childcare, there may be just such a benefit in the *lack* of a precise minimum age for babysitters (or a precise minimum age at which a child may be left alone without a babysitter). Within broad limits, the state has *not* claimed to set a norm for parents. To refrain from setting a precise norm in that way is to assign the responsibility for determining the capacity of a babysitter (or the capacity of children to look after themselves) to parents. A precise norm would to some extent take the responsibility away from the persons who ought to have it. Such an allocation of respons-ibility can itself promote the purposes for which the norm is made.

10. Summary

To understand the value of vagueness, we need to remember that both vagueness and precision *always* bring forms of arbitrariness with them: precision does so because it makes the application of the rule turn on a measure that cannot be perfectly commensurate with the purpose of the rule, and vagueness does so because it leaves the application of the standard to persons or institutions that may act capriciously. The guidance value and the process value of precision need to be reconciled with the arbitrariness of precision.

What is more, precision is very commonly simply impossible. And then, vagueness is valuable as a technique for achieving the general regulation of a widely varying range of conduct. Finally, even though it is true that vague standards allocate power to persons who may act capriciously, that allocation of power may suit the purposes of the law very well, when the persons to whom power is allocated are in a better position than the legislator to articulate and determine the standard (as long as they can be trusted not to be corrupt). And just as the process value of precision may be negligible beside the value of such an allocation of power, the guidance value of precision may be negligible beside the value of leaving private parties to order their relations in a way that obviates the mischief at which the law was aimed.

The arbitrariness of vagueness is that it leaves power to officials who may apply a standard capriciously, or to private persons who may use it for purposes contrary to the purpose of the standard. The corresponding *value* of vagueness is that it allows officials to apply a standard in a way that corresponds to its purpose, without the arbitrariness of precision. It also enables the regulation of activities that simply cannot be regulated with precision, and it can be a useful technique for allocating decision-making power and encouraging forms of private ordering that promote the purposes of the law.

We can sum up these values in the following table:

Table 1. Values of precision and vagueness

In relation to:	Precision has:	Vagueness has:
Persons subject to the rule	Guidance value	Private ordering value
Officials applying the rule	Process value	Power allocation value
Purposes of the rule	Constraint value	Fidelity value

11. Conclusion

If you agree with the claims I have made, you may think that it simply means that vagueness is not always a bad thing, and that it may happen to be useful. These are mere contingencies, and do not tell us anything about the nature of normative texts (except, of course, that they show that it is not a general truth about normative texts that they ought to be precise). But I think that the value of vagueness is a general principle of what Jeremy Bentham[11] called 'the science of legislation'—a general principle, that is, of the understanding of how to craft normative texts. The conclusion is that the use of vagueness in normative texts is a technique of central importance. While it always brings with it a form of arbitrariness that precision could avoid, that form of arbitrariness is often insubstantial. The value of vagueness means that law-makers need it for their purposes.

It would be absurd to make a general aim of formulating legal instruments without vagueness. That is not because it would be aiming too high (seeking a form of perfection that can never quite be reached). It would be aiming at something quite contrary to the project of framing norms to guide persons. That project requires constant attention to the 'compromise between being determinate and being all-inclusive'.

The rule of law *requires* vague regulation in every legal system. The rule of law stands against arbitrary government and against anarchy, and vague rules are essential techniques to oppose both arbitrary government and anarchy. A general refusal to use vague rules would lead to anarchy (by making it impossible to regulate, for example, the use of violence against persons). That is because some forms of regulation cannot be performed at all by the use of precise rules. And even where precision is possible, it can lead to arbitrary government (as it would in a community that used precise rules for the law of spousal support).

What can we say about normative texts in general? Every institution involving the use of normative texts has values analogous to the rule of law. When your mother writes a note to you on the fridge, those analogous values have some of the same import that they have in a legal system. A household may lack many of the techniques for government by rules that a state has—an obvious example is that your mother does not owe you a hearing before an independent tribunal if she suspects you of breaking her hairdryer. But it shares many of the most basic tenets of the rule of law (for example, the value of your mother listening to what you have to say before she jumps to

---

[11] Bentham (1843).

conclusions). Of course, that value may be flouted or ignored to some extent in your household, as it may be in your legal system. Then the normative principle (in your household or in your legal system) is not fully adhered to: the norms are not treated as guides to conduct. If you have rules at all in your household, and if your state has a legal system at all, then your household and your state share the value to be found in the making of norms capable of being followed, the faithful application of the norms according to their tenor, and the consequent upholding of expectations based on the norms. And to pursue all those purposes, vagueness is essential. It is not essential in every norm, because precise rules ('be home by 11 pm', 'speed limit 70') are often the best technique for regulation. But vagueness is an essential part of the science of the legislator, because the project of regulating the life of the community (in your household or your state) demands vague rules in some circumstances.

The normative principle (the principle that the point of a norm is to guide conduct for a purpose) underlies the rule of law, and analogous values in other normative systems and, in fact, in the use of normative texts in general, in quite unsystematic contexts. The principle is opposed to arbitrariness in norms, and arbitrariness arises both from precision and from vagueness in normative texts. So to stand against arbitrariness and in favor of principled, rule-governed conduct, the framers of norms must not generally avoid vagueness. They must be prepared to assess competing forms of arbitrariness, and to judge whether the forms of arbitrariness resulting from a vague norm are more or less damaging than the forms of arbitrariness that result from a precise norm. It is not a general proposition that normative texts should be vague; but the control of human conduct by rules tends to require vague regulation because of the arbitrariness of precision and the simple necessity of vagueness as an instrument for regulating so many forms of human conduct.

3

What Vagueness and Inconsistency Tell Us About Interpretation

Scott Soames

1. Two kinds of vagueness

When signing up for insurance benefits at my job, I was asked, "Do you have children, and if so are they young enough to be included on your policy?" I replied that I had two children, both of whom were over 21. The benefits officer responded, "That's too vague. In some circumstances children of covered employees are eligible for benefits up to their 26th birthday. I need their ages to determine whether they can be included on your policy." She was right; my remark was too vague. The information it provided was insufficiently specific to advance our common conversational purpose.

However, it was not vague, or at any rate not too vague, in the sense in which philosophical logicians and philosophers of language study vagueness. Vague predicates—like 'old', 'bald', 'rich', and 'red'—are those for which there are "borderline cases" separating things to which the predicate clearly applies from those to which it clearly does not. When o is a borderline case for a predicate P, there is, in some sense, "no saying" whether or not the proposition expressed by ⌜he or she/it is P⌝ (said demonstrating o) is true. According to some theories of vagueness, the proposition is undefined for truth, or untruth, and so cannot correctly be characterized either way. According to others, it is true or false—even though it is impossible, in principle, to know which. On still other theories, it is only partially true (or true to some degree). For present purposes we need not worry about which of these theories is correct, or which is most illuminating in discussions of the law. The present point is simpler. The problem with my remark to the benefits officer—the sense in which it was too vague—is not a matter of its susceptibility to borderline cases.

What I stated, on 10 December 2009, was that my two children were then both over 21 years old. That statement is true if and only if both were born on or before 9 December 1988 (which they were). Granted, sticklers may wonder how to classify individuals born on 10 December 1988. Perhaps such individuals are borderline cases of *being over 21 years old on 10 December 2009*. Confronted with such cases, perhaps we should inquire on which side of the International Date Line they were born, or at what hour and minute in which time zone the birth occurred. Perhaps even these inquiries would not settle the matter. If not, my remark may well have been vague in the special, technical sense of logical and philosophical theories of vagueness. However, the borderline cases crucial to so characterizing them are not what made my remark vague in the ordinary sense of that word.

Ordinary vagueness is a contextual matter. Whether or not a remark counts as vague in this sense depends on whether or not the information it provides is sufficiently specific to answer the question, or questions, directing one's inquiry. Since these questions may vary from one context of inquiry to the next, a remark that counts as vague in one context may not be vague in another. Because of this, it is easy to construct examples of remarks that are vague in either the ordinary contextual sense or the technical philosophical sense without being vague in the other sense. If my benefits officer had been a sophisticated computer that measured time in nanoseconds, then my response—"I have two children, but the number of nanoseconds from their birth to the instant at which you receive the electrical impulse encoding this answer is greater than or equal to n", (for some very large n determining a precise instant on 9 December 1988, in Los Angeles)—would have been just as vague, in the ordinary contextual sense, as was my remark to the human benefits officer. This is so although my specification of a lower bound on a length of time in nanoseconds is (we may imagine) perfectly precise in the technical sense of philosophical logic. Conversely, had I responded to my human benefits officer by saying that my children were still toddlers (in a context in which it is known that young children are always included on insurance plans), my remark would count as logically and philosophical vague, despite being fully precise in the ordinary sense of providing all the information required in the context.

So the two senses are distinct, and a context in which a remark is vague in one sense is not always a context in which it is vague in another. Nevertheless, there is an obvious connection between the two senses. If a predicate P is vague in the technical sense, then claims expressed by $\ulcorner$ every/some/the/no F is P $\urcorner$ will be vague in the ordinary sense, *relative to some contexts of inquiry* requiring knowledge of the truth values of these claims at possible scenarios involving individuals that are borderline cases for P.

2. Vagueness and the interpretation of legal, and non-legal, texts

A similar point applies to sentences occurring in legal texts. When a vague action predicate P occurs in such a text—⌜It shall be a felony in the County of Los Angeles of the state of California to P in circumstance Q⌝— there will typically be possible actions in circumstances to which Q applies that are borderline cases for P. When considering such cases, no definite conclusions—(i) ⌜the agent has Ped⌝ is true or ⌜the agent has not Ped⌝ is true, and hence (ii) that the agent has, or has not, committed a felony—will be determinable from a perfect understanding of the text together with a complete knowledge of the facts of the case. Since the information provided by the statute is insufficient for determining the agent's guilt or innocence, the statute counts as vague (in the ordinary contextual sense) in any judicial proceedings convened for this purpose.

Nevertheless, some decision must be reached in such cases, and not just any decision will do. In matters of great importance, flipping a coin will not suffice. Such cases call for principled decisions. But where are the principles to be found, how are they to be justified, and who is charged with finding them? In practice, the answer to the last of these questions is often clear. Those who administer and enforce the law—police, regulatory and administrative agencies, and the judiciary—are often charged with making such decisions on the basis of principles, which, though sometimes only tacit, should be capable of articulation and justification, if challenged.[1] Arriving at these principles is often called "interpreting the law", especially when the legal actors are members of the judiciary. Although interpreting vague statutes is one kind of legal interpretation—which is not entirely unrelated to interpreting other kinds of vague texts and linguistic performances—its function in the law is special, and not merely a sub-case of corresponding interpretations in other genres.

Vague predicates are more regularly used in ordinary discourse, as well as in works of both fiction and non-fiction, than they are in the law. In many of

---

[1] Sometimes it is open to a court to send a case back to the law-making authority for clarification or precisification. However, this is not always possible and, even when it is, it is often impractical. Also, in certain types of cases a rule of lenity may apply, effectively requiring an action to be judged a clear case of the application of a (legally) vague term in order for a negative judgment to be sustained. However, (i) rules of lenity are not always relevant; (ii) since it can be vague in particular cases whether they are relevant, a court may be called upon to exercise its law-making authority at this meta-level; and (iii) even when a rule of lenity is clearly relevant, the court must judge what counts as *a clear case* of the relevant term, despite the fact that *being a clear case* may itself have borderline cases.

these non-legal cases, the purposes of the conversation, inquiry, or artistic endeavor do not require resolving whether or not the predicate applies to borderline cases. Let p be the vague proposition asserted or expressed by an agent (in conversation) or an author (of fiction or non-fiction) who uses such a predicate (without providing any indication of how potential borderline cases are to be treated). In reporting what the agent said or expressed, we (standardly) do not replace p with some precisified substitute p*. Imagine an agent who says, "The pulse of any young man is always quickened by the sight of a beautiful woman." We may be interested in knowing whether two individuals, John, a man who is borderline young, and Mary, a woman who is borderline beautiful, constitute a counterexample to the agent's remark. But if there is "no saying"about John's youth or Mary's beauty, then—since there is no need to come to a verdict about the agent's remark—we would typically admit that there is "no saying"about whether or not they falsify it.

A similar case, which nevertheless takes us a step forward, involves interpreting a text in the history of philosophy. Imagine a philosopher, Brown, who enunciates the thesis ⌜All A's, except those that are also B's, are C's⌝, using vague predicates A and B, where it is clear that he never considered borderline cases of A and B. Upon discovering an individual that is borderline for both to which C does not apply, we wonder whether it is a counterexample to the thesis. Typically, our answer will be that since what Brown asserted was vague, it is simply unclear, or indeterminate, whether or not we have a counterexample. This will remain so, even if we determine that taking both A and B not to apply to the individual makes it possible to extract a comprehensive philosophical system from Brown's total corpus that is superior to any extractable system incorporating a different decision about A and B. The proper verdict is that the preferred system—while heavily indebted to Brown, and properly characterized as *Brownian*—is a precisified reconstruction of the one he actually produced. In this case, the philosophical guidance we receive from our "interpretation" goes beyond our account of what Brown actually said, which is also part of our interpretation.

A real-life example of an interpretation of this sort involves a lacuna in the ideal language of Wittgenstein[2] (which is held to underlie all thought). The Tractarian account recognizes logically proper names, predicates, and a single truth-functional operator of joint denial (of arbitrarily many arguments), plus variables used to express generality (without explicit quantifiers to bind them). This presents a problem of interpretation. On the one hand, the formal devices specified in the text are incapable of expressing what is standardly represented by certain relative-scope possibilities of universal and existential

---

[2] Wittgenstein (1922).

quantifiers in the same sentence. Because of this, the expressive power of the Tractarian ideal language that emerges is severely limited. On the other hand, Wittgenstein, who claims that every proposition is expressible in that language, clearly intends it not to be so limited. The interpretive task is made more difficult by his discussion of what he calls "the general form of the proposition", which is a schematic account of how every genuine proposition is constructible as a truth function of the totality of elementary propositions. Alas, the account is so abstract as to be compatible with both a narrow interpretation (which yields the restricted set of propositions expressible in the scopeless quantified language) and a broader interpretation (which makes for a richer totality, while leaving room for the addition of scope-indicating devices not explicitly mentioned in the text).

The text is vague in the ordinary sense, and so indeterminate, between these two interpretations, with some passages seeming to favour one and some seeming to favor the other. Philosophically speaking, however, there is no contest. The broader interpretation is clearly best, in the sense of producing a superior philosophical system, which Wittgenstein would have favored had the issues been made explicit. However, they are not made explicit in the text, and there is no evidence that he clearly saw them. As with my earlier example involving the fictitious Brown, so in this example about Wittgenstein, the correct interpretation of the text (the *Tractatus*) identifies a powerful formal system—properly characterized as "Wittgensteinian"—while noting that it results from augmenting what Wittgenstein explicitly says in ways that his text is silent about. Here, what is called 'interpreting' an important philosophical text includes both strict historical description and the normative search for philosophical insight.[3]

The use of language to make requests, give orders, provide instructions, specify the scope of someone's authority, or, more generally, to guide action, brings us closer to the legal case. If (i) you are advised, instructed, or ordered ⌜Do P in circumstance Q⌝, where both P and Q are vague predicates; (ii) it is important that you follow the advice, or comply with the instruction or order; and (iii) the action about which you need to make a decision (or the circumstance in which you are called upon to act) is a borderline case for P (or for Q), then you will search for guidance that may go beyond both the strict semantic content of the sentence uttered and the content literally asserted, or stipulated, by the utterance to which you are responding. A natural first step in many such cases is to inquire into the intentions of the person giving the advice or issuing the instructions or orders. By 'intentions', I do not here

---

[3] Discussed in (i) Fogelin (1976) at ch 6; (ii) Geach (1982) at pp 168–71 and Soames (1983) at pp 573–89; and (iii) Fogelin (1987) at ch 6.

mean the speaker's assertive or stipulative intentions. These will already have been identified when you came to understand what was (literally) said, asserted, or stipulated. Rather, the intentions in question concern the reason, or larger purpose, that the agent said, asserted, or stipulated what he did.

Consider the homely example of a father who says, "Never accept a ride from a stranger", to his teenage daughter, Susan, in the course of warning her about recent sexual assaults against girls who had accepted rides in cars from boys from out of town. Some days later, hurrying to her after-school job at the Mini Mart, for which she is late, Susan is stopped by a motorist asking directions to that establishment. The motorist—a sweet little old lady whom Susan has never spoken to, but has seen and nodded to several times around town—offers her a ride to work in return for pointing the way. Susan accepts, thinking, "I know Dad told me not to ride with strangers, and I'm not really sure whether or not this lady is a stranger—*but I know he didn't mean people like her.*"

In so doing, she interprets her father's remark correctly—which is *not* to say that accepting the ride strictly conformed to the injunction he laid down. Since, as we will assume, the motorist is a borderline case of *being a stranger (to Susan)*, there is no saying whether or not her behavior conformed to what her father (literally) told her to do. However, it did accord with his reason for instructing her as he did. This is what Susan grasped, and expressed in her thought about "what he meant". Recognizing the insufficiency of the information provided by the content of her father's remark, she looked to *his reason* for making the remark, and rightly acted in accord with it.

This model can be applied to the interpretation of some vague legal texts. Continuing the simple example, suppose that the town council responds to the outbreak of sexual assaults by adopting a statute: "It shall be a misdemeanor in the Township of Plainsboro for children on their way to or from school to accept rides in automobiles from strangers." Suppose further that a policeman observing Susan accepting a ride stops her as she gets out of the car. After determining that she did not know the driver, he wonders whether to arrest her for violating the new ordinance.

On the one hand, he may reason as Susan did about her father's injunction: although it is not clear whether or not the driver was a stranger to Susan, surely the town council did not mean to prohibit this kind of innocent activity. To reason in this way is to interpret the vague statute to yield a result not determined by the content of the statute itself. If the policeman acts on this interpretation, and his fellow officers consistently follow suit in similar cases, the result will be a de facto change in the law as applied in this sort of case. A statute that previously had clearly applied to certain acts (making them criminal offenses), clearly not applied to other acts (leaving them unregulated),

particular cases, so too can many parents in conforming their behavior to it. This too, is part of the rationale for using a vague, general, and multi-dimensional term like 'neglect'.

The final value I will mention is specific to directives that are vague in either the ordinary contextual sense or the technical philosophical sense (or both). In some situations, directives that are vague in this way lead those whose behavior one wishes to influence to *oversubscribe* to the goals of the directive in an attempt to reduce the dangers of noncompliance (or increase the benefits of compliance).[8] Imagine, for example, a college administrator faced with a financial crisis requiring immediate across-the-board cuts in the budgets of the college's departments. Each, he believes, could make a 10 per cent cut, if pressed, which is the minimum that might allow the college to survive. It would, we may imagine, be better to secure greater cuts, which he believes some departments could probably afford. However, he has to act quickly and does not possess enough detailed information to identify which departments fall into this category, or to set differential targets. He therefore limits himself to two alternatives: (i) ordering all departments to cut at least 10 per cent, on penalty of losing their graduate programs if they fail to comply, vs (ii) ordering all departments to make the maximum reductions possible, indicating that those who are not sufficiently forthcoming will lose their graduate programs.

The first potential directive is precise and specific, while the second is deliberately vague. Depending on the background circumstances, either one might prove to be the more effective. However, there are clearly some circumstances in which the vague alternative would be superior. In such cases, chairmen of the poorer departments, fearing the penalty for making cuts smaller than what the administrator will find minimally acceptable (which they may guess to be around 10 per cent), will struggle to make slightly larger cuts to leave themselves a modest margin of error. While their counterparts in richer departments will reason in the same way, their extra resources may well lead them to make even larger cuts, amounting to affordable extra insurance against what would otherwise be a catastrophic loss. In this case, the vagueness of the standard leads relevant actors to overfulfill the requirements that would have been imposed on them by a more precise directive.

Vaguely formulated laws—for example, those criminalizing, or providing penalties for, various forms of neglect, negligence, abuse, and fiduciary irresponsibility—may display similar advantages over more precisely formulated alternatives. In such cases, the positive value of vagueness in the law typically leads to a corresponding delegation of authority to judges and

---

[8] This point is related to the discussion in ibid at p 27.

administrators who are called on to interpret the law, and sometimes to a positive change in the behavior of those whom the law regulates.

4. Consequences for textualism

This discussion of vagueness throws light on contemporary disputes about the doctrine of interpretation known as 'textualism'. Roughly put, the doctrine states that the content of a legal text—the law in the case of a statute—is what the law-makers say, assert, or stipulate in adopting the text. Although this is, I think, the best rough-and-ready formulation of the doctrine, it is not the most common one. Instead, textualism is typically identified as the doctrine that the content of a legal text (the law it enacts) is the meaning— sometimes "the ordinary meaning"—of the text. Elsewhere (Soames (2009a)), I have argued that this is confused. Contemporary philosophy of language and theoretical linguistics distinguish the meaning of a sentence from its semantic content relative to a context, both of which are distinguished from (the content of) what is said, asserted, or stipulated by an utterance of the sentence. Although in some cases the three types of content coincide, while in still others the final two do, there are a variety of cases in which the third differs from the other two.[9] In every legal case in which there is such a difference, it is the third—asserted or stipulated—content that is required by any defensible form of textualism. Failure to recognize this—due to confusing the three types of content with one another—has led to errors in the law itself, as well as to theoretical errors about the relation of the law to its authoritative sources.[10]

This observation is related to the vexed question of the place in legal interpretation accorded by textualists to legislative intent. Some leading textualists, most notably US Supreme Court Associate Justice Antonin Scalia, maintain that since the job of the courts is to discover the content of statutes and other legal texts, which Scalia identifies with "their ordinary meanings", an inquiry into legislative history to discover the intent of the law-makers in enacting such legislation does not advance the interpretative task. Worse, he worries, epistemological problems inherent in such inquiries are often so great as to leave jurists virtually free rein to read their own policy preferences into the texts they purport to interpret.[11] While one can appreciate these worries, as well as Scalia's desire to limit judicial law-making and to encourage deference

[9] Soames (2010a) at ch 7.
[10] *Smith v United States* 508 US 223 (1993), discussed in Soames (2009a) at pp 412–15.
[11] Scalia (1998) at pp 16–18.

to legislatures and other democratic rule-making bodies, his view about the relevance of legislative intent is seriously flawed.

Most fundamentally, it fails to distinguish illocutionary intentions—to say, assert, or stipulate that P, in part by virtue of one's audience recognizing one's intention to do so—from broader perlocutionary intentions—to cause or bring about something as a result of one's having said, asserted, or stipulated that P.[12] In my simple example discussed earlier, members of the Plainsboro Town Council intend to reduce the risk of sexual assault against the town's schoolchildren by enacting a law discouraging them from accepting rides from strangers. They enact the law by adopting a text with the illocutionary intention that their linguistic performance be recognized as asserting or stipulating that, henceforth, accepting such rides shall be a misdemeanor. Since it is this intention that gives the law its content, no theory of legal content, or of legal interpretation, can afford to dismiss it. Any defensible form of textualism must recognize the importance of the illocutionary intentions of law-makers.

Any doctrine that aspires to be a theory of legal interpretation also cannot afford to dismiss the larger, perlocutionary, intentions of law-makers when the application of a vague statute to a borderline case is at issue. The decision of the Plainsboro court, that Susan acted lawfully in accepting a ride, illustrates the point. Since the content of the statute, together with the facts of the case, failed to determine her guilt or innocence, the court based its decision on the public policy the town council intended the legislation to advance. The court's focus on legislative intent, far from being an excuse to substitute its policy for that of the council, reflected its deference to the council as the town's primary law-making body. Since the task before it was to make determinate something that had been indeterminate in the original statute, deciding the case on the basis of the council's legislative intent rather than its own policy preferences was an act of deference, not usurpation.

A further lesson is evident from this case. Although textualism may well be a plausible theory of legal content, it cannot serve as a comprehensive theory of legal interpretation—where 'interpreting the law' is understood as what courts properly do in adjudicating cases, including those which count, for one reason or another, as "hard cases". As a theory of content, textualism tells us that the content of a legal document is what is said, asserted, or stipulated by the relevant legal authors, or enactors, of the document—which is fine, provided that judges, along with legislators, are included among the relevant legal actors, and that their recorded opinions, along with legislative texts, are included among the relevant legal documents. However, to view things in this

---

[12] Austin (1962) distinguishes between illocutionary and perlocutionary acts.

way one must recognize that interpreting a vague law often involves not only figuring out what its (pre-existing) content is, but also revising that content by precisifying it.

5. Extending the lesson to the resolution of inconsistencies

The same is true of situations in which the facts of a particular case bring two or more existing laws into conflict. In such cases, the combination of facts and law yield a contradiction—eg that the agent is, and is not, guilty of a crime; that a tariff of precisely \$X, and of precisely \$Y, is due (where $X \neq Y$); or that a particular course of action both is, and is not, legally required. As with vagueness (when law plus facts yield no determinate result), so with conflict (when inconsistent results are determined) it is often proper for courts charged with resolving the case to look beyond the contents of existing laws to the legislative purposes they were designed to serve, to arrive at a justifiable change in the law.

As before, it is worth noting that this type of conflict resolution, so important in legal interpretation, has an analogue in the interpretation of non-legal texts. For a philosophical example, one need look no further than Donald Davidson's classic article, 'Truth and Meaning', and related works.[13] There, Davidson holds (i) that a Tarski-style theory of truth—which generates a T-theorem, ⌜'S' is a true sentence of L iff P⌝ for each sentence S of L (where P is a metalanguage paraphrase of S)—may play the role of an empirical theory of meaning for L; (ii) that it may do so because knowledge of that which it states (including knowledge of what the T-theorems state) provides all one needs to understand the sentences of L; and (iii) that the notion of truth employed in the theory is the "semantical concept of truth" that Tarski defines. The problem posed for interpretation is that (i)–(iii) are jointly incompatible with the fact that when Tarski's truth predicate is substituted (in accordance with (iii)) for the ordinary truth predicate in the theorems guaranteed by (i), the propositions they express are knowable a priori, and contain no empirical information about the meanings of sentences of L (in violation of (ii)). In short, the theses (i)–(iii) enunciated in 'Truth and Meaning' and related works are jointly incompatible with the obvious facts about the Tarskian truth predicates they discuss.[14]

Since this inconsistency is now widely recognized, any interpretation that did not mention it would be remiss. However, an interpretation that failed to

---

[13] Davidson (1967) at pp 304–23 and Davidson (1973) at pp 313–28.
[14] Soames (1999) at ch 4.

resolve the inconsistency would be equally remiss. As just about everyone (including Davidson) eventually came to recognize, the best way to do this, while maintaining maximum fidelity to the most important features of Davidson's corpus, is to replace (iii) with the thesis that the notion of truth in Davidson's purported theory-of-truth-as-theory-of-meaning is our ordinary one.[15] This resolution of Davidson's inconsistency parallels our earlier precisification of Wittgenstein's vague text. In both cases, a proper interpretation of a philosophical text includes an historical description of what the text strictly and literally says, plus a normative improvement of that content designed to maximize the philosophical insight extractable from the text's leading ideas. The reason we are not satisfied with the former, but insist also on the latter, is that both the original text being interpreted and the later text interpreting it share a common aim: to increase our understanding of the philosophical subject matter at hand.

As in philosophy, so also in law (up to a point).[16] Legislators, administrators, and members of the judiciary have a common interest that the laws they enact and enforce be coherent, and not lead to flatly inconsistent results when applied to particular cases. Since the body of laws in any modern jurisdiction is extraordinarily large, and mind-numbingly complex, the task of maintaining consistency is enormous and never-ending. Remember, the inconsistency we are most concerned with is not that of two laws flatly contradicting one another—so that *no possible pattern of covered behavior* could ever conform to both. Although such cases may occur, the most prevalent and worrisome problem arises from the incompatibility of two or more laws *with some possible behavior*. Since the range of humanly possible behaviors that could, if they occurred, determine inconsistent results by falling under different legal provisions is without foreseeable bounds, no legislative process— no matter how careful or deliberate—can assure that courts will not be called upon to resolve inconsistencies arising in particular cases. Since courts are designed precisely to mediate between the immense variety of possible behaviors on the one hand, and the legally codified general principles designed to regulate them on the other, this is just as it should be. Given the complex network of conceptual connections relating each law to other laws, and the multiplicity of nuanced adjustments to such networks capable of being

---

[15] Soames (2003a) at ch 12, Soames (2008a), Davidson (1990), and Davidson (2005) at chs 1–2.

[16] Whereas in philosophy, we typically wish to learn as much as possible from the error or inconsistency in the text we are interpreting—which sometimes leads to a sweeping criticism, or elaborate reconstruction and defense, of its leading ideas—in the law the most pressing issue is often the resolution of the conflict for the case at hand, by means of what the court takes to be a minimal change, or reconstruction, of the existing body of relevant law.

generated by different possible actions and circumstances, no legislative body concerned with broad matters of policy could possibly perform the day-to-day task of making the fine-grained adjustments in effective legal content that would be needed to rationalize and harmonize our body of laws. For this we need judicial interpretation.

Of course, not all judicial adjustments to effective legal content prompted by the occurrence of unforeseen particular circumstances are really changes in (the content of) the law. However, as in the earlier example involving the interpretation of vague law, adjustments aimed at removing inconsistencies can amount to changes in (the content of) the law—if made by the court of last resort, or if an adjustment in one case is followed by corresponding adjustments in similar cases, resulting in a consistent pattern of such interpretations. To put the point another way, both precisifying and inconsistency-resolving judicial interpretations are valuable elements of common law in extensive systems of modern positive law.

A different, though related, sort of case in which judicial interpretation resolves an inconsistency involves those in which the inconsistency brought out by the particular facts of the case is not between the contents of different statutes, but between what the law literally says and the transparent purposes for which it was introduced. In these cases, the law as it exists, plus the facts of the case, generate unforeseen results, the wrongness of which seem evident. Consider, for example, a variation of Susan's case in which the obviously undangerous motorist clearly is a stranger, whom Susan has never seen before. In such a case, it is not far-fetched to suppose that the same verdict of 'not guilty' should be rendered as was rendered in the earlier version that turned on the vagueness of the term 'stranger' in the ordinance. In this new version, however, the court is not precisifying content that the town council originally left vague. Instead, it reaches a result that flatly contradicts the one dictated by the facts, together with the law as actually passed. Here, a set of particular facts about an agent generates an unexpected conflict not between two or more laws, but between the content of a single law and the purpose it was meant to serve.[17]

Real-life examples of this are not as hard to come by as one might imagine. Indeed, some come from the highest profile arena of judicial interpretation—constitutional law. The provision in the First Amendment to the Constitution of the United States specifying that, "Congress shall make no law...abridging the freedom of speech, or of the press" is an example. Despite its breathtaking sweep, there are plenty of laws restricting defamatory and libelous speech, commercial speech, publication of state secrets injurious to national

---

[17] Brief discussions of both kinds of conflict are found in Soames (2009a).

security, incitements of violence (including the use of "fighting words"), and false and dangerous speech (falsely shouting "Fire!" in a crowded theater). There are now even certain legal restrictions on political speech, in the form of campaign-contribution restrictions and restrictions on the content of messages aired during political campaigns by certain groups. Although the correctness of some of these exceptions is certainly arguable, and the scope of any of them could be challenged, there is, I think, no serious argument supporting the conclusion that what the First Amendment requires is precisely what its words seem, explicitly, to state—namely that there shall be no law restricting the freedom of speech or of the press in any way.

Might it be argued that we arrive at the correct content by focusing not on what the words of the First Amendment mean in English, independent of their use in any particular context of utterance, but rather on what the framers and ratifiers took themselves to be using those words to assert in their context? The idea here is that they meant something quite specific by their use of the quantified phrase 'no law' (together with the qualifying clause 'abridging the freedom of speech, or of the press'). Perhaps the apparent exceptions to the amendment fall outside the contextually presupposed *domain of quantification* determined by the content they asserted. Whenever one uses a quantified phrase ⌜all/some/no/many/most Fs⌝ in a sentence to say or stipulate something, the content of one's assertion or stipulation depends on the class of things one intends to talk about. The presence of the predicate F explicitly restricts the class to be one each member of which has the property it expresses. However, it is common for further restrictions to be implicitly incorporated into asserted, or stipulated, content by virtue of assertive or stipulative intentions that the speaker presupposes to be recognized by his audience in the context.

For example, if I say to the incoming class of first-year graduate students in my department, "No student who does not pass Philosophy 500 with a grade of B+ or better will receive a PhD", I am not talking about all students everywhere. Rather, the content of my assertion includes a restriction to students *in the PhD program in philosophy at USC*. This extra restricting content is provided not by the words I utter, but by an intention I correctly believe to be recognized by my audience—namely to use those words to assert what is more explicitly expressed by "No student *in this program* (said referring to the PhD program in philosophy at USC) who does not pass Philosophy 500 with a B+ or better will receive a PhD", or, "No student *in the PhD program in philosophy at USC* who does not pass Philosophy 500 with a grade of B+ or better will receive a PhD".

To apply this idea to the First Amendment is to suppose that its framers and ratifiers had some implicit content in mind limiting the type of laws restricting freedom of speech, or of the press, that were to be prohibited—where the mutually understood limitations coincided with those that are now (let us suppose correctly) regarded to be exceptions. To put the point most starkly, the suggestion is that what the framers and ratifiers understood themselves to be saying was, essentially, what is explicitly asserted by uses of:

Congress shall pass no law abridging the freedom of speech, or of the press, *except for those governing commercial speech, defamatory and libelous speech, publication of state secrets injurious to national security, incitements of violence (including those involving fighting words), or false and dangerous speech (such as falsely shouting "Fire!" in a crowded theater).*

To put the view this baldly is, perhaps, to unfairly suggest its absurdity. But absurd or not, it is clearly incorrect.[18]

Its chief problem is that it requires a grossly unrealistic level of detail and transparency—not just in *the verdicts that the framers and ratifiers would have given had they foreseen the different potential challenges to a blanket ban on laws regulating speech and the press*—but also in *what they, in fact, recognized themselves to be strictly and literally saying in adopting the amendment.* Surely it is a fantasy to suppose that they had all this in mind in the sense that I have the graduate program in philosophy at USC in mind, when I say to the incoming class 'No student who…'. Remember, our interpretive problem is to reconcile the apparent content of the legal provision adopted—in this case, one aspect of the First Amendment—with all the seemingly incorrect verdicts capable of being generated by strictly and literally applying that content to the totality of *different possible cases* that might arise in the future. If, as seems natural, there is no foreseeable end to the variety of such possible cases, then an interpretive strategy which, in effect, requires them to have been foreseen, and present in the minds of those who framed and ratified the amendment, is a non-starter.

As if this were not bad enough, the same strategy would have to be repeated for each of the clauses of the First Amendment, the full text of which is:

Congress shall make *no law* respecting an establishment of religion, or prohibiting the free exercise thereof; or *abridging the freedom of speech, or of the press*; or the right of the people peaceably to assemble, and to petition the Government for a redress of grievances. (Emphasis mine)

---

[18] There are some complications worth noting. As Andrei Marmor pointed out to me, it could be argued that the terms 'freedom', 'speech', and 'the press' are vague, and may have been used with partly precisified contents by framers and ratifiers of the amendment. Even if this is so, however, it does not, I think, save an interpretive strategy predicated on an imagined, implicitly understood restriction on the domain of quantification. Nor does it substantially alter the positive conclusions to be drawn about this case.

When applied to the freedom of speech provision, the strategy would have us identify the assertive content of the relevant portion of the amendment, as used by the framers and the ratifiers, with the enrichment of the semantic content of that portion that results from adding extra content (present in their minds) to the content expressed by the compound quantified phrase consisting of 'no law' plus the relevant accompanying clause 'abridging the freedom of speech, or of the press'. Repeating the analysis for the clauses covering religion, assembly, and the redress of grievances, multiplies the implausible complexity and specificity of the story we have already told several times over. Surely we can do better.

The way to understand the First Amendment, and its subsequent interpretation, is, I suggest, to see it as a vastly more important and complicated version of what we saw when we applied the imaginary ordinance, 'It shall be a misdemeanor in the Township of Plainsboro for children on their way to or from school to accept rides in automobiles from strangers' to the case in which Susan accepted a ride from an obviously sweet, distinctly undangerous, little old lady whom she did not know. Since, in that case, a literal application of the law would have led to a finding that did not serve the purpose that the law was designed to advance, the court ruled in a way that narrowed the legal content of the ordinance (assuming the decision to be precedent setting).

Why, one might ask, did the town council formulate the law as it did? One plausible scenario is this. Being well aware that their purpose was to diminish the danger that schoolchildren would be victims of sexual assault, they considered various formulations explicitly referencing the danger—eg 'It shall be a misdemeanor in the Township of Plainsboro for children on their way to or from school to accept rides in automobiles from *dangerous* strangers.' Such formulations were rejected on the sensible grounds (i) that asking the children at whom the law was directed to make judgments about who was dangerous and who was not might easily turn out to be counterproductive, and (ii) that including such a vague and contentious term in the statute would make for uncertainty in enforcement and difficulty in prosecution. Better, the council members reasoned, to leave the language unadorned, and let the court be guided by their evident intention—to reduce unnecessary risk to the town's schoolchildren—to sort out cases in which the ordinance should apply from those in which it should not.

The effect of this policy is to put anyone accepting a ride from a stranger on notice that he or she will be subject to a judgment that could lead to criminal penalties. The council members knew that innocent exceptions to the ordinance would come to be recognized, and, eventually, would lead to a narrowing of its content by carving out special classes of cases. However, they also realized that the ultimate scope and precise identity of those exceptions would be unforeseeable, and that whatever carve-outs came to be recognized would be piecemeal. They were, therefore, aware that the boundaries between such cases and those in which one's behavior in accepting a ride might leave one vulnerable to legal penalty would remain vague, ragged, and usefully unpredictable. In short, they knew that the passage of the ordinance would lead to a strong, but rebuttable, presumption against the behavior to be discouraged. The fact that the presumption is sweepingly expressed, open ended, and pervasive provides motivation to avoid any behavior that might fall into that category. The fact that the presumption is rebuttable in court reduces the disadvantages of the (overly) general description of that behavior in the ordinance itself. All in all, the council members thought, a good bargain.

A similar—though admittedly hypothetical—story can be told about a line of reasoning open to the framers and ratifiers of the First Amendment. What was wanted, we may imagine, was a strong, but rebuttable, legal presumption against the passage of laws by Congress regulating the freedom of speech, or of the press.[19] The sweeping, open-ended content of the amendment was, we may suppose, reasonably intended to put present and future members of Congress on notice that any law restricting freedom of speech, or of the press, risked being judged unconstitutional (and so invalid).[20] We may further suppose that it was anticipated, at least by some, that, over time, reasonable exceptions to the prohibition would come to be recognized, with a consequent narrowing of the legal content of the amendment's guarantee. This is not to say that the precise scope and contents of these exceptions could be foreseen. What could be foreseen was that the process by which the exceptions would come to be recognized would be piecemeal, and that the boundaries between them and the laws to which the prohibition would apply would remain vague, ragged, and usefully unpredictable. In short, the First Amendment provision on freedom of speech, and of the press, would amount to a strong, but rebuttable, legal presumption discouraging the sort of legislation the framers and the ratifiers wished to limit.[21] Not perfect perhaps, but, again, not a bad bargain.

Although this discussion of the content, and interpretation, of the First Amendment barely scratches the surface, the analytical framework employed

---

[19] In the interests of simplicity, I here put aside the other freedoms covered by the amendment.

[20] Who might make that judgment, and what its consequences would be, are, of course, historically complicated matters, since when the First Amendment was ratified judicial review did not yet exist. For purposes of rational reconstruction, I put this complication aside.

[21] Here, and throughout, I use the terms 'legal presumption' or simply 'presumption' in their ordinary senses, which are looser than their technical understanding in the law as designating a rule shifting the burden of legal proof. In the sense in which I use the term, a legal presumption is a policy to be followed by relevant legal actors (which need not concern the burden of legal proof).

is, I believe, one that applies to many instances of constitutional interpretation. Often, constitutional provisions are stated in language the broad purpose of which is quite plain, even though the semantic or assertive content of that language is, by design, overly general. The intent is to articulate a reasonably clear, enduring normative goal the advancement of which, over time, will involve concrete implementations that cannot be foreseen. The overly general content of the constitutional provision keeps the normative goal clearly in mind, while signaling to relevant actors that although care must be taken to adhere to the goal, the actions counted as doing so may not always be those that strictly conform to the literal content of the provision, as originally adopted, but rather are, to a certain extent, up for negotiation. The foundational feature of the law that is exploited in this complex process, and accorded its greatest scope, is the necessary and recognized role of interpretation in resolving conflicts that arise when the purposes that a law, ordinance, or constitutional provision are designed to serve clash with literal applications of its existing content in new cases.[22]

Having come this far, we are now in a position to extend the lessons about textualism drawn from the interpretation of vague texts to cover cases in which interpretation is required to eliminate inconsistencies—either between two or more different laws (together with the facts of a given case), or between the literal application of the law in a particular case and the purpose the law was designed to serve. The precisification of vague legal texts and the resolution of legal inconsistencies make up a large proportion of the "hard cases" about which theories of legal interpretation are offered as guides to proper conclusions. Since what courts are called upon to do in all such cases is to change, rather than ascertain, existing content, it is a category mistake to think that textualism—which is first and foremost a theory of content—is capable of playing this role.

6. A note about legal positivism

There is a corresponding lesson about legal positivism. In some cases, the court properly makes substantive evaluative judgments in coming to a decision that determines what the law is. Since legal positivism says that one can determine what the law is without making any such judgments, there may seem to be a conflict here. Of course, there is not. Legal positivism would be

---

[22] Though this foundational feature of the law is often exploited in constitutional interpretation, it is not the only feature operative in such cases. For example, the resolution of vagueness is also important.

patently absurd if it held that evaluative judgments and evaluative reasoning do not guide those who make the laws. Since judges sometimes do this, any proper understanding of positivism will make room for the idea that the task confronting them in interpreting the law sometimes goes beyond the descriptive task of ascertaining the content of existing law by tracing its authoritative sources. When judges fill in gaps in a vague law, revise existing laws by removing previously unnoticed or unimportant inconsistencies, or override the content of an existing law because its literal application in a particular case clearly conflicts with the fundamental purpose the legislation was designed to serve, the judicial action has a law-making role the proper exercise of which may, in some cases, involve limited normative, or evaluative, reasoning on the part of the judges.

7. Purpose and normativity

The point here—that much judicial interpretation is law-making and hence normative—should not lead one to jump to the conclusion that all such interpretation has this character. It is, of course, true that a great deal of adjudication, consisting in the routine application of pre-existing legal content to normal, run-of-the-mill cases, involves little, if any, real interpretation. However, there are also cases in which substantive, non-normative interpretation is required to identify pre-existing legal content which, together with the facts of the case, fully determine the legally correct result. In these cases the legal content in question—which is that asserted or stipulated by law-makers in adopting a text—outstrips the semantic content of the text used for that purpose. These cases divide into (at least) three subtypes: (i) those in which the assertive or stipulative intentions of law-makers fill a gap in the semantic content of a text that is nonspecific on a crucial point,[23] (ii) those in which law-makers partially precisify the content of a vague term by explicitly applying it (or its negation) to an item that would normally be regarded as a borderline case,[24] and (iii) those in which law-makers innocently misdescribe, or misstate, the content of their own (primary) assertion, due to readily explainable ignorance of the extension of one or more of the terms they employ.[25] In these cases, the interpretive task of sleuthing out what the law-

---

[23] See the discussions of *Smith v United States* in Soames (2009a) and Neale (2007). More on the supplementation of semantically incomplete or nonspecific content can be found in Soames (2010a) at ch 7.

[24] Soames (2009a) at pp 418–9.

[25] For discussion of *Nix v Hedden* 149 US 304 (1893): Soames (2009a) at pp 407–10.

makers actually said or asserted, and, in so doing, determining the legal content to be applied to the facts of the case, require nuanced and sophisticated judgments that are primarily descriptive rather than normative in character.

A further deflationary point can be made about many cases in which interpretation is required to resolve an inconsistency between the purposes of a piece of legislation and its literal application in unforeseen circumstances. If, as seems reasonable, identifying the purposes of the legislation is primarily a descriptive task, so too should be the determination of whether the literal application of its content to the facts of a new case would accord, or conflict, with those purposes (or perhaps be orthogonal to them). After all, one does not have to share someone's purpose to know that he has it, or to know what conflicts with, or advances, it. Where, then, is the normativity?

In cases of conflict—or of orthogonal non-advancement that would impose other costs—a judgment must be made about the costs and benefits of carving out an exception. Do these potential benefits outweigh the potential diminution of the legislation's purposes that may come from narrowing their scope? In many cases this will involve judgments not just about the size of the hit to the values the legislation was designed to promote, but also about the identity, extent, and relative importance of other values brought into play by the potential exception. This is the locus of normativity in cases of interpretation in which the purposes of a legal provision conflict with the literal application of its content in novel circumstances. Similar points apply to the adjudication of cases in which the contents of two or more legal provisions (neither of which has inherent priority over the other) are jointly inconsistent with the facts of the case. In such situations, the court has no choice but to limit the scope of at least one of the relevant provisions. Typically, this will involve not only identifying the purposes served by each, and assessing the likely effects of different possible restrictions, but also of assessing the relative importance of the different values served by different resolutions, and weighing the costs and benefits of each against those of the others. There is no denying the normative elements of this enterprise. However, the scope legitimately afforded these elements is far from unlimited, but rather is tightly constrained by the web of pre-existing legal contents, and accompanying legislative purposes, that interpreters are called upon to rationalize.

Much of what I have said rests on the assumption that interpreters are often able to discern the purposes of a piece of legislation, or other legal provision, and that doing so is primarily a descriptive matter that need not involve subscribing to those purposes themselves. This combination of views is, I think, more controversial than need be. One source of avoidable contention is unclarity about what different authors mean, when speaking about interpretation, by the "purposes" of a law or other legal provision. What I mean here is *not* the causally efficacious factors that motivated the required number of law-makers to enact the law or provision. In addition to being private, and often difficult to discern, these may be as individual and various as the actors themselves. An individual law-maker may be motivated by personal or political self-interest, a desire to advance the economic interests of friends or former associates, devotion to the political fortunes of a particular faction or party, or identification with a privately held, or publically expressed, ideology. Any attempt to aggregate these, and identify the dominant motivators of the relevant group or majority, will, typically, face severe epistemic obstacles. Whether or not these obstacles can ever be overcome in interesting cases, the attempt to do so in the service of interpretation of the sort at issue here is a fool's errand. The purposes of a law or other legal provision, sought in the adjudication of hard cases, are not the causally efficacious motivators that produced the law or provision, but the chief reasons publicly offered to justify and explain its adoption.

In our simple fictional case involving the Plainsboro Town Council, the purpose of the ordinance against accepting rides from strangers was to reduce the risk of sexual assault on children going to, or returning from, school. This, we may imagine, is what the local newspaper agitated for, and how the council members explained and defended their action. Whatever private personal or political motives they may have harbored are irrelevant. The same is true of complicated real-life cases, like the health care bills that passed in the US Senate and House of Representatives in 2009. Among the motivators of individual law-makers were political payoffs in the form of special benefits for their states or districts; political contributions from groups favoring, and companies profiting from, the legislation; fear of retaliation from the presidential administration and its allies; a desire to advance the fortunes of their party and the agenda of their new president; as well as an ideological commitment to expanding government control over the economy and ushering in a more socialistic system of medicine and political economy. However, none of these were among the purposes of the legislation, in the sense relevant here. Rather its chief purposes were (i) expansion of health insurance among the previously uninsured; (ii) reduction of the total amount spent on health care without jeopardizing quality; (iii) reduction of its cost to most citizens, including the poor who would be more heavily subsidized; (iv) equalizing access to health care and insurance; and (v) making both more reliably available by severing their connection to employment.

Since these were central elements of the public rationale offered for the bills, the bills' purposes are easily discernible, and recognizing them does not presuppose endorsing them. In short, knowledge of legislative purposes is (here) unproblematic and non-normative. Normative issues can be expected to arise when details of implementation collide with presently unappreciated facts in ways that bring either the chief purposes of the bills, or the more specific, subsidiary purposes behind particular sections or clauses, into conflict with the contents of the bills' many provisions. At that point normative decisions will be required in implementation and administration, as well as in likely judicial challenges. However, the normativity involved is hardly excessive, and easily conforms to the limitations recognized by our model of interpretation.

No doubt, some will worry that the limited normativity, and appeal to legislative or constitutional purpose, here recognized to be legitimate will provide the sort of excuse all too frequently used to cover what are really unjustifiable judicial rewritings of laws and the Constitution. Though I sympathize with the worry, I do not sympathize with views that falsify what legitimate legal interpretation is, out of confused anxiety to protect citizens from abuses of a legal system based on the correct account. Any system can be gamed, and it is no argument against the limited, but legitimate, normativity of some interpretation that the uncomprehending, or unscrupulous, may abuse it.

When it comes to recognizing the purpose of legislation, more can be said to guard against such abuse. In addition to identifying such purpose with the legislation's public rationale, it is also necessary to specify the level of abstraction required. Since the purpose of the Plainsboro ordinance was to reduce the danger of sexual assaults against the town's children, the ordinance may also be said to be aimed at reducing the danger of harm to its residents. However, only the more specific of these two designations of purpose— rather than the more general designation, which provides a merely partial specification of the aim of the legislation—is relevant to interpreting hard cases. For example, even if the Mini Mart, where Susan worked, were in a dangerous part of town, and so a likely target for armed robbery, no one could reasonably argue that she should be held guilty for accepting a ride to work—even though the motorist was both undangerous and merely a borderline case of being a stranger—on the grounds that precisifying the vague legal content of the ordinance in this way would further its purpose of reducing the danger of harm to residents. On the contrary, since the purpose of the ordinance, in the sense relevant to deciding the case, is its complete purpose (given by the more specific designation), a ruling in her favor would be correct.

Though the example is fanciful, what it illustrates is not. On the contrary, the standard criticism of the landmark decisions reached in *Griswold v Connecticut*[26] (concerning laws restricting the sale of contraceptives) and

---

[26] 381 US 479 (1965).

Roe v Wade[27] (concerning laws restricting abortion) can be understood as involving reasoning of the same general sort. According to US Supreme Court Associate Justice William O. Douglas, writing for the majority in *Griswold*:

[The guarantees in] the Bill of Rights have penumbras, formed by emanations from those guarantees that help give them life and substance. Various guarantees create *zones of privacy*. The right of association contained in the penumbra of the First Amendment is one, as we have seen. The Third Amendment in its prohibition against the quartering of soldiers "in any house" in time of peace without the consent of the owner is another facet of that *privacy*. The Fourth Amendment explicitly affirms the "right of the people to be secure in their persons, houses, papers, and effects, against unreasonable searches and seizures." The Fifth Amendment in its Self-Incrimination Clause enables the citizen to create *a zone of privacy* which government may not force him to surrender to his detriment. (Emphasis mine)

The standard criticism of this decision is that whereas it is true that several amendments to the Constitution were adopted to establish particular privacy rights, no general right of privacy covering contraception (or abortion) were thereby established. Putting this objection in the analytical framework outlined here, we acknowledge that the provisions mentioned by Douglas were adopted for the purpose of establishing strong, but rebuttable, legal presumptions against the passage of laws infringing the particular privacy rights specified. We further acknowledge that the original assertive or stipulative contents of the relevant Constitutional clauses adopted for these purposes were not intended to settle, for all time, precisely which prospective laws would be constitutionally prohibited. Our earlier discussion of the First Amendment guarantee of freedom of speech, and of the press, emphasized legitimate future narrowings of the content expressed by language recognized to be overly expansive in certain ways. A similar point can be made to allow for a limited expansion of that content extending the guarantee to some forms of expression, which, though not strictly speech, share with speech the primary function of communicating ideas. Even recognizing all of this, Douglas's conclusion cannot be reached. Although the contents of the constitutional guarantees he mentions may, legitimately, evolve over time to better serve their motivating purposes, and although each may correctly be said to have been aimed at securing privacy (of a certain sort), such a characterization of purpose is incomplete, and insufficiently specific. Once this defect is eliminated, and the purposes governing the constitutional provisions are fully and specifically stated, the resulting set of privacy rights—though open ended and subject to continuing change—does not encompass any general right to privacy that prohibits laws

---

[27] 410 US 113 (1973).

against contraception or abortion. In sum, the proper role of normative considerations in the interpretation of hard cases—including the most sweeping constitutional provisions—is highly circumscribed, and does not provide anything like a blank check for rewriting laws or the Constitution.[28]

---

[28] Thanks to Andrei Marmor for his many valuable comments.

4

Vagueness and the Guidance of Action

Jeremy Waldron

1. Introduction

'The desideratum of clarity', said Lon Fuller, 'represents one of the most essential ingredients of legality'.[1] And Joseph Raz gives us the reason: 'An ambiguous, vague, obscure, or imprecise law is likely to mislead or confuse at least some of those who desire to be guided by it.'[2] Raz lists clarity as one of the key principles of the rule of law, and he associates it (as he associates all such principles) with what he calls 'the basic intuition from which the doctrine of the rule of law derives: the law must be capable of guiding the behavior of its subjects'.[3]

Like Fuller, Raz thinks that this commitment to *guiding action* and the requirement of clarity that is founded upon it are not just technical or formalistic ideas. They are ways of respecting human dignity. Instead of manipulating a person psychologically or securing a reflex recoil with a scream of command, they approach governance in a way that takes seriously the capacities associated with ordinary human agency: capacities for practical reasoning by reference to norms that the agent can grasp and understand. Law, as H.L.A. Hart acknowledged, 'consists primarily of general standards of conduct communicated to classes of persons, who are then expected to understand and conform to the rules without further direction'.[4] Fuller's position is that embarking on this 'enterprise of subjecting human conduct to rules involves...a commitment to the view that man is...a responsible agent, capable of understanding and following rules'.[5] And Raz agrees:

A legal system which does in general observe the rule of law treats people as persons at least in the sense that it attempts to guide their behavior through affecting the

---

[1] Fuller (1964) at p 68.   [2] Raz (1979) at p 214.   [3] ibid.

[4] Hart (1994) at pp 206–7. Also ibid 38 (specifically on action-guidance by the criminal law).

[5] Fuller (1964) at p 162.

circumstances of their action. It thus presupposes that they are rational autonomous creatures and attempts to affect their actions and habits by affecting their deliberations.[6]

The question I would like to consider is whether the presence in the law of provisions that may be described as vague or unclear or imprecise is necessarily at odds with this commitment.

2. *State v Schaeffer*

An old case from Ohio, *State v Schaeffer*, gives us a couple of examples from traffic law to work with.[7] We are told in this case that, in 1917, the Ohio General Code contained the following provision:

§12604: Whoever operates a motor cycle or motor vehicle at a greater speed than eight miles an hour in the business and closely built-up portions of a municipality, or more than fifteen miles an hour in other portions thereof, or more than twenty miles an hour outside of a municipality, shall be fined not more than twenty-five dollars.

But it preceded that with a provision of quite a different character:

§12603: Whoever operates a motor vehicle or motorcycle on the public roads or highways at a speed greater than is reasonable or proper, having regard for width, traffic, use and the general and usual rules of such road or highway, or so as to endanger the property, life or limb of any person, shall be fined not more than twenty-five dollars.[8]

The difference is stark: §12604 worked with precise numerical speed limits: 8 mph in some areas, 15 mph in other areas, and 20 mph on the open road. The limits strike us as absurdly low, but this was 1917—and at least a driver would know what was expected of him. However, §12603 approached the matter in an entirely different way. It did not use numerical speed limits; instead it spoke of 'a speed greater than is reasonable or proper'. Compared to §12604, §12603 is vague and imprecise, and because of that it seems likely, in Raz's words, 'to mislead or confuse at least some of those who desire to be guided by it'. True, §12604 is not a paragon of precision. The phrase 'in the business and closely built-up portions of a municipality' is not a precise specification of a zone of application for the 8 mph limit; those who know anything about urban geography know that business districts have vague edges and the term 'built-up' has its own vagueness. §12603 avoids those forms of vagueness by applying universally to any public road or highway, but it more than makes up for that in the vagueness of the speed limit it lays down.

---

[6] Raz (1979) at p 222.   [7] *State v Schaeffer* 117 NE 220 (1917).   [8] ibid 222.

A driver—a Mr EE Schaeffer—ran over and fatally injured a 3-year-old boy known as Buley Csaki who was playing in the street in a built-up area with a large number of other children. The state said he was driving at 25 to 30 mph; Schaeffer denied this, saying he was going no faster than 8 mph.[9] Perhaps to avoid the factual issue, the state proceeded against him with a manslaughter charge based on an alleged violation of §12603. Schaeffer was convicted and, on appeal, he complained 'that section 12603 ... is unconstitutional and void, for the reason that it is too indefinite and uncertain in its terms'. His claim was that

the words 'reasonable' and 'proper' are so general, comprehensive, and variable that it would be impossible for the defendant to know, or for the jury to fairly determine what was a violation of the statute; that juries in one case would hold a speed to be reasonable, while the same speed under the same circumstances might be held by another jury in the same county, at the same time, to be unreasonable. In short, it is urged that the statute should definitely fix what is a reasonable speed and a proper operation of a car.[10]

Constitutional doctrine provided then, as it provides now, that statutes can be struck down as void for vagueness, either because they fail to comply with the US Constitution's Sixth Amendment requirement that the accused 'be informed of the nature and cause of the accusation' or because their vagueness represents a failure of due process.

But the Supreme Court of Ohio unanimously rejected this complaint, and Mr Schaeffer's conviction was upheld. I believe it was rightly upheld. More important, I think the Ohio court's reasoning in the vindication of §12603 helps us see the complicated ways in which a vague or imprecise provision can still succeed in guiding the actions of those subject to it. What the court said was this:

The Legislature ... in this instance, saw fit to fix no definite rate of speed for the car. ... Some statutes have undertaken to fix a rate of speed which would be prima facie dangerous, but a rate of speed dangerous in one situation would be quite safe in another situation, and if the rate of speed were definitely fixed, naturally it would have to be the minimum speed at which cars might be safely driven, because that speed would have to be a safeguard against every possible situation which would be perilous even at a speed of six or eight miles an hour. There is no place in all the public [roads] where a situation is not constantly changing from comparatively no traffic to a most congested traffic; from no foot travelers to a throng of them; from open and clear intersections, private drives, and street crossings, to those that are crowded; from free and unobstructed streets to streets filled with crowds of foot travelers and others getting off and on street cars and other vehicles. In order to meet these varying situations, and impose upon the automobilist [*sic*] the duty of anticipating them and guarding against the dangers that arise out of them, this statute was evidently passed in the interests of the public safety in a public highway.[11]

---

[9] ibid 221–2.   [10] ibid 228–9.   [11] ibid 225 and 226.

The court went on to say that it is precisely the statute's 'adaptability to meet every dangerous situation' that commends it as a valid enactment:

Absolute or mathematical certainty is not required in the framing of a statute. Reasonable certainty of the nature and cause of the offense is all that is required. Some offenses admit of much greater precision and definiteness than others; but it is quite obvious that in the case at bar the statute must be sufficiently elastic and adaptable to meet all the dangerous situations presented, to adequately safeguard the travelling public, whether foot passenger, horse, or motor vehicle. Section 12603 is as definite and certain on the subject-matter and the numerous situations arising thereunder as the nature of the case and the safety of the public will reasonably admit.[12]

The court was not convinced by the complaint that different juries might apply §12603 in different ways: this, it said, 'is inevitable under any system of jurisprudence on any set of facts involved in a criminal transaction'. In all sorts of areas of the law, courts use what is called 'the rule of reason'—from *reasonable doubt* in the ordinary charge to a jury in criminal cases, to *reasonable grounds for believing that one is in danger* in a case of self-defense. And the Ohio court added this about the provision in question:

The careful, conservative driver need have no fear of it. The reckless, wanton speed maniac needs to be kept in fear of [§12603]. The life of the humblest citizen must be placed above the gratification of the motor maniac, who would turn the public highways into a race course.[13]

This last point is well worth emphasizing, indicating as it does that there are different postures a person can strike, different attitudes one can have, toward the sort of guidance offered by law. I shall take it up at the end of this chapter in section 9.

In the sections that follow, I want to consider these issues in a more abstract way; I want to explore the complexity of the idea of a legal provision guiding the action of those subject to it. Like Raz—indeed like almost everyone writing in jurisprudence today—I accept that *guiding action* (or *guiding conduct* or *guiding behavior*) is the mode of governance distinctive to law. (I do not think it is right to say—as some do—that guiding action is the function of law.[14] Rather it is the distinctive way in which law performs whatever functions

---

[12] ibid 236.   [13] ibid 236.

[14] Jules Coleman seems to attribute this formulation to H.L.A. Hart, or to H.L.A. Hart on Stephen Perry's or Scott Shapiro's understanding of Hart: Coleman (2001) at p 206. But Coleman also provides a more accurate formulation when he writes: 'Hart notes not only that law can serve a variety of important and legitimate human interests, but that it does so in a distinctive manner through rules that guide conduct' (ibid 144).

are given to it by law-makers.)[15] But I believe we need to approach the question of unclarity, vagueness, and imprecision in law[16] with a more sophisticated notion of guidance than the one we often use. Having one's action guided by a norm is not just a matter of finding out about the norm and conforming one's behavior to its specifications.[17] It can involve a more complex engagement of practical reason and practical deliberation than that. So that is what I shall explore in the pages that follow.

3. The model of rules

Let us begin with a simple question about the ordinary case. What is it for action to be guided by a rule? On the most straightforward model—a model corresponding roughly to the last part of Ohio's §12604—the action of a person P is guided by a legal provision L_1, when the following conditions are met:

Model (i)
(1) L_1 contains a requirement that some type of behavior B_1 is to be performed (in some type of circumstance C_1).
(2) P is capable of understanding and remembering L_1.
(3) At any given time, P is capable of noticing whether he is in a circumstance of type C_1.
(4) When P notices that he is in circumstance C_1, he is capable of monitoring his behavior to see whether he is performing B_1 or not.
(5) If he finds that he is not, he is capable of modifying his behavior so that he is performing B_1 in circumstance C_1.

In the case of Ohio's §12604, circumstance C_1 might be 'driving outside of a municipality,' and behavior B_1 might be 'driving no faster than 20 mph'. P's action can be guided by this ordinance in a way that is perfectly familiar to every driver. We keep an eye out for where we are (in the country or in the city, for example), we pay attention to traffic signs, we glance at our speedometer, and we slow down or speed up accordingly. By its presence, by our understanding of its provisions, and through the connection between that

---

[15] Analogously, on Max Weber's account, the monopolization of legitimate force is not the function of the state—Weber says it is impossible to attribute a function to the state as such—but rather the mode in which it performs whatever functions are assigned to it: (1970) at p 77.

[16] In this chapter, I shall not pursue the distinctions that are sometimes needed as between different kinds of indeterminacy, such as ambiguity, vagueness, and contestability. I set these out in Waldron (1994) at p 509.

[17] cf Shapiro (2001) at pp 169–82.

understanding and our own practical agency, the traffic law guides our actions.

Notice that this model of action-guiding is quite different from any idea of P's simply responding to, as though galvanized by, a command to do B_1. Model (i) highlights distinctive features of human agency: the ability to internalize a norm,[18] to monitor and control one's behavior on the basis of that norm, and the ability to notice the features of one's environment and circumstances and relate those to the other abilities just mentioned in the service of compliance with the internalized norm. Possession of these capacities is an important aspect of human dignity: Fuller and Raz both emphasized this and I have tried to give it prominence in my own recent writings about the connection between dignity and the rule of law.[19] Though model (i) uses the term 'behavior' to characterize what is required of P, it is not a 'behaviorist' model; it takes seriously the mental and epistemic aspects of full-blooded human agency. And it does seem to presuppose a clarity requirement. The kind of self-monitoring and self-control indicated in conditions (3), (4), and (5) assumes that P has clear sense of the circumstances that L_1 makes salient and the form of behavior that L_1 seeks to elicit in those circumstances. P is supposed to be able to match his perception to the clear indication from L_1 that it matters whether he is in circumstance C_1 (as opposed to some other circumstance); and he is supposed to be able to match the monitoring and control of his behavior to the clear indication from L_1 that it matters whether he is performing B_1 in that circumstance or not. With the best will in the world (by which I mean the best attitude toward law and its requirements),[20] he may be in difficulty so far as the relation between the law and his agency is concerned, if the specification of the relevant circumstance or the specification of the required behavior is indeterminate.

4. The model of standards

Though the simple model I have just given indicates ways in which the imposition of straightforward legal requirements respects human agency, the capacities that model (i) presupposes are not the only practical capacities that

---

[18] I mean 'internalize' in the straightforward sense given by condition (2); I do not mean anything more deeply psychological than that, nor do I mean, necessarily, that the person comes to endorse the norm in question.

[19] Fuller (1964) and Raz (1979); also Waldron (2010a).

[20] cf Hart (1994) at p 40, on 'the "puzzled man"...who is willing to do what is required if only he can be told what it is'; and Finnis (1980) at pp 316–7, on the idea of 'the law-abiding citizen'.

individuals have. Consider a more complicated model, corresponding to Ohio's §12603:

Model (ii)

(1) L_2 contains a requirement to the effect that there should be some appropriate modification of one's behavior whenever circumstance C_2 occurs.

(2) P is capable of understanding and remembering L_2.

(3) At any given time, P is capable of noticing whether circumstance C_2 has occurred.

(4) When P notices that circumstance C_2 is occurring or has occurred, he is capable of considering what behavior is now appropriate.

(5) Pursuant to that judgment, P is capable of monitoring his action to determine whether he is behaving in what he judges to be an appropriate way in circumstance C_2.

(6) If he judges that he is not behaving in an appropriate way in circumstance C_2, P is capable of modifying his behavior so that it does become appropriate for circumstance C_2.

In our example, C_2 may be any of the factors alluded to in §12603, such as the narrowness of the roadway, the amount of traffic, or the presence of other factors (such as small children playing on the road), which may make one's ordinary driving—one's usual speed, for example—a potential danger to life or property. And the legal provision requires us to drive at a speed no greater than is 'reasonable or proper' for those circumstances.

What is distinct about this model is the failure to *specify* the action that is to be performed when P is in the new circumstance C_2. It is up to P to figure out what action is appropriate. For example, traffic laws often require drivers to lower their speed, below the posted speed limit, when bad weather (a blizzard or a severe rainstorm) strikes the freeway or when they become aware that an accident has taken place ahead of them. The legislature may not specify a lower speed limit for these circumstances, because what is an appropriate speed may vary so much depending on what else is going on (how much traffic there is, for example, or how bad the accident is) that it makes more sense for drivers to be left to figure this out for themselves. This does not mean that the law endorses whatever the driver decides to do; P may still be cited for driving at an unreasonable speed in the circumstances, because a police officer judges that P's calculation at step (4) is culpably mistaken; and he may be convicted if a judge accepts that view. But just because he can be second-guessed by a police officer does not mean that one might as well specify a speed limit for C_2; all it means is that the particularized calculation required at step (4) is capable of being assessed by law.

Like the Ohio Supreme Court, I believe that L_2 guides action in model (ii). True, it does not do so by precisely specifying an action to be performed, but it offers input into P's agency nevertheless, directing his practical reason to a problem to which the law draws his attention, and requiring him to come up with and implement a solution.

We sometimes say that what distinguishes model (ii) from model (i) is that in (ii) the legal provision is presented in the form of a standard rather than a rule. And when we distinguish rules from standards, we sometimes say that the difference is that a standard is a norm that requires some evaluative judgment of the person who applies it, whereas a rule is a norm presented as the end product of evaluative judgments already made by the law-maker. A posted speed limit of 55 mph represents a value judgment already made by the legislature that that speed is appropriate for driving in the designated area. A legal requirement to drive at a 'reasonable' speed, by contrast, looks for a value judgment to be made downstream from the legislature; it indicates that the legislature has not decided to make all the requisite value judgments itself, but has left some to be made by the law-applier. That characterization of the difference between rules and standards is helpful here, but only if we remember that the first law-applier is not the police officer who pulls the driver over and issues a citation or the judge in traffic court who decides whether or not to enter a conviction. The first law-applier is P, the driver himself.[21] Aware of the norm, he takes it on-board—internalizes it—and makes for himself the evaluative judgment that the norm requires him to make, and monitors and modifies his behavior accordingly. He may do so well or badly; and if he does it badly, he may be liable to citation, conviction, and penalty; and this too he is aware of. All of this adds up to the distinctive way in which P's action is guided by L_2 in model (ii).

Notice that the mode of action-guidance in model (ii) is also compatible with the commitment to dignity that I mentioned in section 1 and at the end of section 3, and to forms of governance that respect human dignity and take seriously the agency of those to whom legal norms are addressed. The dignity of a human agent does not just consist in his estimable capacities for normative comprehension, self-monitoring, and the moderating of his own behavior; it also consists more broadly in his capacity for practical deliberation in both structured and unstructured ways. An open-ended standard of the kind we are considering invokes that capacity and relies on it. It credits the subject with the sophisticated ability to adapt his agency to his own practical thinking when this is required of him, and it indicates the kind of circumstance in

---

[21] For the idea of self-application as a most important moment in the legal process, see Hart and Sacks (1994) at p 120.

which that ability is required. Such a requirement may be more onerous than a simple requirement to comply with a numerical rule, but it certainly treats people as having the dignity to respond positively to this task.

By the way, I am not saying that what L_2 instructs P to do is 'pull over and ponder' (so to speak) as though it were dictating the actual implementation of P's engagement of his powers of practical reasoning. The authorities do not care what sort of thinking process P actually goes through or how long it takes him; what they want him to do is drive at a reasonable and proper speed. They expect that he will respond to this instruction using his powers of practical reasoning oriented to the circumstances he is in. But practical reason can be exercised in all sorts of ways, some of them quick and implicit, some of them sustained and reflective. The law is indifferent about that. (In everything that follows, I am using 'practical reason' in a way that reflects the force of this point.)

5. Judgment and guidance

I can imagine a pedant saying that my analysis of model (ii) unhelpfully elides the distinction between judgment (of what action is appropriate) and the guidance of action on the basis of that judgment. In as much as the law requires the former, it is not *action* that it is guiding. The pedant may bolster this position by developing the following contrast with model (i): model (i) assumes that the legislature has reached a value judgment about the desirability or moral necessity of B_1 (eg driving at a certain speed) in circumstance C_1. That was something the legislators had to do—at what we might call the evaluation stage of the law-making process—before they could finally draft, enact, and promulgate L_1. Maybe this was something they argued about, did research about, felt unsure about, and so on. But they did not begin the process of guiding the action of those subject to their authority until they had completed all that thinking and debating at the evaluative stage. Once that was done—but only then—they were in a position to guide the action of people like P. Similarly, the pedant might say, in model (ii), a legislature that leaves it up to P (and those reviewing P's behavior) to formulate the appropriate speed for circumstance C_2 is not guiding P's action; by leaving the evaluative stage to P, it is casting him in the legislative role, leaving it up to him to guide his own action only after he has determined for himself, in his capacity as a delegated law-maker, a speed limit for the circumstances. In other words, in model (ii), the pedant will say, step (4) is not an instance of action-guidance.

I think the pedant's point is misconceived. Model (ii) as we have presented it does involve some determinate guidance offered to P by the law-maker.

True, it is not a case of the law-maker saying, 'Do precisely this.' But the law-maker identifies a salient type of circumstance or pairing of circumstances, indicates that some adjustment of behavior is appropriate when the circumstances are overtaken by the other, attempts to focus P's practical reason on what that change of behavior should be, and indicates by whatever penal provision is attached to L_2 that P should take this whole business seriously. That is guidance. The law in model (ii) guides P's practical reasoning through certain channels and in certain directions. It evinces a certain faith in that reasoning, in the sense that it empowers P's practical reasoning rather than seeking to dominate or supersede it. But what it indicates will *not* be tolerated is a failure on P's part to orient his practical reasoning to the circumstances specified by the law-maker.

Maybe we can quibble about words and debate whether this is a case of guiding action rather than guiding the use of practical reason. For myself, I see little daylight between the two ideas. But if our pedant wants to insist on the contrast, then we should respond by revisiting the initial premise of our account, namely that law's function is to guide action. There is, after all, nothing canonical about the phrase 'guiding action'. If a sharp contrast between (a) 'guiding action' and (b) 'engaging practical reason' is causing difficulty here, then we should reconsider the proposition that 'guiding action' is how law characteristically proceeds. We may want to say that that is what was intended in a broad inclusive sense—a sense that might include (a) and (b)—not in a narrow sense that focused on (a) to the exclusion of (b). We might want to say that everything valuable and important about the premise that law characteristically proceeds by guiding action is secured by the broader sense of 'guiding action' and nothing of importance is lost by rejecting the narrow sense.

6. Raz on authority

Our pedant might have put his point in terms of Joseph Raz's theory of authority.[22] He might say that, according to Raz, law claims authority and law can only claim authority if particular legal directives represent somebody's view of how somebody else should behave. This is because a claim to authority over P is always a claim that P would be better off following the guidance

---

[22] Raz (1986) at chs 2–3.

of the person claiming authority than trying to figure things out for himself. So—on this interpretation of Raz's approach—nothing which does not represent such a view can have authority attributed to it. And nothing can plausibly count as an exercise of authority if its net effect is to leave P in the position of having to figure out the issue for himself. Model (i) seems to satisfy this set of requirements, but—the Razian pedant will say—model (ii) does not. In model (ii), P has to do all the figuring out for himself and the view to which he subjects himself—the view expressed in L_2—is simply that it is incumbent on him to do this.

I actually believe that Raz's position is (or can be made) more accommodating than this.[23] And certainly, as I have already indicated, the guidance given in L_2 is not quite that indeterminate. Though Raz does in some places use the language of the law's representing the judgment of someone else on what exactly P ought to do, in other places he phrases his position more abstractly. One thing he says is that a law 'must represent the judgment of the alleged authority on the reasons which apply to its subjects'.[24] Now a person may have certain reasons for action, and a person may also have certain reasons for thinking (I mean reasons for practical thinking).[25] We sometimes say of a person who we think made a hasty decision: 'He ought to have taken more time and care to think this decision through' or 'He had reason to deliberate on this matter more carefully than in fact he did.' Having a reason to deliberate carefully means having a reason to pay particular attention to the reasons that one has for acting.[26] One can be guided on the former set of reasons (reasons to deliberate) as well as on the latter (reasons to behave in a certain way). Often we form our own view of how much deliberation to expend on a given decision that we face, and sometimes we make mistakes about this. An advisor may say to us, 'I don't know what you should do about the decision you face, but I am certain that you should take more time over it

---

[23] I see no point in getting into a debate about what precisely Raz meant. He has used a number of formulations in different books and essays, and it is his general position in this matter, not any particular formulation, that is useful for jurisprudence.

[24] Raz (1994) at p 219.

[25] I am not drawing the familiar distinction here between practical and epistemic authority; instead I am distinguishing between practical reasons for acting in some matter and practical reasons for deliberating (in a certain way or in a certain set of circumstances or for a certain time) over how to act in that matter.

[26] I could use the language of 'second-order' reasons here, but I think that would be a mistake, at least as an interpretation of Raz's view. According to Raz, a second-order reason is a reason to act (or not act) on a reason: (1999) at p 39. That is not what I am talking about. I am talking about reasons to pay attention to reasons, reasons to think or deliberate about reasons. This too is a second-order idea, but it is a different sort of second-order idea (ibid 184, distinguishing exclusionary reasons from reasons 'to avoid thinking, considering, or attending to certain matters').

than you are proposing to take.' If we accept that advice, we are in some sense accepting authority: we are submitting ourselves to the judgment of the advisor on reasons that apply to us—the set of reasons for and against taking a given amount of time to deliberate on an issue. It would be quite wrong to say that this cannot count as an exercise of authority simply because the advisor does not give us his bottom-line view on what we ought, finally, to do.

If this is correct, then Raz's conception of authority does not support the pedant's position. In model (ii), L_2 does represent the legislature's view of reasons that apply to P, but it is the legislator's view about reasons that apply to P's deliberating. The legislator has taken a view about when P's deliberating on the possibility of a change in his behavior is appropriate or requisite. The legislator says, 'Such deliberating is appropriate or requisite when circumstance C_2 occurs. You had better deliberate carefully about what to do when this happens, and, since you may be second-guessed by a police officer and a court, you had better take this seriously.'

So a law like the one presented in model (ii) *is* an action-guiding norm, once one recognizes the complexity and multi-layered aspect of action-guidance. It mobilizes some or many of the resources of practical reason or practical intelligence possessed by the norm subject—a mobilization that might not take place if the law-maker had not promulgated L_2—and it puts those resources to work in determining what the subject is to do. And it does so in a way that channels and directs the use of practical reason, without specifying what its outcome is to be. This is an important guidance function, and if it is our view that law aims to guide action, we should not disqualify norms like this from counting as law, simply because they do not fully specify the action that is to be performed. L_2 does communicate to P what is expected of him: the difference is that what is expected of P in this case is something different in kind or level than what is expected of P in model (i).

In characterizing Raz's position, some people attribute to him the view that law, if it is to be authoritative, must be such that those subject to it can figure out what it requires without recourse to moral judgment on their own part.[27] This formulation needs to be treated very carefully. It is true that P cannot figure out what behavior to engage in, pursuant to L_2, without making a moral judgment. But what L_2 in effect says to him is something like, 'Now is the time for you to engage your practical reason to figure out what difference circumstance C_2 should make to your behavior.' In our driving example, §12603 said to Mr Schaeffer that the dangers an automobile evidently posed to children playing in the street indicated the need for practical deliberation about his speed (either quick and implicit deliberation in the case of a skilled

---

[27] eg Dworkin (2002) at pp 1671–5.

and responsive driver or more sustained reflection in the case of a driver not habituated to deliberation of this kind). And *that* instruction—'Now is the time to deliberate'—can be identified without moral deliberation. True, the instruction is to deliberate, and once we have identified it we cannot follow it without engaging in moral reasoning; but the moral reasoning is not essential to figuring out that that is what the driver is being instructed to do.

7. Minimal guidance?

Someone might object that the guidance element in model (ii) is minimal. Simply to show that there is *some* action-guiding element in L_2 is not enough. Almost any vague provision will direct the norm-subject's attention to his own behavior in some way: even 'Do the right thing' can be construed as an instruction to 'Watch what you are doing', so that it elicits some slight change of orientation in the practical reason of the person to whom it is addressed. But—goes the objection—this is not the same as saying that the provision succeeds in guiding action. A law must let a person know what is expected of him; it is not enough to simply alert P to the fact that something is expected of him and to gesture in a vague ballpark sort of way toward the area of action (eg driving or the speed at which one is driving) with which that expectation is concerned.

The objection proceeds from the fact that it is possible to guide action to a greater or lesser extent. But that is also the basis of our answer to the objection. The behavior that is elicited by a given directive can be specified in more or less detail: so §12604 tells drivers to lower their speed from 20 mph to 15 mph when they enter a municipal area, but it does not tell them what gears to use as they lower their speed, or how sharply they should brake to bring this about. Is this an objection to §12604? Must every legal provision be as precise and specified as it is possible to be?[28] No; legislatures differ in what they are trying to achieve so far as the fine texture of action-guidance is concerned and, usually by their terms, they can indicate that to the citizen. So in the case of the Ohio speed limit, it is evidently no part of the legislative intention to guide the choice of transmission mode (when to down-shift etc) at which the slowing to the lower speed is achieved. Within reason, a lowering of speed to 15 mph is acceptable by whatever means the driver chooses to use. The provision makes it clear that it is the velocity rather than the mode of

---

[28] cf the discussion of detail and abstractness in Hayek (1960) at pp 150–3. Hayek believes that specifying action in fine detail is typical of the rule of custom, whereas abstract, coarse-grained guidance is typical of the rule of law.

achieving the velocity that it is concerned with. Something similar is true of §12603. A commonsense approach to the language of the provision indicates that the legislature has deliberately chosen a certain strategy of flexibility and it has communicated *that choice* to the citizen as part of the impact it expects to have upon his agency. As the Ohio court observed, 'it is quite obvious that in the case at bar the statute must be sufficiently elastic and adaptable to meet all the dangerous situations presented, to adequately safeguard the travelling public'.[29] The statute presents itself to the citizen in that spirit.

Again, the objection we are considering (and answering) here can be restated in Razian terms. In a recent paper, Raz poses this rhetorical question: 'If it is the purpose of the law to make a difference to our life, does it not follow that its realization of its purpose depends on its ability to exclude morality?'[30] He thinks the answer is 'Yes', and, although that does not imply that law has to require something of us which is quite different from what morality requires of us—law, he says, often 'modifies rather than excludes the way moral considerations apply'[31]—still it seems to suggest that there is something problematic about a statute which does little more than reiterate what morality requires anyway.

So consider §12603. Drivers are already subject to the requirements of morality, and, even before law intervenes, morality requires those who operate motor vehicles do not drive them at a speed greater than is reasonable or proper, having regard for width, traffic, use, and the general and usual rules of such roads or highways, and so on. Even in our broader sense of action-guidance, morality requires drivers to consider how reasonable their driving is in various circumstances. All this is something that a conscientious driver would figure out without the aid of §12603. So what, if anything, does §12603 add in the way of practical guidance? What practical difference does it make?[32] With §12603, we know what the law adds: a determinate speed limit or set of speed limits that moral reasoning by itself would not necessarily yield. But all that §12603 does is, in effect, to repeat the demands of morality.

I must say that I do not see this as a problem. All sorts of laws repeat the demands of morality: a law prohibiting murder does that. Laws reiterating the demands of morality serve an important function. They give public expression to important values and requirements. They help in moral education. They authorize sanctions for moral violations. And above all they guide the behavior of those who might not otherwise attend to moral requirements. Sure, moral requirements are incumbent on everyone; everyone ought to be

---

[29] *State v Schaeffer* 117 NE 220 (1917) at p 236.   [30] Raz (2004) at p 8.
[31] ibid 9.   [32] Coleman (2001) at pp 137–48.

guided by them without further ado. But some are not guided by morality because they are badly brought up or indifferent to moral considerations, and some are not guided consistently by morality in particular situations because of weakness of will or forgetfulness or the poor quality of their moral reasoning. So a law like §12603, which merely reiterates the demands of responsible driving, has a very important ancillary role to play. In playing that role it makes two sorts of practical difference: it helps morality to make the practical difference that morality makes, and it makes the practical difference of forcing people to focus on the moral demands incumbent upon them.

8. Thick predicates

Model (ii) concerned the legal use of all-purpose evaluative predicates—like 'reasonable' or 'proper' or 'appropriate'. I have argued that such norms (such standards) are action-guiding, though what they guide in the first instance is the element of practical deliberation involved in the exercise of agency. I think the same can be said about standards that use thick moral terms like 'inattentive' and 'aggressive'. They too guide practical reasoning (and action based on that reasoning), but they provide additional structure and channeling for the practical deliberation that they elicit. Suppose the Ohio General Code had complemented the provisions we have already studied with the following further (but imaginary) provision:

Section 12605: Whoever operates a motor vehicle or motorcycle in an aggressive or inattentive manner on the public roads or highways shall be fined not more than twenty-five dollars.

Had there been cell phones and texting in 1917, the code might have included specific prohibitions on taking calls or sending text messages. Had there been road rage back then, it might have prohibited the loud use of particular curse words. But we are imagining, instead, broader, more abstract prohibitions.

A term like 'inattentive' or 'aggressive' singles out a particular kind of evaluation that it invites us to make, relative to our conduct or (if one is a police officer) relative to the conduct of someone else. By a *kind* of evaluation, I mean an evaluation that pays attention to a subset of all the features of a situation that might be thought relevant from the broadest evaluative point of view. A given episode of driving might be evaluated in all sorts of ways— ranging from its speed to its necessity (as in the wartime slogan 'Is your journey necessary?'), but inattentiveness focuses evaluative attention on just some of those features, namely the driver's awareness and alertness to the surrounding circumstances, including the road, the conditions, and actions of the other road users, as well as to the information that his own automobile presents in terms of speed instruments, noise, etc. The prohibition on inattentive driving starts us off down some paths of evaluation and not others. So, for example, a police officer given the task of pulling over inattentive drivers will be zeroing in on some particular aspects of driving, such as where the driver's gaze is directed, or at behavior (swerving etc) likely to result from undue distraction. And equally the driver himself, confronted with §12605, will remind himself of the importance of attentiveness and include this among the dimensions on which he plans and monitors his behavior. True, the standard does not tell him precisely what to do—where to look when, how often to glance at his dashboard or to the right and to the left at what is happening in other lanes— but it instructs him to begin thinking about what actions are required *under this heading*.

The same is true of the prohibition on aggressive driving. Before he became aware of this rule, it may not have occurred to the individual driver that he should develop modes of evaluation of his own conduct along this dimension of aggressiveness. He might have been thinking, 'The more aggression the better', provided he takes sufficient care; nobody wants undue timidity on the road. Or he may not have given the matter any thought at all, just routinely driving too close to cars that he wants to overtake or using his horn when someone is in his way. But now the law indicates to him that aggression is a bad thing and that he had better engage his practical reasoning to figure out what a prohibition on this aspect of driving behavior might reasonably be thought to involve in the various circumstances in which he finds himself. The law assumes that he is capable of this—ie capable of initiating and engaging in the forms of practical reason that flow from an awareness (perhaps an awareness for the first time) that there is a problem with aggressive driving. It assumes he is capable of reflection on this matter and capable too of mapping the results of such reflection onto the monitoring and modification of his own driving habits. So, this too is *law guiding action*, only the guidance now demands an even more complicated and constrained structuring of practical deliberation.

9. Inchoate rules?

Henry Hart and Albert Sacks, in their great work, *The Legal Process*, refer to a category of norms that they call 'inchoate rules'. An inchoate rule is a norm that has the appearance of something that seeks to manage and control all aspects of its application, but for some reason fails to do so, leaving it in effect for the courts to settle the precise nature of the directive that is given. They say, '[a]n inchoate rule is, in effect, a partial postponement of the authoritative determination of public policy as to the matters left uncertain'.[33] In the account that they give, an inchoate rule does not become a complete rule until the courts have contributed significantly to our understanding of it by 'reasoned elaboration'. Hart and Sacks explain this process in a section of their book entitled 'The Process of Reasoned Elaboration of Purportedly Determinate Directions'.[34]

Of the provisions we have been examining, it is arguable that §12604 is inchoate in this sense because it specifies speed limits but not precise delimitations of where they kick into operation. As I noted earlier, the phrase 'in the business and closely built-up portions of a municipality' is not a precise specification of a zone of application for the 8 mph limit; those who know anything about urban geography know that business districts have vague edges and the term 'built-up' has its own vagueness.

Are norms like §12603 and §12605 inchoate rules? I do not think so. They are not purportedly determinate; they are, to use another phrase from Hart and Sacks, 'avowedly indeterminate'.[35] As I said in sections 5–6 and as the Ohio court noted, the legislature made clear its intention to communicate a flexible standard in §12603, and I am stipulating that the same sort of intention is evident from our imaginary §12605. The legislature does not want these norms pinned down to a precise and exact meaning that will govern all future cases; that would detract from the very elasticity that it is aiming at and it would detract from the sort of active consideration by citizens that it is seeking authoritatively to elicit.

I fear that it is harder for jurists to see this in a case like §12605 than it is in the case of §12603. If someone asks about the meaning of 'reasonable' or 'appropriate', all we can do is indicate that these are flexible, all-purpose predicates of evaluation that invite us to consider a number of possible factors in an open-ended way. But for terms like 'aggressive' and 'inattentive', it is tempting to think that the law-makers must have had something more specific in mind and it is tempting to try to identify what that is and call that the legislative meaning of the term. This has been the history of 'originalist' approaches to the use of thick evaluative terms like 'cruel' in the American Constitution (in the Eighth Amendment).[36] Instead of reading a prohibition on 'cruel punishment' as an invitation to engage in structured practical deliberation along the subset of dimensions of evaluation that 'cruel' indicates, the temptation is to treat the word as a cipher for the particular practices that the framers of the constitutional provision must have had it in mind to condemn.

---

[33] Hart and Sacks (1994) at p 139.   [34] ibid 145–50.
[35] ibid 150.   [36] eg the discussion in Scalia (1998).

Or, in the case of some modern human rights provisions, like the prohibition on inhuman and degrading punishment in Article 3 of the European Convention on Human Rights, the temptation is to substitute an array of particular decisions by an authoritative court—shackling is degrading, corporal punishment is inhuman, etc—for the structured deliberation that is invited by the ordinary-language meanings of these terms.[37] Both these approaches treat the norm in question as an inchoate rule, and one way or another their strategy is to flee as soon as possible from the indeterminacy occasioned by an acknowledgment that these are evaluative terms inviting evaluative judgment. By contrast, the approach that I have taken looks for what Ronald Dworkin has called a 'moral reading' of these provisions, which involves judges trying to figure out in their own voice as a matter of moral judgment what punishments are cruel (or inhuman or degrading) and what punishments are not.[38]

Maybe there are good political reasons for treating provisions like the Eighth Amendment as inchoate rules. Constitutional originalism, for example, is sometimes motivated by a distrust of judges exercising the sort of independent moral evaluation that would follow from their taking the moral reading seriously. The worry is that judges will indulge their own subjective policy preferences if they are asked to say in their own voice whether, for example, capital punishment is cruel. Maybe that fear of judicial independence or judicial subjectivity justifies the originalism approach. But what does not justify it is the proposition that the Eighth Amendment, on the moral reading, fails to give the judges any guidance. It *does* give them guidance; only what it guides is their decision whether to engage in moral deliberation on this matter in the way that the meaning of the term 'cruel' invites.

10. Chilling behavior

I have tried to answer the objection that standards like §12603 and our imaginary §12605 fail to guide action and that this is why their imprecision is objectionable. An alternative objection is that such imprecise standards provide altogether too much in the way of action-guidance, because they chill and deter not only the behavior to which they are eventually applied, but also a lot of behavior in the vicinity, as people strive to avoid the risk of being caught out by these indeterminate provisions. A numerical speed limit deters only the behavior that exceeds 8 mph or 15 mph or whatever the limit is. But

---

[37] Also Waldron (2008).   [38] cf Dworkin (1996).

a requirement to drive at a reasonable speed or a requirement not to drive aggressively may deter much behavior that might not eventually be found by a court to be unreasonable or aggressive simply because the agent plays it safe to avoid the risk of prosecution. This objection is very common, and it may be justified in the case of an inchoate rule—where the legislature has managed to indicate that behavior up to some specified limit is permissible but has failed to provide a determinate indication of what that limit is. However, it is not usually justified in the case of standards like the ones we are considering.

Think back to what the Ohio Supreme Court said about §12603 in *State v Schaeffer*:

> The careful, conservative driver need have no fear of [the provision]. The reckless, wanton speed maniac needs to be kept in fear of it. The life of the humblest citizen must be placed above the gratification of the motor maniac, who would turn the public highways into a race course.[39]

The court's position seems to be that 'chilling' the behavior of '[t]he reckless, wanton speed maniac' may be a good thing; it may be a good thing if the formerly inattentive driver becomes hyper-vigilant or if the formerly aggressive driver is led by §12605 to become extremely, perhaps even unnecessarily, polite.

The underlying point here is that guiding action need not be conceived as an exact enterprise. Chilling action is also a way of guiding action. It brings a person's action under legal control within a broad and vaguely defined range rather than by reference to a specific act-type (such as driving at an exactly specified speed). The instruction to 'Slow down', for example, guides action and it does so even though the recipient of the instruction knows pragmatically that dropping his speed by 1 mph does not satisfy the requirement and knows too that dropping his speed *to* 1 mph may be taking things too far. Somewhere in between these extremes there is an area of behavior that the instruction guides him toward. But it is a vague area and, from the law's point of view, it probably does not matter if the desire to avoid sanctions biases things toward the lower end of the scale. Much the same, I believe, may be said of §12603.

If there is a serious objection to chilling action in this sort of way, it is probably better phrased in terms of a background concern for liberty rather than a background concern for guiding action as such. For example, in First Amendment doctrine, we sometimes worry that restrictions on speech in a particular area will 'chill' speech in the surrounding area, and we think that

---

[39] *State v Schaeffer* 117 NE 220 (1917) at p 234.

this is a problem because we have a strong general commitment to freedom of speech in all but the areas where we can say with confidence that a specific restriction is needed.[40] The US Supreme Court has sometimes said that '[b]ecause First Amendment freedoms need breathing space to survive, government may regulate in the area only with narrow specificity'.[41] But it is not clear that any such assumption is warranted in the driving case. Do we really want to say that because the freedom to drive fast (or as one pleases) needs breathing space to survive, government may regulate in the area only with narrow specificity? I do not think so, and I think there are a great many cases like this. Often the use of model (ii) is justified in areas where we think there is no strong background right to liberty: no background interest in freedom that requires an unchilled breathing space. We think it is justified in areas where a person's actions already warrant the watchfulness of the law and where eliciting the person's own watchfulness—even if that takes the form of general chilling caution—is by no means objectionable. Driving, at least in 1917, was just such a case.

Beyond that, the other objection that a legislature needs to confront is an apprehension of unfairness in the disparity that may sometimes occur between the citizen's idea of what is reasonable and the authorities' view of what is reasonable when the citizen's action is reviewed by the police or by the courts. We are not now concerned with the reckless, wanton speed maniac who says, 'I am shocked—shocked!—to find out that I was expected to slow down so much in a built-up area with children playing in the street.' What about the responsible driver who is just unsure about whether his good faith estimate of reasonable speed is going to coincide with that of the police? I am thinking here about the person who worries whether his own good faith calculations will be regarded by others as idiosyncratic, or the person who worries that he may be confronted with a judge or a magistrate who has an idiosyncratic view of the matter that differs from his own. Once again, this is not a concern about action-guidance, but it may be a real concern nonetheless.

I do not believe that this concern is answered, in the way philosophers are often tempted to answer it, by appealing to a notion of objectivity—that is, by saying that so long as there is an objective right answer to the question of what is a reasonable driving speed in a given set of circumstances, no one can complain about unfairness when his own subjective calculation is corrected

---

[40] eg *Citizens United v Federal Election Commission* 130 S Ct 876 (2010) at p 892: 'Applying this standard would thus require case-by-case determinations. But archetypical political speech would be chilled in the meantime.'

[41] *National Ass'n for the Advancement of Colored People v Button* 371 US 415 (1963) at p 433, quoted in *Citizens United* at p 892.

by a court. There can be an objective right answer and still people can come up with widely disparate estimates, and so the question does have to be confronted:[42] is it fair to subject P's estimate to review in terms of someone else's estimate, in circumstances where with the best will in the world—objectivity or no objectivity—the two of them widely diverge?

To avoid this concern, one might want to confine the use of model (ii) as a form of action-guidance to areas of conduct where we have reason to believe there is not going to be a wide divergence in estimates of appropriate behavior. Driving, it seems to me, is such an area. In *State v Schaeffer*, although there was a factual disagreement about how fast the defendant was driving, there seemed to be little disagreement about how fast it was appropriate to drive when large numbers of children were playing on the street. Responsible drivers and responsible law-enforcement officials were likely to converge around a fairly low number, in 1917 perhaps somewhat below the 8 mph limit laid down for built-up areas in §12604. In areas where there is likely to be greater divergence—whether because of different cultures in regard to the activity in question or because of different patterns of perception of what is and what is not a circumstance that promises danger—something more along the lines of model (i) may be appropriate. This might lead us to reconsider our imaginary §12605, or at least the part that relates to aggressive driving. Cultures of driving may have developed so disparately that we can no longer rely on a sort of background consensus to obviate the unfairness of subjecting one person's view of what is and is not aggressive to another person's view on that matter (with possible heavy penalties as a result). It is possible that an otherwise good driver might say, *not* disingenuously, 'I am shocked to find that driving closely behind a vehicle that is travelling below the usual speed in the fast lane and flashing my lights to indicate that I want to overtake is treated as aggressive driving.' It may be better to do what most states now do,[43] which is to authoritatively define aggressive driving in terms of certain specific practices. This represents, in effect, a shift from model (ii) to model (i).

On the other hand, cultures of driving do not come out of nowhere. They grow and develop as people begin to take less and less responsibility for the considerateness of their driving patterns. We imagined an honest driver being surprised to learn that his attitude toward overtaking was regarded by the police or the courts as aggressive. But it might be more realistic to imagine

---

[42] Discussed in Waldron (1992) at pp 158–87; reprinted in Waldron (1999) at pp 164–87.

[43] Florida's definition is typical: aggressive driving means 'At least two of the following: speeding, unsafe or improper lane change, following too closely, failure to yield right of way, improper passing, failure to obey traffic control devices' (<http://www.ghsa.org/html/stateinfo/laws/aggressivedriving_laws.html>, visited on 26 March 2010).

such a driver being slightly defiant about his driving and resistant to the pro-
cesses of practical reasoning that the law aimed to elicit: 'I don't need anyone
to teach me how to drive. Those slowpokes in the fast lane need to learn to
pull over and let those of us by who know how to drive at speed.' The early
stage of emergence of this sort of attitude represents, in effect, an assault on a
certain consensus about reasonable and safe driving and an attempt to replace
it with a different, perhaps more Darwinian, approach. The attitudes (and the
driving) of such a person may or may not be admirable, but we may have less
sympathy with his complaint about unfairness when he finds his actions
authoritatively reviewed in terms of more prudent standards than those he is
trying to inculcate.

Obviously there is much more to be said on these matters of fairness and
consensus, on the one hand, and stronger or weaker background commitments to liberty, on the other. I have not provided a full treatment of these
points. My aim here is to illustrate simply the way in which the real concerns
that they raise differ from the concerns about the action-guiding aspect of
imprecise legal provisions.

11. From traffic to torture

Believe it or not, my main concern is not about traffic rules. I have come to
these issues through a different, more serious, and much darker route: the
problem of legal provisions that prohibit torture.[44] The US anti-torture
statute (18 USC §2340A) makes it an offense punishable by up to 20 years'
imprisonment (or death if death results) to commit, conspire, or attempt to
commit torture.[45] Now, 'torture' is a vivid term, and for most of us it sum-
mons up grisly and distressing images of practices that fall indisputably within
its sphere of reference. But its boundaries do seem to be contestable. Is sleep
deprivation torture? What about forcing people to stand in a stressed position
for many hours? Is waterboarding a form of torture? All these questions have
been debated. The anti-torture statute actually provides a definition:

'torture' means an act committed by a person acting under the color of law specifically intended to inflict severe physical or mental pain or suffering...upon another
person within his custody or physical control.[46]

Unfortunately, this definition does not remove the indeterminacy; it just
helps to identify its source. Torture is vague in part because the phrase 'severe

---

[44] Waldron (2005) at p 1681; and Waldron (2010b).
[45] 18 USC §2340A.   [46] 18 USC 2340 (1).

physical...pain or suffering' is vague. Severity of pain or suffering is a continuum but, by the use of the word 'torture', it seems to presuppose that we can say, of a given episode of pain and suffering, that it either is severe or it is not. In this respect, §2340A is rather like our imagined §12605, prohibiting aggressive driving. It invokes a standard conveyed by a thick term of evaluation, and it engages our practical reasoning in this regard, on the optimistic assumption (which may or may not be justified) that—when prodded by the law—we know and agree about how to apply it.

I believe that the following points drawn from what has been said about our paradigms of traffic law in Ohio can help us think through the difficulties that might arise with regard to the anti-torture statute.

First, the indeterminacy of §2340A, such as it is, does not prevent it from being action-guiding or from making a practical difference to the agency and behavior of those who are subject to it. In as much as it imposes a non-negotiable prohibition and threatens heavy penalties, it constitutes a warning to the community of people likely to be engaged in coercive interrogation that they should give the most careful thought to their choice of interrogation techniques. They are put on notice that the very thing that might attract them to a technique—its painfulness and people's inability to resist it—are themselves the locus of the gravest legislative concern. So, for example, even though the law as written does not settle in a determinate way whether waterboarding is torture, it does tend to guide their agency away from such techniques.

Second, the fact that a relatively indeterminate prohibition might 'chill' interrogative activity is hardly a cause for concern. For suppose it is the definition of 'severe pain or suffering' that is giving pause to our imagined interrogator. He is in the business, let us say, of deliberately inflicting considerable pain on detainees already and he just wants to know where exactly the severity line is, so that they can push up against it but not be seen to cross it. He already has the electrodes plugged in and the dial turned up to 4 or 5; he wants to know how much higher he can go. I think we are unlikely to say of this case what we observed the Supreme Court saying about speech, that '[b]ecause the practice of deliberately inflicting pain in interrogation needs breathing space to survive, government may regulate in the area only with narrow specificity'.[47] Instead, we might see the context of coercive interrogation as being a prime case for legislative watchfulness and we may have no difficulty with the idea that the watchfulness that the law in turn elicits from interrogators may lead to an excess of caution.

Sure, opinions may differ on this. Some will say that we need to avoid chilling interrogative activity because we need the results of interrogation in

---

[47] See above text accompanying note 41.

our pursuit of the war against terrorism. (An analogy would be the opinion that we need fast, efficient driving, so it is important not to chill that with vague safety-oriented ordinances like §12603 and §12605.) But now at least we have located the nub of the dispute. It is not a general concern about vague statutes; it is a concern about the relative seriousness with which we should take the background liberty on which the statute impinges.

Thirdly, we might conceivably identify a problem about fairness, in which an interrogator professes surprise about the way in which his estimation of which practices count as torture (or which episodes of pain count as severe) are second-guessed by a war-crimes tribunal. Whether we like it or not, it is possible that under conditions of modern pluralism, different cultures have emerged that in fact treat these phenomena in quite different ways, so that someone is not just weeping crocodile tears when they say, 'I am shocked—shocked!—to learn that you are going to punish me under the anti-torture statute for setting dogs on prisoners or depriving them of sleep for a month.' That may be so. Alternatively, it is possible that there has been an attempt in recent years deliberately to *create* such a disparity of evaluations, to muddy the waters of human rights law and international humanitarian law so that it appears that the consensus on which §2340 and §2340A were predicated has dissolved. On this alternative account, statements of the 'shocked—shocked!' variety would be part of a campaign, deliberately calibrated to foster this dissensus. If that is the case, I think we should be much less impressed by these complaints of unfairness relative to the ordinary operation of a provision like this. We should probably be less impressed by them anyway, because as the likelihood of actual prosecutions under §2340A is in fact vanishingly small, and the main effect of the attempt to pin down a precise meaning for 'torture' or 'severe' is in fact to furnish a presidential administration with a determinate envelope to push.[48]

12. The lesbian rule

Complaints about vagueness and imprecision are not just abstract concerns in legal philosophy. They afford us an opportunity to think more complicated thoughts in our philosophical conceptions of what it is for a legal provision to guide action, and I have tried to set out in this chapter what some of those complications might be. But we need to remember that it is vague *law* we are talking about, not just vague propositions. That we are talking about vague law means, at the end of the day, we are talking about the auspices under

---

[48] More extensive discussion can be found in Waldron (2005) at pp 1695–703.

which punishments will be meted out and sanctions imposed; and that should alert us to the seriousness of the matter. But we should understand, too, what is at stake in the legislative or regulative enterprise. That is also a deadly serious matter—protecting people from torturers or, in our traffic case, from '[t]he reckless, wanton speed maniac'. In these and similar areas, it is good to focus on the need for legislative flexibility, or what Aristotle once called the 'lesbian' rule: 'For when the thing is indefinite the rule also is indefinite, like the leaden rule used in making the Lesbian molding; the rule adapts itself to the shape of the stone and is not rigid, and so too the decree is adapted to the facts.'[49] The adaptability of law, secured precisely by what others would call its indeterminacy, is not incompatible with law continuing to guide the actions of its subjects. It is a valuable legislative resource and a respectful one too, for it works in tandem with the most sophisticated understanding of people's powers of practical reasoning.

[49] Aristotle (1980) at p 133.

5

Can the Law Imply More Than It Says? On Some Pragmatic Aspects of Strategic Speech

Andrei Marmor

A great deal of the law (even if not all) in any given jurisdiction consists of directives issued by various legal authorities, such as legislatures, judges, administrative agencies, and others. In a fairly clear sense, therefore, the content of the law is determined by what legal authorities communicate. Both lawyers and philosophers of language know very well, however, that the full content of communication in a natural language often goes beyond the meaning of the words and sentences uttered by the speaker. Semantics and syntax are essential vehicles for conveying communicative content, but the content conveyed on particular occasions of speech is often pragmatically enriched by various factors. My purpose in this chapter is to explore some of the pragmatic aspects of legal speech. Some of these aspects are unique. The standard model in the pragmatics literature focuses on ordinary conversations, in which the parties are presumed to engage in a cooperative exchange of information. Unlike ordinary cases of conversation, however, the legal context offers an example of conversation that is strategic in nature. Part of my purpose here is to show that the pragmatics of strategic conversation have certain features that deviate from the standard model.

The chapter proceeds as follows: the first section aims to clarify the conceptual framework, focusing on two main instances of implied communicative content—namely implicatures and utterance presuppositions. I will argue that, in both of these cases, there is an important distinction between implied content that is semantically encoded in the utterance—and therefore forms part of what the law communicatively determines—and implied content that is essentially contextual and thus much more problematic in the legal case. In the second section I focus on the idea of pragmatic commitments and their normative foundations. My main concern here is to explore the normative framework of strategic speech and ways in which it differs from ordinary conversations. Finally, I will try to explain in what sense legal speech is strategic and demonstrate how the pragmatic aspects of strategic speech actually work in the legal context.

1. The implied content of speech

At least three levels of content can be conveyed by an occasion of speech: communicative content may consist of *semantic* content, *assertive* content, and some further content that is *implicated* by the speech in the particular context of its utterance. The semantic content consists of the content that is determined by the semantics and syntax of the expression uttered. Normally, this would consist of the literal meaning of the words used and the syntactical structure of the sentence. The assertive content is the content of the truth-evaluable proposition that is conveyed by the speaker in the particular context of the utterance. It has long been recognized, however, that what a speaker actually says or asserts on a particular occasion of speech often goes beyond what the words and sentences semantically mean, depending on various pragmatic features of the context of the utterance and the speaker's communicative intentions.[1] The relevance of this distinction in the law is something that I will not consider here: I have discussed part of it elsewhere.[2]

The distinction that forms the topic of this chapter concerns those cases in which the content communicated by a speaker goes beyond what the speaker asserts. In many instances of speech, there is some communicative content that is implicated, though not quite asserted, by the speaker in the particular context of his utterance. Generally, the implied content of the utterance of P in context C can be defined as the content that the speaker, in the specific context of C, is *committed to* by uttering P, and the hearers are expected to know that the speaker is committed to, and the speaker can be expected to know this. A speaker can be expected to be committed to a certain implied content if and only if an explicit, *ex post* denial of the implied content would strike any *reasonable* hearer under the circumstances as perplexing, disingenuous, or contradictory. There are several kinds of implied content. The two

---

[1] All of this is well recognized in the literature: see Soames (2009b). Perry suggested calling the pragmatic aspects of speech which determine the assertive content 'near-side pragmatics', as distinguished from 'far-side pragmatics' that concern the ways in which we infer content that goes beyond what the speaker asserted. This chapter is focused on far-side pragmatics of strategic speech.

[2] Marmor (2008) at p 423. Also arguing for a very similar conclusion is Soames (2009a) at pp 403–23.

most familiar cases are implicatures and utterance presuppositions, and these are the cases that I will discuss here.[3]

1.1 Implicatures

Consider, for example, a municipal ordinance requiring restaurants to have clean and well-maintained bathrooms indoors. Even if the regulation does not explicitly say so, surely we would assume that a restaurant that had impeccable bathrooms that are kept locked at all times would violate the ordinance. That the restrooms need to be open for patrons to use is content that is clearly implicated by such an ordinance. It is, as it were, a conversational implicature.

To get a more precise idea of how such implications work, let me briefly review some of Paul Grice's main ideas about implicatures.[4] His main insight is that our ability to understand content of expressions beyond their assertive[5] content is due to a combination of two kinds of factors: general norms of conversation that apply to the relevant speech situation, and specific contextual knowledge that is shared by speaker and hearer in the circumstances of the utterance. In normal conversational situations, when the main purpose of speech is the cooperative exchange of information, certain general maxims apply. Grice helpfully listed and classified these maxims of ordinary conversation, and they are basically as follows:

(i) *Maxim of quantity*—make your conversational contribution as informative as required, namely do not say too little and do not say too much.

(ii) *Maxims of quality*—do not say what you believe to be false, and do not say something if you do not have adequate evidence for it.

(ii) *Maxim of relevance*—make your contribution relevant to the conversation.

(iv) *Maxims of manner*—avoid obscurity and ambiguity, be brief and orderly.[6]

As noted, these maxims apply to ordinary conversations where the purpose of the conversation is the cooperative exchange of information. The maxims are

---

[3] Irony is another example, but I will not discuss it here. Irony is a rather special case, typically implicating that the speaker intends to convey the opposite of the assertive content of his utterance. Some forms of metaphor may also implicate content beyond what is said, and there may be other cases.

[4] Grice (1989).

[5] The question of beyond what, exactly, conversational implicatures operate is somewhat controversial. Grice typically speaks about the distinction between what is said and what is implicated; presumably, by 'what is said', Grice includes assertive (and not just semantic) content. Soames (2008a) however, argues that a great deal of assertive content is also partly determined by pragmatic features of conversation, including implicatures.

[6] Grice (1989) at p 28.

norms that directly instantiate the specific functions or purposes of communicative interactions and facilitate those functions.

A certain content is conversationally implicated by a speaker if it is not part of what the speaker had actually asserted, but nevertheless is implicated by what he said in the specific speech situation, given the conversational maxims that apply. In other words, a speaker S conversationally implicates q by saying p in context C, iff

   (i) S is presumed to observe the relevant conversational maxims in C;

  (ii) the assumption that S meant (or intended that) q is required to make sense of S's utterance of p in context C, given the conversational maxims that apply;

 (iii) S believes/assumes that his/her hearers can recognize condition (ii), and can recognize that S knows that.[7]

As Grice himself emphasized, two main features are essentially associated with conversational implicatures:

   (i) Conversational implicatures are always *cancelable* by the speaker. The speaker can always add an explicit clarification to cancel the implication that would otherwise follow from his utterance. As we shall see, this is an essential feature of conversational implicatures.

  (ii) Conversational implicatures are very context specific; they are not conventionally determined by the rules of language. There is always some derivation, as Grice called it, that leads us to construe the content of an implicature; some story has to be known or to be assumed to make it explicit.

The second condition needs to be qualified, however. In addition to regular conversational implicatures, Grice also identified a category of cases he called *generalized conversational implicatures*. His examples are the following:

Anyone who uses a sentence of the form X *is meeting a woman this evening* would normally implicate that the person to be met was someone other than X's wife, mother, sister or perhaps even close Platonic friend. Similarly, if I were to say X *went into a house yesterday and found a tortoise inside the front door*, my hearer would normally be surprised if some time later I revealed the house was X's own.[8]

---

[7] Note that the last condition, of transparency, is actually rather problematic and controversial. Grice himself was aware of a serious problem here considering the implicatures involved in using disjunction (Soames (2008b)).

[8] Grice (1989) at p 37.

Generalized conversational implicatures are those in which an expression is used that would normally implicate a certain content, unless that implication is explicitly canceled. A speaker can say, 'X is meeting a woman this evening', and immediately add, 'I wonder if the woman is X's wife or not'. Here, the implicature is explicitly canceled by the latter sentence. Now, what Grice seems to suggest is that, in the non-canceled cases, when somebody says 'an A', the expression would normally implicate that one has no specific knowledge about it or that one deems it irrelevant to the context to specify whose A it is. Otherwise the speaker would simply fail to follow the conversational maxim of quantity (do not say too little).

In other words, generalized conversational implicatures are created by a combination of the semantic features of certain standard expressions in natural language—hence the generality—and particular contexts in which the conversational maxims apply. Expressions of the form 'an A' are semantically such that they generate a certain type of expectation; given the conversational maxims that apply in concrete speech situations, this expectation normally generates an implicature.[9]

1.2 Presuppositions

In addition to content that is conversationally implicated by an utterance in a given context, there are many cases in which a given utterance would only make sense if a certain content is presupposed by the speaker in relation to the background knowledge shared by his hearers. A presupposition consists in content that is not actually asserted, but would need to be taken for granted to make sense of the asserted content or its relevance to the conversation. This is the type of content that is either already shared by the conversational participants, or else the hearers would be willing to accommodate for the purpose of the conversation. The interesting cases, however, are those in which we can infer the presupposition from the utterance itself. Soames defines *utterance presuppositions* as follows:

An utterance U presupposes P iff one can reasonably infer from U that the speaker S accepts P and regards it as uncontroversial, either because

---

[9] Cases of generalized conversational implicatures should be distinguished, however, from another familiar type of case in which a certain implicature has been used so frequently that it has actually become an idiomatic expression with a conventional meaning that differs, somewhat, from the literal meaning of the words used. Examples are very familiar. 'Do you have the time?'—which is not normally used as a question about possession but to ask the hearer what time it is. Similarly, 'Can you pass me the salt?' is typically used to make a request, not to ask the hearer about his or her ability to do something. These expressions have long gained a certain conventional meaning, which is no longer a matter of implicature. See, eg Bach and Harnish (1982) at 173. Searle refers to these cases as conventionally used indirect speech acts: (1979) at pp 36–43.

(a) S thinks that P is already part of the conversational background at the time of U; or because
(b) S thinks that the conversational participants are prepared to add P, without objection, to the background.[10]

Consider the following examples:

(1) 'Bill regrets lying to his parents.'
    Presupposition: Bill [believes that he] lied to his parents.[11]
(2) 'Sarah forgot to pick up Jane from the airport.'
    Presupposition: Sarah was supposed (or intended) to pick Jane up at the airport.
(3) 'John's wife is going to the concert tomorrow.'
    Presupposition: John is married.

Some linguists have noted that a speaker's commitment to presupposed content is a matter of degree. In our examples, it seems plausible to maintain that the speaker's commitment to the presupposed content in (1) and (2) is somewhat stronger compared with the commitment to the presupposition in (3). That seems correct. We should also note, however, that some presuppositions are more context sensitive than others. Consider (3) again: in some conversational contexts it might be important to the conversation whether the person spoken about is married to John or not, and, in other contexts of conversation, it might be quite immaterial. At least in part, this context sensitivity can be seen by looking at those cases in which the presupposed content turns out to be false, and then ask how would that falsehood affect the content that the speaker managed to convey. Suppose, for example, that it turns out that John is not married. Would it necessarily defeat the main content of the speaker's utterance of (3)? That depends on circumstances: if both speaker and hearer knew the identity of the woman spoken about, then the fact that she is not really married to John would have made little difference to the main content of the utterance. On the other hand, with respect to utterances like (1) or (2), it would be much more difficult to think of any context where the falsehood of the presupposition would not defeat the main content of the utterance. This follows from the fact that some presuppositions are particularly sensitive to the context of the conversation, and others are less so.

---

[10] Soames (1989) at p 573.
[11] I take it that it is possible for an agent to regret that P, even if P has not actually occurred; it is impossible for an agent to regret that P, however, if the agent does not *believe* that P occurred.

1.3 Semantically encoded implications

Grice suggested in a few famously cryptic remarks that there are cases in which implicated content follows from *the meaning* of the words used in the expression uttered. Implicated content is often *semantically encoded* in the expression that the speaker used. Grice called them *conventional* impli-catures.[12] However, the same phenomenon is often present in utterance presuppositions as well. In both cases, certain content might be implicated in a way that is semantically encoded in the expression uttered by the speaker.[13] So let us look at some examples, disregarding, for now, the dis-tinction between implicatures and presuppositions. Consider the follow-ing utterances:

(4) 'Even X can A' (implicating that there are some others, besides X, who can A, and that X is one of the least likely among them to A).
(5) 'X managed to find A' (implicating that finding A was expected to involve some difficulty).
(6) 'It was X who broke the vase' (implicating that somebody must have broken the vase).
(7) 'X is not coming to the party tonight' (implicating that there must have been some expectation that X would/might come to the party tonight).
(8) 'The Republicans and Senator X voted against the bill' (implicating that X is not a Republican).
(9) 'I cannot join you for dinner, I have to meet with X' (implicating that the two events in question—the dinner and the meeting with X—are simultaneous).

Common to utterances (4)–(9) is that, in addition to the assertive content of the utterance, some content is implicated by the speech, as indicated in the bracketed text. There is, however, this crucial difference: in the utterances of (4), (5), and (6), the relevant implicated content is semantically encoded in the expression used. This is clearly manifested by the fact that the implied content is not cancelable by the speaker. It simply makes no sense to say that 'it was X who broke the vase' and then immediately try to cancel the implication/presup-position by saying that actually nobody broke the vase.[14] On the other hand,

---

[12] Grice (1989) at p 25. The question of whether there is anything really conventional about such semantically encoded implications is a question I have dealt with in Marmor (2009) at ch 5.

[13] Indeed, Karttunen and Peters argued that utterance presuppositions are just conventional implicatures (1979) at pp 1–56. I do not quite agree with their view (Marmor (2009) 115), but this disagreement does not affect my arguments in this chapter.

[14] Notice that semantically encoded implications are typically projectable: the implication remains even when the expression is embedded in negations, conditionals, etc (anaphora might be an exception, though: see the note below).

the relevant implications in (7), (8), and (9) are not semantically encoded. And again, this is attested by the fact that the implied content is cancelable by the speaker. For example, there can be a context in which it would make sense to express (8), even if X is also a Republican. It could have been a known fact, shared by the conversational parties, that Senator X was widely expected to vote for the bill. By saying that the 'Republicans and X' voted against the bill, one may be clarifying something that the conversational parties would have found informative and relevant, given their specific background expectations.[15]

Generally speaking, I will assume here that cancelability is a sound criterion for distinguishing between implied content that is semantically encoded and content implied that is not semantically encoded.[16] If the implication of an utterance is not cancelable, it is because the implication is semantically encoded in the expression uttered. By choosing to use a certain expression, the speaker has already committed himself to the content that is implicated by the meaning of that expression. Implications that are not semantically encoded are such that their content is inferred from the combination of the expression used in a given conversational context and some conversational norms (maxims, in Grice's terminology) that the speaker is presumed to follow.

Now, when we turn our attention to the legal context, particularly in the case of legislation, I think that it should follow quite naturally that implications which are semantically encoded inevitably form part of the content of the law. Precisely because such implications are not cancelable, and they do not normally depend on the particular context of the conversation, we may safely conclude that if an instance of legislative speech saying that P semantically implicates that Q, then Q is part of what the legislative speech actually determines as a matter of communicative content. In other words, semantically encoded implications are basically on par with assertive content.

To be sure, I am not suggesting that a speaker is committed to all the content that is logically or otherwise *entailed* by what he says. People cannot be expected to be committed to content that they could not be aware of.[17]

---

[15] Note that a semantically encoded implication does not necessarily follow from the meaning of individual words; in some cases, different content is implicated by the same word used in different types of sentences. As an example, compare the implication of the word 'too' in these two cases of anaphora: 'Joseph was in the room *too*' (implicating that others were in the room), and 'If Joseph goes to the meeting, the department chair will be there *too*' (implicating that Joseph is not the department chair). The example—though not quite the point of it—is taken from Kripke (2009). This is also discussed in Marmor (2009) at p 113.

[16] This assumption is widely shared in the literature.

[17] Surely all those who have used and expressed the axioms of arithmetic for centuries cannot be taken to have been committed, in any sense whatsoever, to the truth of Gödel's theorems, though, as we now know, Gödel's theorems are entailed by those axioms and some truths about set theory. I owe this example to Scott Soames.

Generally speaking, however, speakers can be taken to be committed to content that is *obviously and transparently* implicated by the semantic features of the expression they have uttered, given normal linguistic competence in the relevant natural language.

Is there any reason to doubt that semantically encoded implications are necessarily part of law's communicated content? If there is any doubt about this, it might stem from the relative lack of specificity of the implied content. Content that is implied by the kind of expressions under consideration here is often somewhat unspecified. The specification of such content is typically context dependent. Nevertheless, even if the relevant expression leaves some content unspecified, the information encoded might be sufficient to make a difference. If a speaker asserts, for example, that 'Even John can pass the exam', the speaker is clearly committed to the following content: (i) that there are others, besides John, in some relevant reference group, who can pass the exam; and (ii) that among those in this group, John is one of the least likely to be able to pass it. Of course the hearers would need some contextual background to know what is the relevant reference group here. In this respect, the content is semantically underspecified. But the rest of the content in (i) and (ii) is semantically entailed by the use of the word 'even' in this sentence, regardless of the particular context of this utterance. And this content is not cancelable. Imagine a speaker who says: 'Even John can pass the exam; after all, he was the best student.' This would be a very perplexing utterance; it is difficult to imagine a context in which it would make sense.

Admittedly, however, the distinction between implications that follow only from the semantics of the expression used, and those in which some pragmatic elements also play a role, is not always so easy to discern. Consider, for example, a speaker S uttering the following sentence:

(10) 'All Xs who are F ought to φ.'

There is a clear sense that in uttering (10), the speaker, S, is committed to the content that *there might be an X who is not F*. Is this an implication that is semantically encoded in (10)? Not entirely. What (10) implies is something like this: *For all that S knows* (in the context of this utterance), there might be an X who is not F. Why is that? Arguably, because otherwise S would have violated the maxim of quantity (do not say too little). Had S *known* that all Xs are Fs, his utterance would have expressed too weak a proposition—it would have said too little, as it were. Therefore, we may safely conclude from the utterance of (10) that for all the speaker knows, there might be an X that is not F. But this implication partly depends on the Gricean maxim of quantity; it is generated by some pragmatic features of the speech. What we have here, I think, is some information that is encoded in the expression used that, together with the assumption that the speaker adheres to the maxim of quantity, generates a certain implicature. It is a case of a *generalized conversational implicature*. Note, however, that generalized conversational implicatures are cancelable, and therefore not quite on par with assertive content.

Let us now return to those cases in which the implication is thoroughly pragmatic. In such cases the content implied is partly derived by assuming that the conversational parties follow certain maxims of conversation. But then the question arises: what are the maxims of conversation that would apply to legislative speech? The normative framework of legal speech may be different from the framework of an ordinary conversation. This is the main topic that we need to explore in the legal context. Once we realize that legislative speech is often a *strategic* form of communication, not necessarily a cooperative one, we will be able to see that the kind of pragmatic commitments that apply in the legal context are different from those that apply in the regular conversational context. Before I try to explain this in some detail, let me clarify a terminological point: I am not going to assume that strategic forms of communication are entirely non-cooperative. A certain cooperative element is probably present in any communicative interaction. I use the term 'strategic speech' only to indicate that there are some important non-cooperative elements in certain types of communicative interactions, and I will try to explore how these non-cooperative elements affect the relevant implications in question.

2. The normative framework of strategic speech

As noted, the maxims Grice identified apply to ordinary conversations where the purpose of the conversation is the cooperative exchange of information. The maxims are norms that directly instantiate the specific functions or purposes of such communicative interactions and facilitate those functions. Now of course, not all speech situations are cooperative exchanges of information. Consider, for example, expressions we use in the context of courtesy or politeness. These are cases in which some form of cooperation is going on, but not typically of the kind that involves a truthful exchange of information. A polite remark or an expression of courtesy is not meant to be entirely truthful or implicate anything beyond what is conventionally regarded as appropriate. (Perhaps in such cases there is a certain commitment to pretend that you say something true, even if the commitment is not to the truth of what you say. I am not sure—sometimes there is not even a pretence, just a compliance with a certain ritual.)

Some types of speech are strategic. Parties to a strategic conversation may wish to employ conversational maxims in ways that generate implications that act to their advantage, without a real intention to be committed to such implicated content. The extreme example is manipulative speech: these are cases in which a speaker asserts something true while deliberately implicating something that he knows to be false. As an example, consider this case: Mr Smith goes to a hospital and, in making some medical enquiries with one of the nurses, he presents himself as 'Dr Smith'. As it happens, Smith's doctorate is in philosophy. Wouldn't the nurse be rather surprised, and quite rightly annoyed, in learning this little detail later? True, Mr Smith did *not assert* that he is a medical doctor but, given the circumstances, it is an implication that would naturally follow. In other words, the asserted content here is true; it is only the implicature that is false.

Such cases of manipulative speech show that an implicature can be abused. But in fact, the abuse or manipulation is made possible precisely because the hearer wrongly assumes that the speaker adheres to the ordinary Gricean conversational maxims. I am not trying to argue that legislative speech is typically manipulative; far from it. My point in raising this possibility of manipulation is much more limited: it is to show that the communicative commitments that we ascribe to a speaker are crucially dependent on the assumptions about the normative framework of the relevant conversation. Manipulative implications are possible only because the hearers are led to assume that the speaker follows the ordinary conversational maxims.

Another lesson can be drawn from this. In an ordinary conversation, the kinds of intentions and commitments that we can rightfully ascribe to the speaker are identical to the content that the hearer would be interested in grasping and acknowledging it as such. However, when the conversational situation is not guided by a mutual interest in cooperative exchange of information, the interests of the speaker and hearer may be misaligned. Manipulative speech is simply the extreme example of this divergence of interests. There are, however, other and more subtle cases of strategic speech where something very similar is going on.

The essential feature of a strategic speech—as I will use this term here—is that the speaker strives to implicate more than he would be willing to make explicit.[18] Consider, for example, two legislators striving to achieve a compromise on a particular legislative act. Each legislator would want to advance a certain agenda that the other might (partly) oppose. If they make their aims very explicit *ex ante*, it is very unlikely that they will reach a compromise. Part of what enables opposing parties to reach a compromise consists in their

---

[18]   cf Peter Strawson's interesting discussion of essentially non-avowable intentions of manipulative speech acts: (1964) at p 163.

ability to conceal, or at least not make very explicit, the overall implications of their collective speech. Compromise often requires, as I will explain shortly, tacitly acknowledged incomplete decisions: parties engage in an act of collective speech in a way that leaves some of the implications of their collective expression undetermined or deliberately vague or ambiguous. It is the nature of such strategic interactions that they allow the parties to make moves within the game, so to speak, without disclosing *ex ante* all their ulterior motives, expectations, or aims.

I am not claiming that strategic communication instantiates norms that dispose of any requirement of truthfulness or relevance. It would be very difficult to have any kind of conversation in which hearers cannot assume that the speaker is committed to some norms of truthfulness and relevance. The point about strategic interactions is that it is always partly a cooperative and partly a non-cooperative form of interaction. But then the question is: what is it that enables this mixture of cooperative and non-cooperative forms of communication? How does it work? The answer I suggest is that there is some inherent uncertainty about the norms that govern the particular conversation that enables the parties to the conversation to make strategic moves in it. Had the conversational maxims that govern a strategic conversation been as clear and determinate as they are in the case of an ordinary conversation, it would have been very difficult to make strategic moves in the conversation. Precisely because there is some degree of uncertainty about the norms that govern the conversation, parties can exploit implications of what they say in ways that they would not be willing to make very explicit *ex ante*.

The uncertainty about the relevant conversational maxims can be of two kinds: sometimes it may not be entirely determinate whether a certain maxim applies or not, and sometimes the uncertainty concerns the level of commitment or adherence to maxims that are taken to apply. For example, there are cases in which it is not entirely clear whether the maxim of truthfulness applies at all: do I really have to tell the truth when the waiter asks me if I liked the food? Or what exactly am I to reply when asked by my wife whether I like the expensive new dress she just bought? Note that there is some uncertainty at play here: had it been obvious that the hearer does not expect a truthful answer, it is doubtful that there would be a point in asking. In other cases, it may be relatively clear which maxims apply, but it is somewhat uncertain or indeterminate how seriously parties to the conversation are presumed to adhere to the relevant maxims. Think about parties engaged in commercial negotiations: how truthful, or how relevant, can the speaker's contribution to the conversation be taken to be assumed? And how much can they be expected to adhere to the maxim of quantity?

Consider another example of strategic speech, and one which is familiar to us in the academic context, about the ways in which we read letters of recommendation. Suppose that you are considering a job candidate who just finished her PhD at another university, and you are reading the letters of recommendation written by her professors. Naturally, you are interested not just in what the letter explicitly asserts but, perhaps even more so, in what the content of the letter implies. You try to read, as it were, between the lines. But you also suspect that the recommender, interested as he may be in the promotion of his student, might try to imply a bit too much. So you try to figure out the implications of what you read in the letter, but you take it with a grain of salt. And of course, the colleague who wrote the letter knows all this, and you know that he does. So how does it work? Are we fooling ourselves? Not quite. It works for both parties, speaker and hearer, precisely because the normative framework of the conversational situation is somewhat uncertain. I think that this is a case where the maxims are known and generally followed: the uncertainty pertains to the level of commitment or adherence to the maxims. Does the speaker really adhere to the maxim of quantity, for example (do not say too much)? That is not a norm that letters of recommendation strictly follow: they would be much shorter if they did.

The relative uncertainty of the norms of strategic communication may result in different forms of indeterminacy of communicative content. In some cases, the result might be that the speaker is committed to—or at least regards himself to be committed to—less than he would otherwise be. (It is as if the speaker says, 'This is a game we are playing here, do not expect me to be really committed to everything I imply.') This would typically be the case when the uncertainty about the normative framework pertains to the level of commitment to the norms. At other times, particularly in cases where the uncertainty pertains to the question of whether a certain maxim applies at all, the result is that the content implicated by the speech is itself somewhat indeterminate or uncertain. It is difficult to generalize about all cases. Different forms of strategic communication may generate different results in this respect.

To sum up so far: two main features of strategic communication distinguish it from an ordinary cooperative exchange of information. First, there is typically a certain misalignment of interests: a speaker's interest in implicating a certain content and the hearer's interest in acknowledging the uptake of that content might diverge, to some extent. The speaker wants to communicate more than she would be willing to make explicit, while the hearer may not have an interest in acknowledging the uptake of such oblique implications. The hearer's interest is often one of maintaining some plausible deniability of the uptake of the implication, acting *as if* he did not grasp or hear it. Second, this mixture of cooperative and non-cooperative elements of strategic communication is made possible by a certain degree of uncertainty about the relevant maxims of conversation or the level of adherence to them that the parties are presumed to follow. It is precisely this lack of complete certainty about the maxims of conversation that enables the success of communication in spite of a certain divergence of communicative expectations or intentions. The lack of certainty leaves some content hanging in the air, as it were, leaving each party to the conversation with an option of understanding the full communicated content somewhat differently.

Admittedly, all of this is very general and imprecise. We need to see how these features of strategic communication actually work. In the next section, I will use the example of legislative speech to demonstrate some of these unique aspects of strategic communication. The account is not meant to be exhaustive. My purpose is to demonstrate some of the difficulties and their possible solutions. Undoubtedly much more work needs to be done to fill in crucial details.

3. Strategic speech in the law

Let us take the example of legislation as a paradigmatic case of legal speech. The enactment of a law is not a cooperative exchange of information. Legislation is typically a form of *strategic behavior*. In fact, the situation is more complicated because legislation consists of at least two conversations, so to speak, not one. There is a conversation among the legislators themselves during the enactment process, and then the result of this internal conversation is a form of collective speech addressed to the subjects of the law enacted, often mediated by the courts (or various agencies).[19] Mostly, however, it is the conversation between legislatures and the courts that I would like to focus on here. It is a good example for our purposes because it is an ongoing conversation that takes place over time and is clearly strategic in nature. Now, of course, the internal conversation among legislatures is very strategic. It certainly does not abide by the Gricean maxims of a cooperative exchange of information. And then, when courts get to hear the legislative speech, as it were, it would be difficult for them to ignore the strategic nature of the conversation that generated the collective speech. Furthermore, this is not a one-sided conversation: the courts respond to the legislature by the ways in which

---

[19] Actually, the situation might be more complicated because sometimes the legislature purports to convey different messages to different audiences. This general phenomenon of legislative double talk is familiar from Meir Dan-Cohen's work on acoustic separation in criminal law (2002) at pp 37–93. I have tried to explain the linguistic relevance of such double-talk: Marmor (2008) 423.

they apply the law and interpret it in doubtful cases. And then the legislature can respond to the courts in various ways, sometimes by overruling the courts' decisions, or by adjusting the legislative discourse to the courts' signals, and so forth. Let me mention some familiar examples to demonstrate these points, and then try to draw some general conclusions.

The most familiar aspect of legislation is that it is almost always a result of a compromise. Compromise often consists in what I would like to call *tacitly acknowledged incomplete decisions*—that is, decisions that deliberately leave certain issues undecided.[20] This is closely tied to the fact that legislation is an instance of collective agency:

X would want to say that 'P' intending to implicate Q.
Y would want to say that 'P' intending to implicate not-Q.
X and Y act collectively, <u>*intending* their collective speech in saying P</u> to remain undecided about the implication of Q.

The general problem is that the underlined *intending* is often not so clear; in fact, the typical case would be one of conflicting and incompatible intentions, hopes, expectations, etc, namely both X and Y intending—or hoping, or expecting—their intentions to prevail. In some cases, this may not be problematic: it is certainly possible that both X and Y would have conflicting intentions or expectations about the implication of Q, without intending their *collective* speech to implicate anything about Q. This kind of compromise is often achieved by settling on a wording in the bill that is more vague (or ambiguous) than would be otherwise required. In such cases, the legislators basically agree to a delegation of power, leaving the specification of the vague term to be settled by the courts. But it would be unrealistic to assume that this is always, or even typically, the case. More often than not, legislators would like to have their legislative agenda realized in practice; they would want to achieve certain goals that are better served by an application of the bill they enact in ways in which they want it to be understood. In other words, the typical case would be the one in which both X and Y expect or at least want that the *collective expression of P* would implicate (or not) that Q.

As an example, consider two legislators agreeing to the following formula of an anti-discrimination provision: 'It is unlawful to discriminate against persons on the basis of gender, race, ethnicity, or nationality'. Now suppose that one of the legislators assumed that 'to discriminate against a person' clearly implies that discrimination would be unlawful if, and only if, it is *intentional*. But the other legislator may not have shared this intended implication. After all (she thought), people can engage in discriminatory practices

---

[20] There is nothing new in this idea; it has been noted by numerous writers.

even if they are not aware of the discriminatory effect of their conduct. And similar divergence can be present with respect to the question of whether the list of grounds for discrimination in the legal provision is exhaustive or not; does this law allow discrimination if it is not based on the listed grounds? (I will say more on this type of implication below.) Once again, it is certainly possible that the collective expression is intended to be indeterminate about these questions (which is typically tantamount to an intention to delegate the decision to the courts). But it is equally possible that legislators simply intend to implicate different content by their collective expression.

Now of course, when this kind of collective action involves numerous agents, sometimes hundreds of legislators, with different political agendas and intentions about bills they enact, and different roles they play in the legislative process, the difficulties are evident. In Gricean terms, the problem in such cases is twofold: first, there is a considerable indeterminacy about *who* counts as a relevant party to the conversation—eg the initiators of the bill, the less-than-enthusiastic supporters, those who voted against?[21] And, second, there is an inherent uncertainty about *what* counts as a relevant contribution to the conversation that different parties are allowed to make. Remember that part of what enables legislators to reach compromises is the fact that they do not have to make their motives, intentions, or expectations all too evident.

Let me pause to take some stock. I have tried to show that unlike regular conversational contexts, where the parties to the conversation aim at a cooperative exchange of information, a partly non-cooperative form of communication is present in the legislative context. The process of legislation itself is plagued with strategic behavior that tries to overcome the lack of initial cooperation between the relevant agents. And then, once we have the result of this process, it becomes very difficult to determine which aspects of it are relevant to determining the content of the legislative speech, and which aspects ought to be ignored.

Assuming that I am correct about this, the following question arises: if the set of maxims of conversation that Grice identified do not necessarily apply to the context of legislative speech, are there other norms that apply instead? Or can we identify which of the Gricean maxims of conversation would apply to the kind of strategic behavior manifest in legislative speech situations, and which would not apply? The answer is rather complex: it partly depends on the normative, that is, moral-political, understanding of the role of legislation in a legal system, and partly on the interpretative practices that courts actually follow. However, as the argument in the previous section suggests, we should

---

[21] For an excellent analysis of the political dynamics of legislation and the differences between various groups of legislators, see Rodriguez and Weingast (2003).

not expect such norms to be fully determinate in any case. Let me try to explain these points.

Abstractly, the idea is this: one might think that just as we draw conclusions about the maxims that apply to an ordinary conversation from the basic cooperative objective of ordinary conversations, we should be able to draw some conclusions about the maxims that would apply to legislative speeches from the nature and objective of such communicative interactions. Can we not simply observe the main objectives of legislation and then draw some conclusions about the relevant conversational maxims that would instantiate those objectives? Perhaps we can think about it in a way that is very similar to a competitive game. Games typically manifest certain forms of strategic behavior. The rules of the game determine what counts as the point of the game, and what kind of skills and abilities one would need to exhibit to play the game and play it successfully. Typically we can draw some conclusions from the purpose of the game about different forms of conduct in it that would be deemed permissible, and others that would not be permissible. Consider chess, for example. Since it is an intellectual kind of competition, we should be able to conclude that chess players are not allowed to use physical intimidation as part of their tactics in the game.[22] In other games, however, such as boxing, and perhaps even football, physical intimidation might be perfectly acceptable. In other words, we can draw some normative conclusions about the kind of moves players should be allowed to make simply from the nature of the game and its general purposes. Can we extend this analogy to legislation, and try to deduce some maxims of conversation that would instantiate our conception of what kind of 'game' legislation is, so to speak?

Two main considerations count against such a possibility. First, the problem is that any conception of the nature of the 'game', which would be sufficiently thick to generate the kind of normative conclusions we are after, is bound to be controversial. People tend to have very different moral-political conceptions of the appropriate division of labor between legislative and adjudicative institutions in the relevant political system. There is, for example, a well-known debate about the role of legislative intent in statutory interpretation. People hold very different views about the appropriate roles of legislative intent in statutory interpretation, ranging from those who advocate great deference to intentions of legislators to those who hold the view that such intentions are completely irrelevant. Now this is just an example of the kind of debate that reflects deeper controversies about the institutional role of a legislature in, say, a constitutional democracy. The question of

---

[22] An actual case of this kind is nicely discussed by R Dworkin (1977) at ch 3.

whether we should take into account, and to what extent, the particular intentions of a legal-political authority in interpreting its directives partly depends on one's views about the legitimacy of such authorities, and their moral-political rationale.[23] And these views tend to be very controversial.

Furthermore, as I have tried to argue here all along, this kind of partial uncertainty about the norms that apply to legislative communication is not incidental. In fact, it is precisely a certain level of uncertainty about the relevant conversational norms that enables the parties to engage in a strategic form of conversation—that is, both during the enactment process and during the ongoing conversation between courts and the legislature. There is, however, one caveat that needs to be mentioned. Over time, the norms of statutory interpretation that are actually followed by the courts may partly determine some conversational maxims of legislation. In following certain norms about the ways in which courts interpret statutory language, the courts could create some kind of Gricean maxims for the legislative context. For example, the extent to which courts are willing to hear evidence about statutory history would partly determine the norms of relevance about legislative implication. Such norms would partly determine what counts as a relevant contribution to the conversation between legislators and the courts, so to speak. Thus, to some extent, and greatly depending on the interpretative culture of the courts, some maxims of conversation might be specified for the legislative context.[24] Note that the reliability of such norms crucially depends on the actual consistency, over time, of the interpretative practices of the courts. If the courts do not consistently adhere to the relevant interpretative practices, the legislators would not have clear signals about what would count as a relevant contribution to the conversation between them and the courts and, therefore, inevitably, even between the legislators themselves. But again, if my argument about the uncertainty of norms of strategic conversation is correct, we should realize that neither the courts nor the legislature would necessarily have a strong incentive to have norms of interpretation that are followed very consistently.

Let me give a couple of examples to demonstrate these points. Consider first this familiar example of implicatures in legislative speech: suppose that the law asserts that 'All Xs ought to φ unless X is an F, a G, or an H.' (Or, which is the more typical case, the law asserts that 'all X's ought to φ', followed by

---

[23] I have explained this in much greater detail in Marmor (2005) at ch 8.

[24] In the United States, courts have adopted numerous canons of statutory interpretation, some of which may look like quasi-Gricean maxims specific to legislative speech. The problem is that these canons, numbering well over 100, often come into conflict, and thus the courts often get to pick and chose which one prevails under the circumstances.

another section prescribing an explicit exemption to those who are F, G, or H.) Now, this kind of utterance would normally implicate that the mentioned exceptions are exhaustive, namely that *all* Xs who are not (F or G or H) ought to φ. Note that this implicature is cancelable; the legislature can easily indicate that it does not consider the exceptions to be exhaustive. However, absent such indication, it would be natural to assume that the legislature has implicated that F, G, and H are the only permissible exceptions to the requirement of Xs to φ. (This is an instance of a generalized conversational implicature.)

Every first-year law student learns, however, that courts are not very consistent in applying such implicatures. Judges tend to be rather skeptical, and perhaps rightly so, of the legislature's ability to determine in advance all the possible justified exceptions to rules they enact. Sometimes, therefore—but, crucially, not always—courts simply ignore the implicature: they treat a list of exceptions as illustrative or incomplete rather than exhaustive.[25] In such cases, the courts are hearing, so to speak, the assertive content of the legislative speech while ignoring the communicative content that was not quite asserted but only implicated by it. And notice that part of what makes this possible is a certain level of uncertainty about the relevant maxims of conversation; uncertainty that is generated by the courts' selective and not quite predictable application of the relevant maxims (the maxim of quantity, in this case). Given the strategic interests of both parties in this interaction—namely the courts and the legislatures—a certain level of uncertainty about the extent of the courts' willingness to infer implicatures is understandable. It allows both parties to make various strategic moves in this game, so to speak.

My second example is about presuppositions. One interesting pragmatic aspect of presuppositions, noted by Soames in the definition I cited above, is the phenomenon of accommodation. When a speaker utters a sentence in a given conversation, the speaker would normally assume that there is some content that is already shared by his hearers and therefore does not need to be asserted. However, sometimes an utterance involves a presupposition that adds some information to the conversational background—information not previously shared by the conversational parties. In such cases, the speaker acts on the assumption that his hearers would be willing to add the presupposed content, without objection, to their shared background. Consider, for example, the utterance of (2) 'Sarah forgot to pick up Jane from the airport.' It is quite possible that the hearer of this utterance was not aware of the fact, or may have not known, that Sarah *was supposed* to pick up Jane from the

---

[25] A famous case in point is *Holy Trinity Church v United States* 143 US 457 (1892).

airport. If the speaker is willing to utter (2) as stated, it is because he would assume that the hearer is willing to add this information to her background knowledge without any particular difficulty. So *now* she knows that Sarah was supposed to pick up Jane from the airport, and she is willing to add this information to her background knowledge in this conversation.

In the legal case, however, accommodation does not always work so smoothly, and for understandable reasons. Let me illustrate this kind of accommodation failure with the famous case of *TVA v Hill*.[26] This was a lengthy and complicated litigation about the construction of the Tellico Dam by the Tennessee Valley River Authority. Environmental organizations wanted to halt the construction of the dam, claiming that it would endanger the habitat of a small fish, called the snail darter, in violation of the newly enacted Endangered Species Act.[27] As it turned out, however, after the environmental issues had come to the public's attention, Congress continued to fund the construction of the dam in its annual appropriation bills. Now, one would have thought that if Congress appropriates funds to the construction of a certain project, the presupposition is that the project is legally authorized.[28] Nevertheless, the Supreme Court decided that these appropriation bills could not be taken to have implicated that Congress legally authorized the construction of the dam in face of the environmental opposition that was salient by that time. In effect, the court refused to accommodate the information that was conveyed by the presupposed content of the appropriation bills. By refusing to accommodate this fairly obvious presupposition, the court explicitly ignored content that the legislative speech is committed to.[29] I am not suggesting that the court was wrong (or right) to do this; I mention this case only to demonstrate how the pragmatic commitments of legislative speech— which were very clear in this case—do not necessarily form part of the uptake that the court is willing to accommodate, and perhaps legitimately so.

There is another point I wish to make by mentioning the *TVA* litigation: this is one of those cases in which the strategic nature of legislative speech is demonstrated very clearly. When Congress enacted the appropriation bills, it

---

[26] 437 US (1978) 153.

[27] The protection of the snail darter was not quite the main reason for the opposition to the dam; the issues involved were very complex; partly environmental and partly economic.

[28] In particular that there was a looming unsettled question about the application of the Endangered Species Act to the Tellico Dam because the construction of the dam had started years before the act came into effect. Many legal commentators assumed at the time that the act should not be applied to projects that were underway by the time it came into effect.

[29] For more details on this case, see McCubbins and Rodriguez (2005) at p 699. (I do not quite share the authors' negative view about the court's decision in this case. I do think that they are right, however, that the court relied on questionable information about the deliberative quality of appropriations procedures in Congress.)

was already apparent that there was serious environmental opposition to the construction of the dam and that the construction might be halted if the snail darter were added to the endangered species list (as it was). However, instead of making the unpopular move of explicitly overruling the Endangered Species Act and authorizing the construction of the dam (or explicitly over-ruling the Fish and Wildlife Service's (FWS) decision to list the snail darter as an endangered species), Congress hoped to achieve the result more obliquely by continuing the appropriation of funds to the construction. One can only surmise that there was not enough support in Congress to face the environmentalists head-on. Now, as I have tried to argue here, the more strategic the nature of the relevant conversation, the more likely it is that the pragmatic commitments of speakers and the interests of hearers in the uptake of those commitments may diverge. Which is to say that the divergence of interests between speakers and hearers about implied content is likely to vary according to differences in legal areas and the types of legislative speech that are characteristic of different types of legal regulation. The more strategic the legislative context is, the less we should expect to see an alignment of the speaker's intended implications and the hearer's interests in acknowledging the uptake of those implications and vice versa, of course.

For example, in areas of regulatory legislation, particularly in areas in which the regulation is based on expertise, it is less likely that courts will have an incentive to ignore pragmatic implications of legislative speech.[30] In fact, the *TVA* decision itself nicely demonstrates this. One way to see the dilemma here is in terms of a conflict between two different types of legislation: on the one hand, there was the Endangered Species Act and the ensuing regulatory decision of the FWS that added the snail darter to the list of endangered species. On the other hand, there were the appropriation bills enacted by Congress. Basically, the court decided that the expert regulatory legislation prevails. Once again, my point here is not to justify the court's ruling; the point is to demonstrate that the courts are quite sensitive to the distinctions between different types of legislative speech, and that judges largely follow the principle that the more strategic the legislative context is, the less they are willing to hear more than what the speech actually asserts.

I hope that my discussion shows that, as a general policy, this makes a lot of sense, and not only for the courts but for the legislature as well. As long as

---

[30] The US Supreme Court explicitly recognizes greater deference to expert agency regulations. This is called the *Chevron* doctrine, based on the decision in *Chevron USA, Inc v Natural Resources Defense Council, Inc* 467 US 837 (1984). As commentators have noted, however, the *Chevron* doctrine is itself discriminately applied, depending on the level of confidence that courts have in the relative expertise of the agency in question.

both parties have an interest in maintaining a strategic conversation, both would have an interest in some level of opacity about the norms governing their conversation. Expert agencies, on the other hand, are typically not in the business of making strategic moves; they are under much less pressure to conceal their strategic aims, and they need less strategic flexibility and more clarity. Therefore, in the case of agency regulations, we should expect greater alignment between the speaker's pragmatic commitments and the hearer's willingness to grasp those commitments as such. Thus, generally speaking, the more strategic the nature of the interaction, the more we should expect a divergence between what the speakers strive to implicate and what the hearers would be willing to uptake or accommodate. And vice versa: the less strategic the legislative context is, the closer it comes to the standard Gricean model of ordinary conversations. [31]

[31] I am grateful to Scott Altman, Marshall Cohen, Joseph Raz, and Scott Soames, for helpful comments on a draft of this chapter.

6

Textualism and the Discovery of Rights[1]

John Perry

Excessive bail shall not be required, nor excessive fines imposed, nor cruel and unusual punishments inflicted.

US Constitution, Eighth Amendment

Mr Livermore:...No cruel and unusual punishment is to be inflicted; it is sometimes necessary to hang a man, villains often deserve whipping, and perhaps having their ears cut off; but are we in the future to be prevented from inflicting these punishments because they are cruel? If a more lenient mode of correcting vice and deterring others from the commission of it would be invented, it would be very prudent in the Legislature to adopt it; but until we have some security that this will be done, we ought not to be restrained from making necessary laws by any declaration of this kind.

1 *Annals of Congress*, 782–3 (1789)

1. Introduction

1.1 Textualism

Textualism is the view that the content of a statute—basically, what actions it mandates, forbids, or protects—is determined by the original meaning of the text of the statute. The original meaning is determined by the words of the text and the meanings they were commonly understood to have had at the time of enactment. Textualism is the view espoused by US Supreme Court Associate Justice Antonin Scalia;[2] sometimes he calls it 'textualism-originalism', but I will just call it 'textualism'.

---

[1] I am grateful to Anne Gardner, Scott Soames, Andrei Marmor, and students in the Soames–Marmor fall 2009 seminar on law and language at USC for helpful discussion.
[2] Scalia (1998a).

In this paper I distinguish between two understandings of textualism, which I will call 'meaning-textualism' and 'conception-textualism'. Meaning-textualism strikes me as commonsensical and attractive; conception-textualism as confused, implausible, and unworkable.[3]

Meaning-textualism is the view that the content of a statute is determined by the words in the text of the statute, given the meaning that those words had at the time of enactment or ratification, or, in the case of ambiguity, those meanings or *senses*,[4] among those the words had at the time, which the enactors intended to exploit and the ratifiers understood the text as written to be using.[5] Of course, the writer may spell out a special meaning for a term in the text itself. If the writer only spells out the special meaning in his own notes or diary, the meaning-textualist should regard this, prima facie, as only of historical interest.

Conception-textualism is the view that the conceptions that the enactors had of the states, conditions, phenomena, and the like referred to by their words, used with their commonly understood meanings, in the operative senses, are determinative. Here by 'conception' I mean 'the way a thing is perceived or regarded,' or more broadly what is believed about a thing—that is, about an object, kind of object, condition, activity, kind of activity, and so forth. In giving us the meaning of a word, the dictionary basically tells us what condition, phenomena, etc the word refers to, either in other words, or with familiar examples, or a combination. This provides some small amount of agreement that is necessary for different individuals to use the word with the same meaning, but it does not determine a conception of the thing in question. You may love tomatoes, think they are vegetables, nutritious, and best served uncooked. I may hate them, think they are fruits and for that reason not vegetables, and think that they are poisonous if served uncooked. Still, we can talk about tomatoes, argue about tomatoes, and perhaps agree on a policy that forbids our city or state from importing tomatoes grown elsewhere. Samuel Livermore, the senator quoted above, may have thought that hanging was cruel, and so would be banned by the Eighth Amendment, while others with whom he was debating did not share this opinion. Still, they use the same word, with the same meaning, in the same sense, in conducting their debate.

---

[3] Rakove (1996) has a useful set of distinctions among kinds of textualism, somewhat more historically nuanced than the one I make.

[4] I use 'sense' when a word has more than one meaning, and speak of the *sense exploited* by the speaker and *understood* by those hearing or reading and interpreting the words as *operative*.

[5] Ordinary statutes are enacted by legislative bodies. Constitutions, amendments, and the like are typically ratified by groups that were not responsible for writing them. The US Constitution was ratified by the state legislatures. James Madison argued persuasively that in the case of the Constitution it was the understanding of the ratifiers, not the writers, that should be authoritative. So the distinction is important. Nevertheless, I will usually just say 'enactors'.

Sometimes Scalia seems to advocate meaning-textualism, at other times conception-textualism, and sometimes it is hard to tell exactly how he is thinking of things.

'Meaning' of course has many meanings, and can be used for both meanings and conceptions, and a number of other related things, from the intentions of agents to the significance of an event.[6] I use it in the sense in which dictionaries give us the meanings of words. They do not tell us what a given utterance meant historically (its significance in the grand scheme of things), or what the speaker or speakers meant (intended to achieve in uttering it). For descriptive nouns, verbs, adjectives, and adverbs at any rate, the dictionary tells us what conditions an object of the appropriate sort has to meet to truly be described by the word. Many, perhaps most, words can be used for different conditions, corresponding to different senses. If we look up 'irritate', for example, we find two senses: to irritate is to make someone annoyed, impatient, or angry; or to cause inflammation or other discomfort in a part of the body. As I understand meaning-textualism, it is the *sense* of the words that was originally operative, which will typically be among the meanings a good dictionary of the time will explain, that is at issue. It is what we learn about a word in a specific text by looking up the meaning of the word in a dictionary, and, if more than one meaning is given, by figuring out which one was being employed. This latter issue is often, although certainly not always, fairly clear from the linguistic and communicative contexts. If the dictionary is accurate, this procedure will tell us what the writers, signers, ratifiers, etc took the meaning of the word to be, if they were 'semantically competent', and what they assumed the semantically competent contemporary readers of the statute would take it to mean.

Meaning-textualism seems like common sense to me because it seems to apply to statutes the same apparatus we use to determine what some individual *says* when they are talking to us, which is a somewhat different question than what they intend to achieve or imply. If my wife, who knows a lot about where things are but can be confused about right and left when things are happening fast, tells me 'turn left at the stop sign', and I turn left, I have done what she *said* I should do, even if, in fact, she wanted me to go to the right. If I suspect she is confused, and turn right, then I have done what she meant to tell me to do, but I have not done what she said to do, given the meanings of the words she used. We have a fairly robust concept of what a person says. Meaning-textualism takes it that statutes prohibit or allow what the person who uttered the words, at the time they were enacted, said was prohibited or allowed. And that seems like common sense.

---

[6] Rakove (1996) has a good discussion of this from a historian's point of view.

But more importantly, perhaps, is that meaning-textualism seems necessary for understanding how people of diverse opinions about matters can nevertheless agree on principles, rules, policies, and laws, and expect the principles, rules, policies, and laws to be followed by others with different conceptions about things. People can use words with the same meaning, and intend the same meaning, while disagreeing about very important issues concerning the things the words refer to. Members of a philosophy department may agree about the meaning of 'philosophical' and the meaning of 'talent' and the meaning of 'philosophical talent'. They may agree, say, that it is a trait that some people have and others do not, such that those who have it are more likely, other things being equal, to do well in rigorous philosophy programs and produce good works of philosophy. Within that agreement about meaning, they may have considerable disagreement about philosophical talent. Some may think that the mathematics Graduate Record Examination (GRE) score is the single best indicator of philosophical talent; others may think it is of virtually no value at all. Some may think that great logicians exhibit the highest kind of philosophical talent; others may think that most of them are deficient in it. Some may think that many leaders of the field completely lack philosophical talent, while others may think that these same individuals are philosophically very talented. What I mean by a person's conception of a thing (property, relation, kind, condition, phenomenon, trait, etc), referred to by a term T, is basically what they believe more or less firmly about it; the beliefs that guide them are determining which things are or are not, or probably are, or probably are not, correctly described with the term T.

Without some agreement in or overlap of conceptions of what is referred to by a term T, people cannot use T with the same meaning. They must be able to arrive at some acceptable definition, or agree on a range of examples that exemplify the trait, to be talking about the same phenomenon at all. But considerable disagreement in conception is compatible with agreement in meaning. If it were not, most departmental policies would never be enacted. If we agree on what we mean by 'philosophical talent', it makes sense for us to pass a policy statement stating that our department, in considering graduate applications, will make the decision solely on the basis of expected philosophical talent. We might pass the policy, publish it in the catalogue, and remind ourselves of it each year when we consider which students to admit. This agreement in policy, and what the meaning of the text of the policy is, will not at all preclude vigorous debates about which students exhibit philosophical talent, what good signs of it are, and whether those most talented are more or less likely to go on to successful careers.

Conception-textualism, as a philosophy of interpretation for documents, such as constitutions, statutes, policy statements, committee reports, and all sorts of other things that are prepared by groups of people with the intention of communicating with and regulating the behavior of themselves and others, seems to me a rather bizarre and hopeless idea. If one finds in the policies of a philosophy department the statement that only philosophical talent shall be used as a criterion for the admission of graduate students, one should not assume that the department members who enacted this policy shared a conception of philosophical talent. Most likely they had different opinions about who had talent, what the nature of philosophical talent mainly consisted of, and what good tests for it were. All we can conclude is that a majority thought that philosophical talent should be the sole criterion for admission. If they take the policies of the department seriously, future department members should either use philosophical talent as the sole criterion for admission, or change the policy.

Even if there were a conception of philosophical talent shared by the writers and original enactors of the policy, that would not mean that their conception is authoritative and binding on later department members. If a philosophy department was dominated by logicians at the time the policy was adopted, they may have expected and intended that by passing the policy they would guarantee that future graduate classes will be made up of logically sophisticated students. If with time the department comes to be dominated by historians of philosophy, existentialists, and social and political philosophers, the remaining logicians may be sorely disappointed. They can argue that the policy is not being followed, because the people being admitted are not being admitted on the basis of what really is philosophical talent but on the basis of other traits that their incompetent colleagues confuse for philosophical talent. Their colleagues can argue back that many of the students the writers of the policy admitted in years past were in fact completely without philosophical talent. That argument is fair enough. But the logicians cannot legitimately argue that, because they wrote the policy, their conception of philosophical talent is authoritative. Their argument has to be conducted on the issue of what the best evidence for philosophical talent is, not on the basis of what they hoped to achieve.

So, I think there are two forms of textualism, and I like one and not the other, and I think both are espoused in different places by Scalia.

1.2 Discovering rights

The general question I wish to explore is whether the discovery of previously unrecognized rights makes sense within a textualist framework. It seems to me that it surely does make sense within the framework of meaning-textualism, but it may not in the framework of conception-textualism.

In a collection of Scalia's opinions, *Scalia Dissents*, the editor Kevin Ring notes the peculiar history of the right to sodomy. In 1986 the US Supreme Court decided that sodomy was not protected; the Constitution does not mention it and there was no history of protection of it, and in fact all states prohibited it until 1961. In 2003, the Supreme Court ruled that it was a constitutional right. According to Ring, this sort of thing may make sense for advocates of a 'living constitution', but does not make sense for textualists: 'For textualists like Scalia, the result does not change unless the law, that is, the text, changes.'[7]

I will call this 'Ring's Principle'. If the facts of the lack of protection of sodomy are fixed, the words of the text are fixed, and the original meanings are fixed, what then can have changed between 1986, or 1789, and 2003, so that sodomy was not a constitutionally protected right for such a long time, but then became one?

If one is a meaning-textualist, there seems to be at least the possibility of an answer: something has been learned about sodomy that was not previously known, and this fact shows that sodomy falls under one of the general protections in the text of the Constitution. If one is a conception-textualist, Ring's Principle seems unassailable (or at least pretty plausible).

Consider the open sentence (1), where 'A' is a variable for actions broadly construed, that is, anything from expressing one's ideas to committing sodomy to living without being executed, and 'S' is the name of a particular statute:

(1) The right to A is guaranteed by statute S.

Could (1) be *discovered* to hold for some action A, at some date after the statute was enacted? It seems this might happen in two ways. First, it could be for some reason or another action A did not qualify for protection at the time the statute was enacted and some period of time thereafter; then things changed and from then on the action did qualify for protection. The discovery involved is simply the discovery that relevant facts have changed. I will call this the 'Change Model'.

A second possibility is that the relevant facts do not change, that A was protected from the moment statute S was enacted, but for some reason this fact was not *discovered* until some time later. I will call this the 'Knowledge Model'. Do either of these possibilities make sense if one stipulates that the text of the statute, with its original meaning, determines what is and is not protected?

---

[7] Ring (2004) at p 7.

1.3 Meaning-textualism and the death penalty

I will focus on the death penalty. Given meaning-textualism, could we discover now or at some point in the future that the death penalty was unconstitutional? That is, that we have the right to live out our lives without being executed, no matter what crimes we commit? Scalia finds it especially absurd to suppose that the right not to be executed could be found in the Eighth Amendment to the Constitution, since the promulgators clearly contemplate this punishment in the Fifth Amendment, which required due process before one could be deprived of 'life, liberty, or property'. As Dworkin puts Scalia's point:

The 'framers' would hardly have bothered to stipulate that 'life' may be taken only after due process if they thought that the Eighth Amendment made capital punishment unconstitutional anyway.[8]

Scalia says:

No textualist-originalist interpretation that passes the laugh test could, for example, extract from the United States Constitution the prohibition of capital punishment that three nontextualist justices have discovered.[9]

Dworkin, however, thinks that it at least makes sense that the death penalty could be discovered to be unconstitutional. There is no contradiction, he says, in claiming that the framers' original meaning was that punishments that are cruel should be forbidden; that they did not think that the death penalty was cruel and did not intend to forbid it; and that it turns out nevertheless to be cruel.

Dworkin offers the following example as an analogy:

Suppose some legislature enacts a law forbidding the hunting of animals that are members of an 'endangered species' and then, later in its term, imposes special license requirements for hunting, among other animals, minks. We would assume that the members who voted for both provisions did not think that minks were endangered. But we would not be justified in concluding from that fact that, as a matter of law, minks were excluded from the ban even if they plainly *were* endangered.[10]

Dworkin's analogy suggests the Change Model.[11] Although what is at issue is a prohibition, rather than a protection, of a kind of action, we shall see that the Eighth Amendment itself suggests cases of this type involving rights.

---

[8] Dworkin (1998) at p 120.   [9] Scalia (1998b) at p 132.
[10] Dworkin (1998) at p 121.
[11] Although it does not require it, for, as he words it, minks may have already been endangered at the time the statute was enacted.

2. Two models for discovering rights

2.1 Preliminaries: meaning, reference, extension, and conception

I begin by making a number of distinctions drawn from the philosophy of language, which seem necessary for a clear understanding of what meaning-textualism implies. I will not explain them in their full generality, but focus on issues relevant to phrases of the sort that occur in the Eighth Amendment: 'excessive bail', 'excessive fines', 'cruel and unusual punishments'. One such phrase is 'endangered species', which occurs in Dworkin's example, and I will start with that.

Consider a simple sentence:

(1) Red-eared frogs are an endangered species.

This sentence appears to work in the following straightforward way. The term 'red-eared frogs' stands for a certain group of frogs. The word 'species' stands for the set of all species. 'Endangered' is an adjective, applied to species. Its effect is to narrow what 'endangered species' stands for: it stands for a subset of the set of species. The statement is true if the group of frogs that 'red-eared frogs' stands for is a member of that narrowed-down set; that is, if that group is an endangered species; that is, if red-eared frogs are a species, and are, in addition, endangered.

If we look up the words 'species' and 'endangered' in the dictionary, we will not find a list of the members of all the species, nor a list of things that are endangered. Rather, we will find conditions, explained in other words, that things must satisfy to be members of those sets. A species is a group of living organisms that meets the condition that its members can interbreed. Something is endangered, in the relevant sense, if it is threatened with extinction. Now we might also say that the words 'species' and 'endangered' stand for these conditions. We need to distinguish between these two intuitive uses of 'stands for'.

Following standard usage in the philosophy of language, I will call the *set* of species the *extension* of the word 'species.' I will call the condition of *being a group of living organisms that can interbreed* the *reference* of 'species'. (The word 'reference' is not always used this way.) The extension of the word 'endangered' is a function, which takes us from a set to a subset of that set. The extension of 'endangered species' is a set, the set that results from applying this function to the set of species. 'Endangered' refers to the condition of *being near extinction*. 'Endangered species' refers to the condition of *being a group of living organisms that can interbreed and is near extinction*. All of this should strike readers as an elaborate way of telling them something they already know.

This picture, however, will not quite do. Red-eared frogs were not endangered in 1789, or in 1867 when Mark Twain wrote a famous story about them.[12] They are endangered now, in 2009. Which species are endangered changes with time, and time must somehow figure into our story. The word 'endangered' gives us a *time-relative condition*, so we really cannot simply say that (2) is true or false. It really is not sentences, but statements—uses of sentences on particular occasions by persons or groups of persons to say something—that are true and false, and a statement made with (2) in 1867 would have been false, while one made today would be true.

The meaning of 'endangered' does not really give us a condition on species, but a condition on species relative to time. To narrow down the set of species to the relevant set of endangered species, we need time. The present tense tells us that the relevant time for the statement made in 1867 is that year, and 2009 for the statement made today. The same information could have been conveyed by an indexical, like 'now', or an explicit date, like '1867'.

The fact that the extension of a phrase varies with time does not imply that the meaning of the phrase has changed. Bald eagles are now not an endangered species in the very same meaning of the phrase 'endangered species' in which they once were endangered, and red-eared frogs are now an endangered species in the very same meaning of the phrase in which they once were not. If the phrase 'original meaning' in the formulation of textualism comes to 'original meaning', then textualism does not rule out in general that the extension of protected or prohibited actions according to a statute will not vary with time.

It is important, to repeat myself, that we distinguish conditions from the conceptions that people may have about those conditions; that is, mainly, beliefs about which objects meet the conditions, what is good evidence for meeting the condition, what are underlying causes and effects of the condition, and so on.

2.2 The Change Model

It is typical of statutes to confer a status on actions for the indefinite future: 'Excessive bail *shall not be* required.' The time at which excessive bail shall not be *required* is clear: any time in the future. But relative to which time or times should the bail be *excessive*? In 1789, or when the indictment occurs?

---

[12] 'The Celebrated Jumping Frog of Calaveras County.' At least, red-eared frogs were the dominant species when Twain lived in Calaveras County. A jumping frog contest is held each year at the Calaveras County Fair, but red-eared frogs are seldom if ever contestants, since various non-native frogs are much better jumpers.

'Endangered species shall not be hunted.' *When* can they not be hunted? Any time after the statute is enacted. But as of when do they need to be endangered, to fall under the statute's protection? At the time of enactment, or the time of hunting?

We can give the statute either a *fixed* or *functional* interpretation. In the first case, it is the set of species that are endangered at the time of the legislation that cannot be hunted, even if they cease to be endangered, or if other species come to be endangered. If we give the statute the functional interpretation, on the other hand, then hunting for a species is prohibited at each time, if at that time the species is endangered. Thus, hunting for minks might be prohibited, by the original meaning of the statute, even though at the time it was enacted it did not outlaw the hunting of minks, and was even part of legislation that licensed hunting for them.

In his discussion of Dworkin's example, Scalia says that, in my terminology, he would be inclined to interpret the statute with a fixed rather than functional interpretation. However, such an inclination is surely not required by textualism. Language in general is rife with predicates and general terms whose extension varies with time, and many such predicates and general terms make their way into statutes, and the natural interpretation is most often functional. A statute enacted in 1960, say, prohibiting the sale of alcohol to minors, understood as those under 21 years of age, would not prohibit for the indefinite future the sale of alcohol to those persons who happened to be born after 1939; it would be given a functional rather than a fixed interpretation. I assume that in the late eighteenth century a bail of, say, $100,000 would have been excessive for the crime of involuntary manslaughter. Nowadays that would not be excessive bail for such a crime. Does a correct interpretation of the bail clause of the Eighth Amendment fix excessiveness thresholds at their 1789 values, or deem them to be a function of the time of indictment? The latter is surely correct. We seem to have an example of losing a right when the threshold of excessiveness passed $100,000, namely the right not to have one's bail set at $100,000 for involuntary manslaughter.

Still, being endangered, as a condition on species, or being excessive, as a condition on bail, does not seem like a completely apt analogy for being cruel, as a condition on punishments. There seems to be no set of facts, like the varying sizes of animal and plant populations, that would make some punishments cruel at one time that were not cruel at others. Of course, which punishments people *consider* to be cruel, and the conception of cruelty itself, certainly vary, with all sorts of factors—not only time, but social class, culture, familiarity, and the like—and in bizarre ways. A few years ago Americans were aghast when a Californian in Singapore was sentenced to caning for chewing gum on a subway. In spite of the sensitivity manifested in this reaction, Americans do not seem to regard sentencing people to overcrowded and dangerous prisons for long periods of time for non-violent offenses such as selling small quantities of marijuana as cruel. In fact, both punishments are cruel.

Scalia's second objection to the mink example is in effect that 'cruel' is not relevantly analogous to 'endangered'. This is a much better objection to Dworkin, I think. The discovery that a given punishment is cruel will not be very much like the discovery that a given species is endangered. However, there is still plenty of conceptual room for such discoveries, even given textualism.

What is required, of course, is not simply a case where the conception of what is cruel has changed. Perhaps some day people in Singapore will agree that caning is a cruel punishment for chewing gum, and Americans will come to see that many of the sentences currently imposed for drug offenses are quite cruel. I myself would be dubious that such changes in opinion would reflect either an abandonment of the current meaning of 'cruel' or a change in the extension of 'cruel' due to some temporal parameter buried in the structure of its meaning. I think such punishments are cruel now, and people who do not realize this are simply wrong.

To make a distinction between change in meaning, and hence the condition associated with a term, and mere change in the opinions people have about the condition, presupposes a certain degree of realism about the condition, allowing for objectivity, and the possibility that opinions can vary from person to person and time to time, although the condition and the facts are the same. There are many kinds of human discourse where such realism might seem implausible. I will argue below that cruelty should be treated realistically.

2.3 The Knowledge Model

Suppose that in 1956 a legislature passes a statute to ban the sale of 'toxic paint', defined within the statute as paint that when dry will expose children who chew and lick the painted surface to dangerous levels of toxins. Now at that time, lead-based paint was widely used for painting houses, windowsills, toys, and all sorts of other chewable and lickable objects. And lead-based paint, when dried, exposes children who lick and chew the painted surface to dangerous levels of toxins. However, this was not known until the 1970s.

One can imagine such a statute being passed in concert with other paint-oriented statutes, perhaps requiring that 60 per cent of the lead in lead-based paint comes from American sources of lead, that make it clear that the legislators did not plan or expect or in any way intend or contemplate that the use of lead-based paint would be banned. Indeed, they may have all been in the pockets of a lead-based paint company, who thought the legislation would clear the market of modern alternatives to their product.

Perhaps it sounds odd to say that the legislature banned the sale of lead-based paint but did not know that it had. This oddness is simply because we expect bans, once made, to be put into effect, and do not think to allow for the case of ignorance of the extension of the relevant predicate. So it sounds odd, but it is correct. At any rate, it seems clear that the statute, with its original meaning, provides the statutory basis for preventing the sale of lead-based paint once it is established that lead-based paint in fact leaves toxic residue. What changes, when this is discovered to be true of lead-based paint, is not the text of the statute, nor the conditions to which it refers, nor an implicit temporal parameter, nor even the extension of kinds of paint that in fact meet the condition for banning. What changes is knowledge of which kinds of paints meet the condition, and, as a result, what steps are taken to put the ban on toxic paints into effect.

This also does not seem to be a perfect analogy with 'cruel punishments', at least at first glance. The issue of whether a type of punishment is cruel or not does not seem to depend on hidden properties of the punishment, analogous to the toxic properties of lead-based paint, any more than it seems to depend on time-sensitive conditions, as 'endangered species' or 'excessive bail' does.

Still, I think that when we look closely at the original meaning of 'cruel punishments', we shall see that both the Change Model and the Knowledge Model have some application.

3. Cruel and unusual punishments

3.1 Introduction

All four words in the phrase 'cruel and unusual punishments' are interesting and problematic. We can start with 'and'. The punishment clause of the Eighth Amendment comes to this: 'Cruel and unusual punishments shall not be inflicted.' Does this mean to prohibit punishments that are either cruel or unusual (the union of the set of cruel punishments and the set of unusual ones)? Or only punishments that are *both* cruel and unusual (the intersection of the two sets)?

Logic teaches us that 'and' means conjunction and 'or' means disjunction, but this does not resolve the issue. Are we interested in the set of punishments that are cruel *and* unusual (the intersection)? Or are we interested in the set consisting of the cruel *and* the unusual (the union)?

Suppose a restaurant has a sign: 'Shirtless and shoeless customers shall not be admitted.' This means the same as: No shoes, no shirt, no admittance. That is, it would exclude shirtless shod people, and shoeless shirted people, as well as barefoot, bare-chested people; not just those in the intersection of the two sets, but all of those in their union, are unwelcome. Similarly, if a more welcoming bar has a sign that says, 'Shirtless and shoeless customers are especially welcome, the shirtless shod and the shoeless shirted should feel as welcome as those both unshod and unshirted.' Not just those in the intersection, but also those in the union, are welcome.

On the other hand, if the sign at the unwelcoming restaurant had said, 'Shirtless, shoeless customers shall not be admitted', it would seem that the shirtless and shod and the shirted and shoeless are welcome; it would not have been quite as unwelcoming. And if the bar had said, 'Shoeless, shirtless customers are especially welcome', we would expect the shirtless to be removing their shoes and the shoeless to be removing their shirts to be welcome.

It seems to me that the punishment clause, as a case of relatively unexceptional English, naturally has the union reading. If it had read, 'Cruel, unusual punishments shall not be inflicted', it would have the intersection reading.

If we take 'unusual' in its normal meaning, of not being habitually or commonly done, then the condition of being an unusual punishment is clearly time sensitive, as well as involving some reference class. That is, the questions: unusual when? unusual where? and unusual among whom? naturally arise. A conceivable hard-nosed interpreter could support a fixed interpretation of 'unusual' and an intersection reading of 'and', and we would not be protected from any punishment, no matter how cruel, if it was not unusual in 1789.[13] A softie might claim that the death penalty is no longer usual in the appropriate reference class, the community of civilized nations, and so is unconstitutional for being unusual, whether or not it is cruel.

In 1789, the phrase 'cruel and unusual' may have suggested methods of executing people that were definitely cruel and also unusual outside of Spain and Germany, and which met with widespread disapproval in the English-speaking world. And they might also have had in mind the arbitrary decrees of earlier English Tudor and Stuart monarchs: the clause is lifted intact from the English Bill of Rights of 1689, following the Glorious Revolution. The

---

[13] In *Harmelin v Michigan* 501 US 957 (1991), Scalia argued that common—that is, not unusual—punishments are not prohibited even if they are cruel, and unusual punishments are not prohibited as long as they are not cruel. These opinions deserve a close analysis, but I am not able to do that here.

death penalty itself, most likely carried out by hanging, may not have been thought by many to be cruel in 1789, although US Senator Samuel Livermore, quoted at the beginning of this chapter, who does not seem to be particularly soft-hearted, clearly thought it was cruel. He thought that cutting off ears and the death penalty, though cruel, were necessary to deter the crimes for which they were used as punishments, and so argued against including the clause in the American Bill of Rights. However, I believe that Scalia is correct that the cruelty of the death penalty as such was not a live issue in 1789, but that certain modes of execution, such as death on the rack, or drawing and quartering, were thought to be cruel.

3.2 Cruel punishments

The meaning of 'cruel'

One possibility that would support Scalia's reasoning and Ring's Principle, even within the context of meaning-textualism, is that in 1789 the word 'cruel', used with its usual meaning, directly picked out a subset of punishments. I will call the subset 'Cruel-1789'. If this possibility were actual, only punishments that belong to this set would be prohibited by the Eighth Amendment. It could be that in, say, 1965, the word 'cruel' used with its usual import at that time picks out a different set of punishments, Cruel-1965. It may well be that execution belongs to Cruel-1965. But that would be irrelevant to whether it is prohibited by the Eighth Amendment. We have very clear evidence (the fact that execution is clearly contemplated as a possible outcome of due process elsewhere in the Bill of Rights) that execution was not, and so is not, a member of Cruel-1789. *If* this were how the meaning of 'cruel' worked, no meaning-textualist could reasonably suppose that in 1965 execution was prohibited by the Eighth Amendment; the set Cruel-1965 is irrelevant. The view would not pass the laugh test.

But descriptive adjectives do not usually work that way, and 'cruel' is no exception. If we compare, say, the 1755 definition from Samuel Johnson's *A Dictionary of the English Language*,[14] Noah Webster's 1828 definition from *An American Dictionary of the English Language*,[15] and the definition from my Apple computer's dictionary,[16] we do not gain the impression that there has been a significant change in meaning, and none of them gives the meaning of 'cruel' by enumerating its extension. Johnson defines 'cruel' as 'Pleased with

---

[14] Johnson (1785).   [15] Webster (1828).
[16] McKean (2005).

hurting others; inhuman; hardhearted; void of pity; wanting compassion; savage; barbarous; unrelenting.'[17] Webster says:

Disposed to give pain to others, in body or mind; willing or pleased to torment, vex or afflict; inhuman; destitute of pity, compassion or kindness; fierce; ferocious; savage; barbarous; hardhearted; applied to persons or their dispositions.[18]

My computer's dictionary defines it as 'having or showing a sadistic disregard for the pain or suffering of others'.

It is extremely important to note that all these definitions define 'cruel' as an attribute of humans, not of actions generally or of punishments, so none of them tells us directly what we need to know to interpret the amendment. The *Oxford English Dictionary* (*OED*) does provide a definition of 'cruel' as applied to actions, clearly derived from its meaning when applied to persons:

1. Of persons (also transf. and fig. of things): Disposed to inflict suffering; indifferent to or taking pleasure in another's pain or distress; destitute of kindness or compassion; merciless, pitiless, hard-hearted.

c. Of actions, etc: Proceeding from or showing indifference to or pleasure in another's distress.[19]

The sense of 'cruel' the *OED* gives for 'actions' seems clearly to pertain to specific acts, and not types of acts. I will reserve the term 'action' for *types* of acts, so I take clause (c) of the *OED* definition to be about particular acts. Whether an *act* is cruel, the *OED* tells us, depends on the attributes of the agent that causes it, or that it shows him to have. In my terminology, the second part of the *OED* quote tells us that acts are cruel if they proceed from the cruelty of the person—that is, the quality, of the person, to be disposed to inflict suffering, and to be indifferent or take pleasure from it.

Consider the *action* of cutting off a child's arm. It is definitely an action that could be done by a cruel person; it does cause pain and suffering, and so might well be the sort of thing that a (particularly) cruel person would do for that reason. However, a given *act* of cutting off a child's arm might not express insensitivity to pain and suffering or hard-heartedness if it were done to stop the spread of gangrene or cancer. In deciding whether a particular act that induces pain and suffering is cruel or not, we want to know why the pain and suffering-inducing action was performed on the given occasion, as a part of the particular act.

---

[17] Johnson (1785).
[18] Webster (1928).
[19] Simson and Weiner (1989).

Acts, actions, executions, accomplishments: action structures

At this point it will be helpful to reflect a bit on the structure of acts. By 'action', as I said, I mean a type of act, while acts are particular events. *Acts* involve agents at times moving their bodies and parts of their bodies in various ways, in the circumstances they are in, and thereby bringing about certain results, and thus performing indefinitely many *actions*. The act that inaugurated this sentence was a moving of my right forefinger, a depressing of a key, a typing of a 't', a disturbing of the air around me, and many other things. *By* moving my finger, while it was perched over the keyboard in a certain way, I depressed the 't' key. Moving my finger is a *way of* depressing the 't' key in those circumstances. If my computer is turned on and functioning properly, by depressing the 't' key I make a 't' appear on my monitor. And so on. Acts have structure, studied in the philosophy of action, and recognized in ordinary ways of thinking and talking about actions, in particular the word 'by' and the phrase 'is a way of'. What we do *by* performing one action in one set of circumstances can be quite different from what we do by performing the same action in a different set of circumstances. For example, making a certain poking movement with my forefinger in certain circumstances is a way of calling an elevator, and thereby inconveniencing its current hurried occupants, who would have preferred to bypass my floor. In different circumstances, the same movement might be a way of poking a short man in the eye, thereby making him angry. In the one case, *by* poking my finger, I called the elevator and annoyed its occupants; in the other, *by* poking my finger, I made a short man angry.

We can distinguish between basic actions or *executions* (no pun intended) and *accomplishments*, the latter being the things brought about by executing movements in circumstances. From certain points of view, one might think that the real act simply consists of a person moving in a certain way at a certain time. For most purposes, however, we think of an act as having a more complex and interesting structure. This will involve the way it was done (what movements were executed to perform the action, in what circumstances) and what it was a way of doing (the actions that were done by performing it, in the circumstances). In the case of intentional actions, the relevant structure includes the reasons for which it was done, and so its intended as well as its actual results. How much of the action structure exemplified by an act will be brought into its description depends on what we are interested in. A statement like 'Fred went to the store to buy pickles', implies that he somehow moved his body, but does not tell us much about how he did it. If he went to the store, he either drove or walked or biked; if he walked, he either started with his left foot or right foot; and so on. Such details are brought in as they are relevant. The description focuses on the actual result (getting to the store) and the goal or intended result (being in a position to buy pickles).

Properties of action structures

Suppose now that someone cuts off a child's arm, simply to demonstrate surgical technique. Such an act would be cruel. What are we saying when we say the act is cruel, and how does the cruelty of the act connect with cruelty as a disposition of persons?

When we bring actions and other things under general terms, we imply that they meet some condition associated with the term, and that this term would be applicable to other things that share this characteristic. (We do not, as Wittgenstein's example of 'game' reminds us, imply that all things to which the term applies share a characteristic: there may be many combinations of characteristics sufficient for an activity to be a game that have a quite complicated relation to one another.)

Having an arm cut off is a cruel fate for a child. But is it a cruel act by the physician? We cannot say unless we know more about the structure of actions that the act exemplified. Part of what we need to know is the goal the physician had in mind: to save the child's life? Or to demonstrate a surgical technique? We also need to know what other means were available to accomplish the same thing. If the goal of cutting off the child's arm is to save the child's life, but this worthwhile goal could have been accomplished in a less painful way, with antibiotics say, and the physician was motivated by sadism or indifference (he did not want to go across town to get the antibiotics), the act could still be cruel. Cruelty is properly attributed to acts in virtue of the action structure they exemplify.

The point mentioned above—that in 1789 (and in much of the world today), execution is not deemed a cruel punishment for certain crimes, but certain methods of carrying it out are considered cruel—is another example of the same general point. Knowing that an act is of a certain type—a cutting off of a child's arm, or an execution—may not give us enough information about the act to say whether it is cruel. We need to know more about the action structure; in the one case, *how* the execution was performed, in the other, *why* the arm was cut off.

The need to look at the whole structure of the act, including the reasons for which it was done, falls out of the connection made in the *OED* definition between cruelty, as a property of acts, and cruelty as a property of people. Cruelty is, according to the *OED*, a disposition to cause suffering and indifference to the suffering of others. A surgeon who cuts off a child's arm to demonstrate a surgical technique shows such indifference and strongly suggests such a disposition. A surgeon who cuts off a child's arm to stop an infection from spreading, but could have achieved the same goal by a more elaborate and time-consuming procedure that would leave the arm intact, also shows such a character trait. So these acts are cruel.

Here then is a provisional definition of 'cruel' as an adjective of acts: acts that cause others pain and suffering are cruel if done to produce pain and suffering, or for no reason, or for a worthwhile goal for which there are other available less painful methods of achieving that the agent knows, or for a goal that is not worthwhile.

An important point that follows from this way of saying what it is for an act to be cruel, and would remain valid if the analysis were made more complicated, is that an act's being cruel is not an observational property of the act. This is not to say that it might not be obvious in many cases, but an act's being cruel or not depends on some factors—such as the disposition of the agent that led to it, his goal, and the alternatives available—that cannot always be simply read off from observing the act.

Consider mid-nineteenth century teachers in charge of 12-year-olds at a residential school. The teachers have been taught that masturbation is quite harmful, and have been trained in what is considered the proper technique of caning as punishment for it. One can imagine a teacher, who is not at all disposed to cause pain in others and gets no pleasure from it, caning a masturbator. The act is not cruel under the above definition. The act causes pain and suffering and is quite misguided. The teacher may be criticizably unreflective and gullible. But the teacher is not cruel, and the act does not show a disposition toward causing pain in others or an indifference to such pain.

Imagine another teacher, similarly trained and indoctrinated, but more reflective and less gullible. Reflecting on his own masturbation, the teacher comes to believe that the practice is at worst harmless and also realizes that caning is unlikely to significantly inhibit it. His goal in caning his masturbating charges is simply to comply with what he is expected to do. However, he canes his masturbators quite vigorously, even though he believes, correctly, that a quite-mild caning would be equally (in)effective. This teacher is indifferent to the suffering he causes, and perhaps even enjoys it; he is cruel, and his act is cruel.

So much for cruel acts. But what of cruel *actions*? It makes sense not only to say that the second teacher's act was cruel, but that caning was and is cruel. But how can caning be cruel, if the first teacher's act was a case of caning but was not cruel?

The question assumes a simple rule for dealing with cases like this one where the same predicate is applied both to specific things and to types of those things. In this case the word 'cruel' is applied both to acts and to actions. The simple rule is that if the predicate applies to the type, it must apply to every act that is an instance of the type. However, this simple rule does not seem to be correct in a wide variety of cases where we apply predicates to types.

Consider, 'Birds fly.' Here we have a predicate, 'fly', that is applied both to individual birds like Tweety, and also to the type or category of being a bird, and also to subtypes of that category: pelicans fly, hummingbirds fly, and so on. 'Birds fly' seems like an unremarkable assertion, and one might suppose that it implied that all birds fly. But penguins are birds, and penguins do not fly.

This phenomenon is called 'non-monotonicity'. If a predicate is monotonic, then if it applies to a type, it will apply to every subtype of that type, and to every instance of that type. 'Flies' applies to birds, penguins are a subtype of birds, but 'flies' does not apply to penguins. So it seems 'flies' is not monotonic.

Some philosophers are inclined to say that non-monotonicity is an illusion: it is really not true that birds fly, it's just close enough to the truth to be useful to say. Computer scientists working in artificial intelligence find such non-monotonic rules to be essential in understanding expert reasoning; they are more inclined to say that the phenomena is real: it is true that birds fly, it simply does not follow that penguins do. I will side with the computer scientists, motivated more by simplicity of exposition than deep conviction.

The important lesson is that we often use truths, or near truths, like 'Birds fly', in reasoning and discourse. The import of the remark seems to be that paradigmatic birds fly; prima facie, if something is a bird, it flies. If it is a bird, assume it flies until you find out otherwise, and so forth. For our purposes, the point is that attributions of characteristics to types are often made and deemed to be true (or close enough), even though not every instance of the type shares the characteristic, and it cannot be attributed to every subtype. Thus one can say 'Cutting off a child's arm *is* cruel', and then consistently allow, 'But of course cutting off a child's arm to keep gangrene from spreading is *not* cruel', and then consistently allow 'But of course cutting off a child's arm to keep gangrene from spreading because one is too lazy to walk across the street and get some antibiotics' *is* cruel, and so on.

Similarly, it would seem true or close enough to deny that lightly kissing someone on the cheek is cruel. Still, if the rest of the action structure that the act exemplifies is of a certain sort, an act of this type could be quite cruel. The person kissed may have been badly burned, so that the act does cause pain, and this could be the reason the agent did it. Or perhaps the act is intended to make the agent's spouse feel emotional pain.

Combining these reflections, the guidance of the dictionary, and some ideas suggested, if not exactly espoused, by Livermore, I suggest that the connection between cruelness as a personal attribute, cruel acts, and cruel actions is this:

(i) A *person* is cruel if he or she is disposed to inflict suffering because of being indifferent to or taking pleasure in the pain or distress of others.

(ii) An *act* is cruel if it proceeds from or shows indifference to or pleasure in another's distress, ie if it is the result of a person's cruel disposition.

(iii) An *action* structure: G-ing by A-ing is cruel (that is, A-ing is a cruel way of achieving a goal G), if:

- A-ing typically causes pain and suffering;
- there are other, equally effective ways of achieving goal G that are typically available and known to agents to be available that cause less pain and suffering.

(iv) Being cruel is non-monotonic: instances of cruel action structures will typically be cruel acts, and subtypes of cruel action structures will typically be cruel, but not always.

In 1789, it seems Americans in general did not think it was cruel to hang people, but they did think it was cruel to draw and quarter them, or to torture them on the rack until they died, or to kill them in an iron maiden. They no doubt realized that hanging caused pain and suffering, but did not see a more humane way of achieving the goal of execution. We can understand this on the present analysis. Death on the rack was more painful than is required to bring about the goal of death, so it was cruel. The pain and suffering involved in hanging, however, was unavoidable.

The attribution of cruelty to types of actions, then, is two steps removed from the robust meaning the dictionary provides for 'cruel', which has to do with dispositions of persons. There is a step from cruelty as a trait of persons to cruelty as a property of individual acts; then there is a further step from cruelty as a property of acts to cruelty as a property of types of actions. There is a lot of play in each step. Does this show that cruelty, as attributed to actions, is not really a matter of objective fact? Or that there is no room for distinguishing between what is really a cruel action, and what people, at a given time, or in a given culture, think of as a cruel action? This no more in the case of 'cruelty' than in the case of other adjectives with a similar range of application, adjectives such as 'intelligent', 'stupid', 'rude', and the like. In all such cases, attributions are non-monotonic: the connection between the adjective applied to the type and the adjective applied to it in some instances is somewhat loose because of some condition of typicality, normality, and the like. This means that such adjectives will tend to be vague rather than precise. But it does not point to anything particularly *subjective* about their use. It does not imply that they are a mere matter of taste, perspective, or inclination. The opposite of 'subjective' is not 'precise' but 'objective'. For example, it is a matter of objective fact that keeping one's receipts to get reimbursed is intelligent and that throwing them away is stupid.

Cruel punishments

The Eighth Amendment prohibits certain types of punishments. Punishment is, according to the dictionary, the infliction or imposition of a penalty as retribution for an offense. 'Penalty' and 'punishment' usually are part of a small circle of interdefined terms, but somewhere in the circle the idea that penalties and punishments are bad for the person punished comes in. What seems to be prohibited by the Eighth Amendment, then, are certain types of action structures, where cruel actions are performed by way of imposing penalties as retributions for offenses.

The term 'retributive' is often used as a label for a theory about the justification of punishment. The theory is basically that the offense justifies the punishment. No further justification, in terms of deterrent effect, removal of the perpetrator from society, or improving of the perpetrator's character, is needed. However, one need not accept the retributive theory of the justification of punishment to accept that retribution is part of the *nature* of punishment, that is, a punishment is *for* an offense.

Webster defined the verb 'retribute', now uncommon, in this way:

To pay back; to make payment, compensation or reward in return; as, to retribute one for his kindness; to retribute to a criminal what is proportionate to his offense.[20]

The parameters of a punishing then are a punisher, a punished, an offense, and what the punisher does to the punished: the punishment. Webster's definition highlights the relation of the nature of the offense and the nature of the punishment. The issue is at least as old as Deuteronomy: an eye for an eye, an ear for an ear, a foot for a foot, and so on. An ear for an eye is disproportionally lenient; an eye for an ear is disproportionally harsh.

There are arguments in Eighth Amendment cases, mostly by Scalia, to the effect that proportionality has nothing to do with the prohibition of cruel and unusual punishments. One argument is that the intent of the authors was not to preclude punishments that were cruel relative to the offenses punished, but only to preclude punishments, like drawing and quartering or execution by the Spanish rack or the German iron maiden, that were cruel ways of executing people no matter what the offense. Another is that if the punishment clause had been meant to treat punishments that are cruel relative to the offense, then the fines clause would not have been necessary, for what are excessive fines if not cruel punishments in the meaning of cruel for the offense?

---

[20] Webster (1828).

But as Webster's definition of 'punishment' points out, although any kind of a penalty, including a fine, can be called a 'punishment', the word usually suggests physical pain. And excessive fines might not be excessive because they are cruel: the motive is more likely to be greed on the part of the government that imposes the fine than enjoyment of the malefactor's pain.

The general tenor of these arguments is that if the authors of the Eighth Amendment had intended proportionality to be an issue, they would have said so; they did not say so, so it is not an issue. This is surely fallacious from the point of view of meaning-textualism. Given the parametric structure of punishments, based on the meaning of the word, and the given long literature on the appropriate relation between punishment and offense, the import of 'cruel punishments' will be not only the exclusion of punishments that are cruel no matter what the offense, but also of those that are cruel relative to the offense. Extra language would be required to exclude the second category, not to include it.

The phrase 'excessive fines' has the same structure as 'cruel punishments'. 'Excessive' picks out a subset of fines. 'Cruel' picks out a subset of punishments. A case of fining needs a finer, a person fined, an offense, and a fine. Does 'excessive' pick out a subset absolutely, say fines that are so large as to be excessive no matter what the offense? Or does it pick out a subset relative to the offense? One naturally understands the latter, and it would take extra language to convey the former. The case is entirely parallel with 'cruel punishments.'

So it seems that the *meaning* of the text of the punishments clause of the Eighth Amendment—as it would have been understood by semantically competent ratifiers in 1789, and by semantically competent readers of the Bill of Rights in 2009—prohibits punishments that are cruel relative to the offense. Let us turn now to the question of whether our two models for discovery of rights, or some combination of them, apply to the case of the right not to be cruelly punished as established by the Eighth Amendment.

The first way for an action to become cruel, without a change in the meaning of 'cruel', is for more humane alternatives to the action to become typically available, so that the same goals can be achieved in less painful ways. Which means for achieving a given end are available, and typically known to agents to be available, clearly depends on time and place in several ways. Less painful methods of achieving a given goal may be discovered at a certain point in time; thereafter they may be typically available and known to be available in some places, to some groups of agents, but not in other places, to other groups of agents. There will be relativity to time and space and other factors, with no change in the meaning of 'cruel'. This falls under the Change Model.

For example, the guillotine and the electric chair were both promoted as more humane alternatives to hanging, the gas chamber was promoted as a humane alternative to the electric chair, and lethal injections as a more humane alternative to the electric chair and the gas chamber. Whether any of these claims are true, I do not know. But suppose (which is certainly not obvious), that hanging imposes more pain and suffering than is proportionate to the crime of premeditated murder, and that death by guillotine is less painful than death by hanging. Then once the guillotine is widely available, known to be available, and known to be a less painful mode of execution, hanging as a way of executing someone for premeditated murder has become what it was not before, a cruel punishment, prohibited by the Eighth Amendment.

Now consider the penalty, common when I was a child, of having one's mouth washed out with soap for using bad words; that is, being required to sit in the bathroom with a bar of soap in one's mouth for some relatively short amount of time, say 10 or 15 minutes. In the movie *A Christmas Story*, a child subjected to this punishment fantasizes that it eventually causes blindness, and imagines his parents' guilt when he returns home as an adult, blind from soap poisoning in his youth.

Although I suppose not now a very common punishment, one might think that washing one's mouth out with soap was an appropriate, proportioned punishment for the offense of using bad words, if one takes into account only the unpleasantness of sitting for 10 minutes with such a vile taste in one's mouth. The mother in *A Christmas Story* apparently thought so, and she seemingly was not a cruel person. But if she discovers that the punishment causes adult blindness, she will discover the punishment she used is cruel.

The use of long-term incarceration in prisons as a secular mode of punishment suitable for democratic republics is a relatively recent phenomenon, which developed over the past century and a half. It was conceived as a humane alternative to corporal and capital punishments for many crimes. I think it is fair to say that experience has taught us much, or should have taught us much, about how much pain and suffering is involved in such long-term incarceration, in the prisons that we can afford to build and maintain, and given the high percentage of the population that, at least in America, ends up in prison. At the same time that the prison system has evolved, there have been important developments in the sciences relevant to assessing pain and suffering, and the effectiveness of incarceration of various lengths as a method of deterrence and improvement of the incarcerated. Thus, it would not be surprising if we were to discover that some punishments regularly employed were cruel even though they were instituted with the intention of providing humane alternatives. Such discoveries would be discoveries that these punishments are unconstitutional, given the clear meaning that the

Eighth Amendment had when it was ratified and that it has now. Meaning-textualism supports rather than undercuts the idea that we can discover that certain punishments that are not unusual are nevertheless cruel, and for that reason, unconstitutional.

4. Moral vision and constitutional interpretation

In the Tanner Lecture that begins his book, *A Matter of Interpretation*, Scalia's explanation of textualism seems to advocate meaning-textualism. In his 'Response', conception-textualism seems to be his view.[21] This is particularly clear in his response to Dworkin, where he waxes poetic about whose moral vision is to guide interpretation of the Constitution. But there is no evidence that the Constitution expresses a moral vision that was shared by the authors or the ratifiers, who ranged from slave owners like Madison to abolitionists, from those who liked Hobbes to those who liked Locke to those who liked Hume and presumably to scores who had never read any of these authors, and who included people of a wide variety of religious and skeptical persuasions. What the Constitution does give us is words that they all understood, and that at least in certain cases, like the Eighth Amendment, seem to have had the same meaning in 1789 that they have today, and which, in the last quarter century, the Supreme Court has consistently refused to follow.

The Eighth Amendment has not attracted much attention over the centuries compared to the First or the Fifth Amendments, or the amendments passed after the Civil War. The bulk of what one finds in constitutional law textbooks is fairly recent opinions authored or co-authored by Scalia. The philosophy of interpretation exemplified in these opinions is best described as opportunistic textualism, the search for some rationale, in text, intention, inferred conception, and elsewhere for not applying the clear meaning of the punishment clause to clearly cruel and disproportionate punishments brought to the court's attention, such as life imprisonment without possibility of parole for three relatively minor thefts, or long sentences for sale of a small quantity of marijuana.

Does the death penalty itself violate the Eighth Amendment? I am not convinced that it does. In present-day America it does seem impossible or at least extraordinarily difficult to employ it without violating the Fifth Amendment of due process. And, because of the difficulties entailed by the jurisprudence on matters of due process, the only *mode* of employing it today seems cruel in a way that the Founding Fathers, or even those of us who

---

[21] Scalia (1998b).

remember an age of relatively quick executions, could scarcely have imagined: keeping people in prison long enough so that many of them are no longer the sort of people apt to commit such crimes, and then executing them. So, somewhat ironically, the Fifth Amendment, which is the basis for Scalia being quite certain that the death penalty is constitutional in spite of the Eighth Amendment, may be the cause of its being prohibited, in the present mode of carrying it out, by the Eighth Amendment.

5. Conclusion

Many of Scalia's writings about textualism strike this philosopher as quite sensible as a philosophy of legal interpretation. These writings describe what I have called meaning-textualism: we should understand the words as having the available meanings and meanings that they had at the time the laws were written, and would have been understood to have by the writers and ratifiers of the law and by the public affected by the law at that time. Meaning-textualism may not provide everything that is needed for interpreting all laws, since laws can be long and complicated in ways that challenge consistent interpretation. But it is surely a plausible starting point, especially for relatively short and simple constructions such as we find in the Bill of Rights.

Even there, however, dictionaries only carry us so far. Dictionaries focus on words; what happens when words are combined in phrases quickly gets complicated. The whole issue of predicating properties of *actions*, types of acts, in virtue of which they are protected or prohibited, raises a number of questions that are interesting and complex. I think philosophers of language can be helpful. My own efforts in this chapter are probably too simple and flawed in other ways. But I think more adequate efforts will only reinforce the naivety of Ring's Principle.

My efforts suffice to show the dangers of slipping from Scalia's plausible view, meaning-textualism, to the totally implausible theory he sometimes favors, conception-textualism, that it is not the meanings of the words the founders used that is crucial, but rather the opinions they had about the properties those words stood for. Whether the founders shared such opinions about cruelty, punishment, and other key properties to such an extent that it even makes sense to talk about *the conception* of *the founders*, much less their 'moral vision', strikes me as beyond dubious. But even if I am wrong about this, it is surely what was said by the words they chose that we ought to worry about.

7

Textualism, Intentionalism, and the Law of the Contract

Gideon Rosen

1. Jurisprudence as the science of legal effects

Law-making is, for the most part, a verbal business. In mature legal systems in which the social and institutional conditions for law have been established, changes in the law are typically produced by the verbal pronouncements of legal actors: legislators, judges, administrative officials and, in the case of popular referenda, individual voters. There may be cases in which the law changes, not as a result of anyone's saying or doing anything in particular, but rather as a result of cultural and political changes of other kinds.[1] But in the paradigmatic case, law is made or unmade when some legal actor, individual or collective, performs a speech act the express intent of which is to modify (or perhaps simply to articulate) the law.

We can think of the law in any given jurisdiction at any given time as a body of true propositions of the form: *According to the law of J, P.* Suppose that in Princeton, New Jersey, on 10 August 2009, the law is *L*, and that some suitably placed legal actor utters a sentence *S*, the effect of which is to change the law. The effect of the utterance may be to add something new to the law without subtracting anything, to subtract without adding, or to modify the law by adding and subtracting simultaneously. In any case we can model the legal effect of *S* as a pair, (S^+, S^-), where S^+ contains the propositions that *S* has managed to incorporate into the law, and S^- those propositions that *S* has managed to delete.

One important job for jurisprudence is to describe the mechanisms that underlie this paradigmatic form of legal change. A theory for this purpose

---

[1] The clearest cases of this sort are those in which a law falls into desuetude through non-enforcement.

will have two parts: an account of the conditions under which some entity (individual or collective) counts as a 'suitably placed legal actor' with authority to make law in a certain area, and a set of principles connecting the verbal pronouncements of such actors with their concrete legal consequences. The aim is thus to provide a general framework for explaining facts of the form:

X's utterance of *S* in context *C* had legal effect (*S*⁺, *S*⁻).

The relevant species of explanation is not historical. The aim of jurisprudence, as distinct from legal history and sociology, is not to explain why *X* said what he said, or why the law developed as it did. The aim is rather to identify the synchronic facts *in virtue of which* this particular pronouncement had this particular cluster of legal effects.[2] More generally the aim is to identify the *principles* that map legal pronouncements, together with background circumstances, onto their determinate legal consequences: the laws of legal effect, as it were.

2. A role for the philosophy of language

Precisely because law-making is a verbal business, it is natural to suppose that the philosophy of language should have something to contribute to this jurisprudential project. It is natural to suppose, after all, that when an utterance has a certain legal effect, it has that effect in part thanks to its *meaning* or, more generally, thanks to its various linguistic features; and one of the aims of the philosophy of language is to provide us with a vocabulary for describing these features.

As an example, consider a view we might call

Simple Textualism: A legal sentence *S*, uttered in a determinate context *C*, expresses a proposition about the law in some jurisdiction. The proposition expressed by *S* depends on *S*'s meaning in the language[3]—a meaning it has independently of any particular occasion of use—and perhaps on objective features of the context, such as the time and place of the utterance, but it does not depend on the private and potentially idiosyncratic

---

[2] For general remarks on explanations of this sort, see Rosen (2010).

[3] We can be noncommittal about what sort of item the 'linguistic meaning' of a sentence is. All that matters for the textualist is that linguistic meanings can be assigned to sentences prior to, and independently of, their use on some particular occasion, and that these sentence meanings are sometimes sufficient, in conjunction with other features of the context of utterance, to determine a proposition that might be added to the law. This may not be true, but it is a commitment of simple textualism as I understand it.

beliefs or intentions of the speaker or his audience.[4] Given suitable background conditions, the legal utterance is a performative whose effect is to add this very proposition to the law, and so to make this proposition true.

Just as a felicitous utterance of 'I hereby christen this ship *Titanic*' has the effect of making it the case that a certain ship has been so christened, so an authoritative utterance of 'It is henceforth a misdemeanor to keep a tiger as a pet in Princeton' may have the effect of making it the case that a certain act is now a misdemeanor.

This simple-minded view represents the purest form of textualism—the view that the legal effect of a legal utterance is a function of the public language meaning of the legal text together with objective features of the context and prior settled law. The most important feature of the view, for our purposes, is that it assigns no constitutive role to the specific mental states of the legislators and their audience beyond their role in determining the identity of the utterance and pertinent features of the context of the utterance. A legislator may utter *S* and, when he does so, he may have any number of hopes, dreams, beliefs, expectations, and intentions as to the legal consequences of his utterance. The textualist's central thought is that these mental states are quite irrelevant unless they somehow play a role in determining which sentence he uttered, or the proposition it semantically expressed when it was uttered.

One stark alternative to simple textualism is *intentionalism*—the view that the legal effect of an authoritative pronouncement is determined by the intentions of its author (individual or collective), and not, in general, by the public language meaning of the words he used. Now it cannot be stressed enough that legal actors may have many different kinds of intentions when they issue their authoritative legal pronouncements. They may have

- *lexical intentions*: the intention to use a certain word or construction. (This is the sort of intention that one fails to realize when one misspeaks.);
- *semantic intentions*: the intention to *mean* this or that by their words;
- *communicative intentions*: the intention to cause certain beliefs or expectations in their audience in a characteristic way;[5]

---

[4] Whether a contract scrawled on the back of a napkin is to be understood as written in English rather than (say) Serbo-Croatian may depend on the draftsman's intention to write in English. Whether a contract binds the promisor to pay $20.00 for the promisee's *cat*, as opposed to $2,000 dollars for his *car*, may depend on which English words the parties to the contract meant to inscribe. The textualist's key thought is that, *once the identity of the text is fixed*, facts about the author's expectations and intentions have no bearing on the legal effect of his utterance.

[5] These are the intentions highlighted by Grice (1989). Note that an intentionalist account of legal effect may invoke these Gricean intentions without maintaining, as Grice did, that they provide the basis for a reductive account utterance meaning.

- *practical intentions*: the intention to cause downstream non-legal effects, eg to promote economic growth, or to motivate donors to contribute to the next campaign.

Perhaps most importantly for our purposes, they may have strictly

- *legal intentions*: the intention to bring about certain changes in the law by means of their pronouncements—eg the intention to see to it that it is henceforth a crime to keep a tiger as a pet in Princeton.

An intentionalist theory of legal change may invoke intentions in any of these categories. The view I call *Simple Intentionalism* focuses exclusively on legal intentions:

Simple Intentionalism. When a legal actor seeks to change the law by means of a verbal pronouncement S, he intends his utterance of S to have certain legal effects, (S^+, S^-). When the pronouncement is effective—when the actor is suitably placed and all proper procedures have been observed—the effect of the utterance is precisely this intended effect (S^+, S^-).

The most important feature of this view is that it assigns no constitutive role to the objective or 'impersonal' linguistic features of the legal utterance. Of course it may be useful to know what a legal sentence meant when it was uttered, since the semantic facts about an utterance may be excellent *evidence* of the speaker's legal intentions. But when we ask, 'In virtue of what did the speaker's utterance of S have the legal effect it had?', the answer will not advert to the linguistic meaning of S at all, but rather to the speaker's subjective intentions as to the legal upshot of his or her pronouncement.[6]

These are only the simplest representatives of important classes of positions. There are hybrid views, and views that are neither textualist nor intentionalist in inspiration, as we shall see. I mention them now for purposes of orientation, and also to alert the reader to a theme in what follows. Proponents of theories in this area sometimes imply that their preferred view is not simply true, but that it *must* be true—that it somehow lies in the *nature* of law or of law-making that when we make law with words in the paradigmatic way, the legal effects of our utterances are determined by the linguistic meanings of our words, or by our subjective legal intentions, or by whatever it is that the theorist's preferred view identifies as the underlying ground of legal effect. This tendency is to be resisted. To the contrary, if textualism or intentionalism or

---

[6] Simple Intentionalism does allow a constitutive role for impersonal linguistic meaning in the special case in which the speaker's legal intention is to add to the law *the proposition expressed by sentence S*, whatever it may be. When a legislator votes for a bill without reading it, her intention might well be captured in these terms.

any other determinate view of these matters is correct as an account of any part of the law—Bolivian criminal law, for example, or US constitutional law—this will be thanks to special features of the relevant field of law and to contingent features of the legal regime in question. To a significant degree, the true principles connecting the linguistic features of legal utterances to their legal effects are a matter of positive legal fact, grounded in the legal history and practice of the community. The nature of law does not settle which of the many possible rules is in fact in place in the same sense in which it does not settle the details of the traffic code.

This means that the philosophy of language cannot tell us what the relation between language and the law actually is in (say) New Jersey in 2010. That is a question for empirically informed legal theory. Nor can the philosophy of language tell us what the relation between language and the law ought to be, since that is a normative question for moralists and normative theorists of social policy.[7] What the philosophy of language can do—and this is not nothing—is to provide us with a vocabulary for formulating various hypotheses about the relationship between language and the law, and so for clearing away certain confusions that might otherwise arise. This chapter approaches these issues indirectly by considering a range of questions from the law of contracts.

3. Contract law and the law of the contract

It would be extravagant to claim that an ordinary contract changes the law. When I accept your offer to paint your house for $5,000, I do not thereby change the laws of the state of New Jersey. But I do change the legal obligations under which you and I both labor. More generally, like any genuinely legislative act, a valid contract serves to change the legal score. It creates new obligations and claims, but it may also create new powers and privileges, both in the parties to the contract and in third parties. For this reason, we may think of contracting as law-making writ small. The principles that map a contract onto its determinate legal effects are generically similar to those that map a statute or a constitutional provision onto its effects, but they are presumably much simpler, and therefore easier to study.[8]

---

[7] Greenawalt (2005) at 533.

[8] The case of contracts is presumably simpler in part because the number of actors involved in drafting and implementing the legal text is relatively small. Of course there are even simpler cases by this standard, eg the law of wills, in which the legal text has a single author (at least nominally). We focus on contracts for two reasons. First, while there is a genuine controversy in the law of contracts

Following Farnsworth, let us call the legal change effected by a valid contract the *law of the contract*, reserving *contract law* for the general rules that form the background for particular acts of contracting and which are clearly part of the law by any standard.[9] Any general account of the relation between language and the law will have a chapter detailing the rules that map the linguistic features of a contract *C*, together with any other relevant parameters, onto the law of *C*.

Our general point about the limited relevance of the philosophy of language to jurisprudence applies in this case in particular. Systems of contract law may differ radically in their understanding of the relationship between the language of the contract and the law of the contract. Pure intentionalist regimes are possible, as are pure textualist regimes (though this is controversial), and so are countless regimes of other sorts. Which system we actually have is a matter of positive law, and which system we ought to have, is a matter for moral and social theory. The philosophy of language cannot settle which system is ours, or which is best. Our aim, then, is to not resolve these issues but to clarify them. Our question will be:

How *might* the linguistic features of a contract bear on the law of that contract?

Since the range of possible contract regimes is vast, we restrict our attention to possibilities that are broadly consonant with central features of contemporary American contract law.

4. Gaps, default rules, and unenforceable provisions

This requirement of broad consistency with central features of US contract law rules out both Simple Textualism and Simple Intentionalism as we have stated them. Simple Textualism in the theory of contracts would be the view that the legal effect of a valid contract is to impose obligations corresponding to the impersonal linguistic meanings of its overt provisions. Simple Intentionalism would be the view that the legal effect of a contract is to impose the obligations that the parties intended to impose by means of it.

---

about how the laws of legal effect are to be understood, the case of wills is relatively straightforward: to a good first approximation, the legal effect of a valid will is determined by the testator's intentions with respect to the distribution of his property. A strict textualist approach to the interpretation of wills is possible, but it has rarely been taken seriously (Corbin (1952) at p 489). Second, the case of contracts is the simplest case which preserves the most perplexing features of legislation proper: the fact that determinate legal effects are generated by a verbal performance with many 'authors'. For a comparative discussion of the interpretation of wills and contracts, see Greenawalt (2005).

⁹ Farnsworth (2004) at p 413.

Regimes of both sorts may be possible, but neither is consistent with contract law as we have long had it.

When I buy a defective widget from Acme Corp, my contract with the merchant obliges him to refund my money or to supply a working widget, even if the contract has no explicit warranty. When I agree to sell you 1,000 pounds of rice next April at $2/lb and then renege because the market price has risen to $4/lb in the interim, I incur an obligation to pay you $2,000 (the difference between the market price and the contract price) even if our contract is silent about the remedy for its own breach, as most contracts are.

These examples illustrate a familiar point. An ideal contract would specify every legal change effected by it with an overt clause, but real contracts always have gaps—points at which the obligations of the parties under various contingencies are not addressed in the overt agreement. Because Simple Textualism derives the law of the contract from the overt text of the contract in a simple way, it implies that in cases of this sort the contract imposes no obligation. A regime of this sort is possible, but it is not the regime we have. Instead contract law supplies a battery of *default rules*, which imply contractual obligations that do not correspond to any explicit language in the agreement. Contracts for the sale of goods that lack an explicit warranty are construed to include an implied 'warranty of merchantability' (UCC 2-314). Contracts that contain no damages clause are construed to require 'expectation damages'—roughly, compensation sufficient to ensure that the victim is no worse off than he would have been if the breaching party had performed the contract, and so on.[10]

This interaction between contract law and the law of the contract is not a necessary feature of the law of contracts. We can imagine a regime in which the only legal changes effected by a contract are those imposed by some explicit language in the agreement. In a system of this sort, in the absence of an explicit warranty, there would be no warranty; in the absence of an explicit damages clause, there would be no enforceable damages for breach of contract, etc. Contracting would obviously be much more tedious and much more expensive in such a system, and, indeed, one important function of default rules is to reduce the costs of contracting.[11]

The existence of default rules and 'implied terms' rules out Simple Textualism as we have formulated it. But it is easy to see how the view might be modified in response. Contracts (it might be said) do not create legal obligations *ex nihilo*. They do so against the background of contract law (and in some cases against the background of prior contracts). The principles of

[10] American Law Institute, *Restatement of the Law (Second)*, Contracts 2d §347.
[11] For other rationales for default rules, see Ayres and Gertner (1992) at 729–73.

contract law may include conditionals of the form: 'If a contract requires that *X* do *A*, then it requires that *Y* do *B*.' A contract that contains an explicit clause requiring *X* to do *A* may trigger this principle and generate a requirement that *Y* do *B*, even though the contract contains no explicit language on this point. A textualist who wishes to allow for this possibility should therefore say that the legal effect of a contract comprises obligations corresponding to the propositions semantically expressed by the explicit text of agreement, together with the *consequences* of those propositions given the default rules of the jurisdiction and prior settled obligations.

A deeper problem arises when we bear in mind another important fact about all modern systems of contract law. In many cases it is possible to 'contract around' a default rule. If Acme Corp sells me an experimental widget, the company can explicitly disavow any warranty, and if this is part of the contract, the language may override the implied warranty of merchantability. In other cases, however, the default cannot be overridden in this way. Our contract for the sale of rice may include a 'liquidated damages' clause requiring me to pay you $1 million if I fail to deliver the rice as promised. But if t does, this provision will have no legal effect, thanks to a rule of contract law that voids any such clause when the liquidated damages exceed a reasonable estimate of expectations damages.[12]

Rules of this sort entail that an explicit provision in a valid contract may have no legal effect whatsoever. Such 'filters' are ubiquitous in contract law. A contract provision that requires one of the parties to commit a tort or a crime is not enforceable—has no legal effect—as are provisions that are 'contrary to public policy' or somehow 'unconscionable'.[13] This just goes to show that the powers of individuals to alter their legal obligations by means of contract are substantially limited by background contract law, much as the powers of the states to make laws for their citizens are limited by federal law. Again, this feature of contract law is not essential. We can imagine a regime of perfect freedom of contract in which any genuinely contractual agreement would be enforceable according to its terms. But that is very far from the system that we have.

Simple Textualism and Simple Intentionalism as we have stated them are both incompatible with this basic feature of our contract regime. Both views entail that every provision in a valid contract has some legal effect grounded either in its impersonal linguistic meaning or the legal intentions of the parties, and, as we have seen, that is just not true. The only textualist thesis worth discussing is the weaker (but still quite interesting) claim that *when an explicit contract provision has legal effect*, its effect is a function of its impersonal

---

[12] *Restatement (Second)* §356.   [13] *Restatement (Second)* §§ 178–196.

linguistic meaning together with pertinent facts about the context of utterance and settled background law. (This would be analogous to the textualist claim that when a criminal statute or an administrative regulation has effect—as not all do, thanks to constraints imposed by higher law—its legal effect is determined by its linguistic meaning.) Similarly, the only intentionalist thesis worth discussing is the claim that, *when an explicit contract provision has legal effect*, its effect is determined by the legal intentions of the parties. In what follows we focus on these conditionalized versions of textualism and intentionalism and on various alternatives to them, all of which seek to answer the following question:

When a contract provision has legal effect, in virtue of what does it have the particular legal effect it has?[14]

5. Textualism, hypothetical intentionalism, and the objective theory of contract

Textualism in the theory of contract interpretation has affinities for a larger view sometimes called the *objective theory of contract*. This is mainly a negative doctrine according to which the private mental states of the parties have no bearing on whether a contract is in place, or what the legal effects of that contract may be. Textualism is a species of the objective theory to the extent that it grounds legal effect in public language meanings and in features of the context of utterance that are not a matter of private mental states, but which might in principle be ascertained more or less directly by a suitably placed third party. It is unclear, however, whether textualism as we have defined it must always conform to the letter of the objective theory. Suppose that Jones agrees to pay Smith $20 for '*that* barrel of fish'. According to the textualist, his legal obligation depends on the referent of the demonstrative phrase, and

---

[14] This way of framing the issue may suggest that the rules of contract interpretation (ie the rules that assign legal effect to bits of contract language) only apply *after* it has been determined which bits of the contract are to have effect, but that is misleading. In typical cases we must first determine *what the legal effect of a provision would be if it had effect* before we can determine whether it has effect. We may therefore take textualism, intentionalism, and the other approaches to contract interpretation to be discussed below as competing accounts of the *putative* legal effect of a contract provision. Restrictive principles of contract law, like the rule against penalties, then function as filters to determine which of these putative effects is genuine. (Some writers reserve the word *interpretation* for the determination of putative legal effect, as distinguished from *construction*, the determination of actual legal effect.) In a more comprehensive treatment, it would be important to stress that these filters sometimes work by *modifying* the legal effect of a provision rather than by simply voiding it. In that case the ultimate legal effect of a bit of contract language is determined by its putative effect *as modified* by background rules of contract law.

the referent of the demonstrative may depend on which barrel Jones *had in mind* when he produced it. Similarly, if Fritz agrees to pay $200 for *all the beer*, or to deliver the bananas *while they are still green*, it may turn out that the domain of the quantifier ('all') or the extension of the vague predicate ('green') is determined not by objective features of the context, but by the subjective intentions of the parties. If so, textualism is not strictly compatible with the objective theory. And yet the views have a clear affinity. Both hold that mental states that do not contribute in these fairly specific ways to the proposition expressed by a contract provision in a given context play no role whatsoever in determining the legal effect of the contract. In particular, both hold that the parties' subjective *legal* beliefs and intentions—their beliefs and intentions about the *legal consequences of their agreement*—play no such constitutive role; and that is the feature of the views that will matter in what follows.

Textualism is not the only version of the objective theory. One salient alternative is the view that the legal effect of a contract is determined by the legal intentions that a third party apprised of the language of the contract and of relevant background circumstances—though not of the real intentions of the parties—would *attribute* to the parties on the basis of this information.[15] The difference between this view, which we may call *Hypothetical Intentionalism*, and textualism is clearest in cases of scrivener's error. Suppose a contract provides that A 'agrees to sell the horse Beauty to B for $30.75'. If Beauty is a healthy horse, as anyone familiar with the circumstances of the contract would know, then a reasonable third party would conclude that the decimal point was a draftsman's error, and that the real price for the horse under the contract is $3,075. (This would be even clearer if the contract lists prices for many horses all in a range around $3,000 with every other price rounded to the nearest dollar.) If so, then the hypothetical intentionalist will maintain that this *is* the price under the contract. A simple-minded textualist, by contrast, would interpret the contract according to its letter, assigning a price of $30.75.

It is often unclear whether an expression of the objective theory is meant as an endorsement of textualism or instead of some version of the hypothetical intentionalism. Consider a famous statement of Learned Hand:

A contract has, strictly speaking, nothing to do with the personal, or individual, intent of the parties. A contract is an obligation attached by the mere force of law to certain acts of the parties, usually words, which ordinarily accompany and represent

---

[15] There are of course versions of this view that would ground contractual obligation in imputed intentions of other sorts, eg in imputed *semantic* or *communicative* intentions. We focus on imputed *legal* intentions only to keep the discussion manageable.

a known intent. If, however, it were proved by twenty bishops that either party when he used the words intended something else than the usual meaning which the law imposes on him, he would be held unless there were mutual mistake or something of the sort. (*Hotchkiss v National City Bank* 200 Fed 287, 293 (1911))

The first sentence affirms the objective theory. The second suggests that the legal effect of a contract is determined by the intent that is *ordinarily* expressed by the language of the contract—which may or may not be equivalent to what we have called the 'impersonal linguistic meaning'. All of this is consistent with textualism. The last sentence, however, allows for an exception in cases of mutual mistake, which may cover the sort of undetected scrivener's error mentioned above, and which may therefore suggest hypothetical intentionalism rather than simple textualism.

It is unclear whether full-strength textualism has ever been endorsed in the law of contracts. The most flamboyant exponent of the objective theory, Oliver Wendell Holmes, Jr., does say at one point that a contracting party who misspeaks is bound by the letter of his agreement. Discussing a contract for the delivery of cotton aboard a ship called *Peerless*, Holmes writes that 'if the defendant had said "Peerless" by mistake, meaning "Peri," he would have been bound' (to deliver cotton on the *Peerless*).[16] Similarly, Holmes maintains that private conventions of usage have no bearing on the legal effect of the contract, which is to be interpreted according to its public language meaning:

I do not suppose that you could prove, for purposes of construction as distinguished from avoidance, an oral declaration or even an agreement that words in a dispositive instrument making sense as they stand should have a different meaning from the common one; for instance, that the parties to a contract orally agreed that when they wrote 'five hundred feet' it should mean one hundred inches, or that Bunker Hill Monument should signify Old South Church.[17]

This claim was endorsed by Samuel Williston, the most important American contract scholar in the objectivist tradition. But as Williston notes, Holmes's approach is consistent with a form of hypothetical intentionalism.

[T]hough courts say they are seeking the intentions of the parties, the assertion is even more emphatic that this intention can only be found in the expressions of the parties in the writing. In effect, therefore, it is not the real intent but the intent expressed or apparent in the writing which is sought.[18]

---

[16] Holmes (1881) at p 309.   [17] Holmes (1898–9) at p 420.

[18] Williston (1920) 2: §610. Pronouncements of this sort are ubiquitous in the cases. See, eg *Garfinkel v Morristown Obstetrics & Gynecology Associates*, PA 773 A 2d 665, 672 (NJ 2001): 'In interpreting a contract, it is not the real intent but the intent expressed or apparent in the writing that controls.'

Textualism and hypothetical intentionalism will yield the same result in many cases. This is unsurprising, since one of the main sources of evidence available to the hypothetical interpreter is the public language meaning of the contract. The views will yield different verdicts when the hypothetical interpreter has access to evidence that trumps or supplements this linguistic evidence. In some cases of this sort, the public language meaning of the contract is ambiguous or non-specific, and so taken by itself yields no result. The hypothetical interpreter who sets out to impute legal intentions to the parties may have access to evidence that goes beyond this public language meaning, which may support an attribution of intentions that resolves the case.[19] The result is that where the strict textualist may see no contract at all—or a contract that imposes no enforceable obligation given the facts—the hypothetical intentionalist will sometimes see determinate legal obligations. In other cases of this sort, the public language meaning of the contract provision may be sufficient to determine an obligation on textualist principles, but the hypothetical interpreter will have access to information which supports a different set of obligations. In cases of this sort, the textualist will see one determinate obligation—that suggested by the language of the contract—where the hypothetical intentionalist sees another, one grounded in the legal intentions that it would be reasonable to impute to the parties given the totality of the admissible evidence. To see how these options differ in practice, let us consider some examples.

6. Ambiguity

In what is certainly the most famous case on ambiguity in contract language, Raffles agreed to sell Wichelhaus 125 bales of cotton at 17¼ d. per pound to arrive at Liverpool 'ex Peerless from Bombay'.[20] When the goods arrived at Liverpool on a ship called *Peerless* in December 1863, Wichelhaus refused to take delivery and Raffles sued. As it happens, and as neither party knew when they signed the contract, there were two ships called *Peerless* sailing from

---

[19] This can happen in two ways. The hypothetical interpreter may have access to extra-textual evidence involving concrete interactions between the two parties, or he may have access to more general evidence that permits him to resolve ambiguities in the contract that cannot be resolved on purely textual grounds. If the contract involves a clause governing the sale of 'bats' and another governing the sale of 'balls and gloves,' the hypothetical interpreter may be in a position to impute an intention to sell *baseball bats* by bringing to bear his general knowledge. If we allow the textualist access to this sort of evidence for the purposes of resolving ambiguities in the text, the space between textualism and hypothetical intentionalism is narrowed considerably.

[20] *Raffles v Wichelhaus* (1864) 159 Eng Rep 375, Ct of Exchq.

Bombay to Liverpool in 1863, one arriving in October, the other in December. Wichelhaus claimed that he had understood the agreement to concern the October *Peerless*[21] and that Raffles had simply failed to deliver cotton on that ship as they had agreed. (The written contract did not specify a date of delivery.) The question is whether Wichelhaus breached the contract.

The court held that since there were two ships named *Peerless*, the contract was ambiguous, and that given testimony and relevant circumstances it was reasonable to infer that 'defendant meant one Peerless and plaintiff another'. From this the court concluded that there was no *consensus ad idem*—no 'meeting of minds'—and hence no contract.

In somewhat more detail, the court's reasoning in *Raffles* (in so far as it can be gleaned from the terse report) appears to run as follows. The judgment is an application of the Plain Meaning Rule, according to which extrinsic evidence (also called *parol evidence*) is admissible for interpreting a contract when—but only when—the contract is ambiguous on its face. It is a settled principle of contract law that when a contract is completely integrated—ie when it represents the complete and final agreement of the parties about the matters it addresses—extrinsic evidence is inadmissible for the purposes of *varying* or *supplementing* the terms of the agreement. (This is a version of the Parol Evidence Rule.) The Plain Meaning Rule speaks to a slightly different issue, namely whether extrinsic evidence is admissible for the purpose of *interpreting* an overt provision when that provision is not ambiguous on its face. The court's argument in *Raffles* seems to run as follows. The existence and content of a contract is ultimately determined by what the parties had in mind (real intentionalism). We consult the language of the contract to divine these intentions. When the contract language is clear on its face, we may not go beyond the language of the contract (and general background knowledge) for this purpose. But since there were two ships named *Peerless*, the contract is ambiguous and parol evidence is therefore admissible. This evidence supports the claim that the parties had different ships in mind, and that there was therefore no binding contract.

This way of resolving the issue assumes intentionalism, but the result in *Raffles* is consistent with many theories. A hypothetical intentionalist might reason analogously, holding that parol evidence is admissible for the purposes of *imputing* intentions to the parties when the contract language is ambiguous, and that the result in this case is the imputation of incompatible intentions on a material point. Perhaps more importantly, it is open to the textualist to say that when a contract is ambiguous on some material point, and the

---

[21] Perhaps disingenuously, since cotton prices had also fallen dramatically in the interim. See Simpson (1989).

defendant's conduct would count as breach on one resolution of the ambiguity but not another, then any suit for breach of contract must fail. This would be roughly analogous to the rule of lenity in criminal law, according to which any material unclarity in a statute is to be resolved in favor of the defendant. Such an approach might be undesirable, but it is possible, and it is consistent with the textualist's main claim, namely that contractual obligations, when they exist, are grounded in the language of the instrument and not in the real or hypothetical intentions of the parties.

The upshot is that all three approaches can ratify the result in *Raffles*. Substantive differences emerge, however, when we consider a variant in which as a matter of fact both parties had the same ship in mind, say, the December *Peerless*. The court's real intentionalist argument entails that in this case there would have been a contract for delivery on the December *Peerless*, in which case Wichelhaus would have been in breach. Hypothetical Intentionalism yields the same result if *but only* if there exists admissible extrinsic evidence on the basis of which the hypothetical interpreter might have imputed this shared intention to the parties. If there is no such evidence, a court applying an intentionalist standard may find (contrary to fact) that the parties had different ships in mind, and hence that there was no contract. For the real intentionalist, this would be a *mistake*. For the hypothetical intentionalist, it will be a correct account of the legal facts, since on his view, the 'hidden' intentions of the parties are irrelevant.

What should the textualist say about this version of the case? The most simple-minded textualist will have trouble distinguishing the variant from the original, since in both cases the contract contains an ambiguous sentence whose 'impersonal' meaning is insufficient to determine what counts as performance given the facts, in which case there was presumably no actionable breach. If the textualist cannot avoid this result, his view is inconsistent with contract law as we have long had it, since the variant case is not a hard case. If the parties had the same ship in mind, and if extrinsic evidence would show this, there is no doubt that they were contractually obliged to buy and sell cotton on that ship.

As Holmes noted, however, the textualist has a strategy for echoing the traditional 'meeting of minds' result in *Raffles*, both in the real case and in our variant.

It is commonly assumed that such a contract is void, because of mutual mistake as to subject matter, and because the parties did not consent to the same thing. But this way of putting it seems to me misleading. The law has nothing to do with the actual state of the parties' minds.... The true ground of the decision was not that each party *meant* a different thing from the other... but that each party *said* a different thing. The plaintiff offered one thing; the defendant expressed his assent to another. (*The Common Law*, 309)

As he develops his account, Holmes's position depends on a substantive linguistic claim, namely that in legal contexts, at any rate, there is no such thing as an ambiguous proper name. 'A proper name, when used in business or pleading, means one individual thing, and no other, as everyone knows.'[22] The thought seems to be that in cases of apparent nominal ambiguity, there are in fact many different homonymous names—*Peerless*$_{OCT}$, *Peerless*$_{DEC}$, etc—spelled and pronounced exactly alike. Just as the intentions of the parties may be relevant for the limited purpose of determining that they wrote in English, so they may be relevant for determining which of the two homophonic words the parties used. Since the extrinsic evidence suggests that the parties had distinct *lexical* intentions in the real version of the case, it shows that the contract offered by the one was not the same linguistic object as that accepted by the other. In the variant case, by contrast, since the lexical intentions of the parties coincide, there is a contract and Wichelhaus has breached it.

This approach is widely viewed as a desperate measure designed to square Holmes's version of textualism with the result in *Raffles*, which is widely (though not universally) regarded as correct.[23] Still it does raise a number of intriguing questions. First, one may wonder how the analysis is meant to apply to the case. For all we know, there was only one copy of the contract in *Raffles*—a single sheet of paper drafted by one party and signed by both. Is this consistent with Holmes's claim that 'the plaintiff offered one thing; the defendant expressed his assent to another'?[24] If every *token* proper name is unambiguous, and there is only one token in this case, then Holmes's analysis is untenable. The approach makes sense only if one supposes that, in the real version of the case, there were in fact two token names in play—one in the offer, the other in the acceptance— even though these acts were effected by means of a single concrete contract: two tokens occupying a single region of space on the physical page. A metaphysical view of this sort is possible, but it would be *wild*, and it is simply bizarre to think that any serious doctrine in contract law might depend on it.

Second, and more importantly, the account relies on a distinction between *lexical* intentions (to use one word rather than another) and *semantic* or *legal* intentions (to *mean* this or that by one's words, or to change one's legal

---

[22] 'The Common Law, 309'.

[23] See Gilmore (1974) at pp 39–57. Commentators who dispute the result maintain that the identity of the ship was not a *material* term in the contract. If I promise to deliver a gross of widgets from Warehouse A and ultimately deliver a gross of perfectly functional widgets from Warehouse B, I am not in breach of contract. If the identity of the ship is immaterial, then the fact that the parties understood this term in different ways should not void the contract, even if a 'meeting of minds' is held to be required.

[24] 'The Common Law, 309'.

obligations in a certain way by means of one's use of a word). The claim is that lexical intentions are relevant to determining the legal effect of the contract, at least in the special case in which the word in question is a homonym,[25] but that intentions of these other sorts are never relevant. But one might want to know why this subtle distinction should be important. The lexical intention to use the word *Peerless*$_{OCT}$ by inscribing the letters P-E-E-R-L-E-S-S is no more objective or observable than the semantic intention to use a single ambiguous word to mean this rather than that. So in so far as Holmes's reluctance to rely on semantic or legal intentions is grounded in a general squeamishness about allowing subjective mental states to play a role in grounding legal obligations, lexical intentions should be equally beyond the pale. The most we can say about Holmes's view on this reading is that it accords a more limited role to mental facts than the real intentionalist alternatives that he opposes. On an alternative reading, we might attribute a more radical view to Holmes, according to which the 'disambiguation' of a homonym has nothing to do with the speaker's intentions at all, but is rather grounded in objective facts about (say) the causal pedigree of the word-token that he employs.[26] This would be more consistent with Holmes's outlook, but his remarks are too brief to sustain further discussion of the matter.

To see the limits of this gambit, contrast this case with one involving genuine ambiguity rather than homonymy. In *Frigaliment Importing Co v BNS International Sales Corp,*[27] perhaps the *second* most famous case on contract ambiguity, the court found that the word 'chicken' is genuinely ambiguous in the dialect of the poultry business, sometimes referring to any adult bird of the relevant species,[28] and sometimes only to young and tender birds suitable for broiling, but not to older birds good only for stewing. Plaintiff ordered 'chickens'; defendant shipped chickens in the broad sense; and plaintiff sued for non-performance, claiming to have ordered chickens in the narrow sense. Consider a variant in which the extrinsic evidence shows that both parties in fact intended to use the word in the narrow sense. For the intentionalist (real or hypothetical) this would entail judgment for the plaintiff. For the Holmesian who admits extrinsic evidence only for the purpose of determining that the parties *used the same word*, this would not follow. After all, they clearly *did* use the same word. The trouble is that, since that word is ambiguous, it is unclear what counts as performance under the contract. A strict Holmesian textualist may be forced to say that the plaintiff has not met his

---

[25] As we have seen, Holmes implicitly denies that lexical intentions are relevant when one of the parties simply misspeaks, saying 'Peerless' when he means to say 'Peri': Holmes (1881).

[26] As in Devitt (1981).

[27] 190 F Supp 116 (SDNY 1960).

[28] As one expert testified: 'Chicken is everything except a goose, a duck, and a turkey.'

burden to show that the defendant has breached the contract, and hence that his suit must fail. This is what the court in fact said in the real version of *Frigaliment*, where extrinsic evidence suggested that the parties had materially different understandings of the contract; but in the hypothetical variant in which the parties in fact had the same understanding, this is clearly the wrong answer.

The question is whether the textualist can secure the right answer in cases of this sort, and here we note only the possibility of a response. It is open to the textualist to allow intentions as a somewhat broader role. Just as Holmes himself appears to allow *lexical* intentions a role in fixing the content of a contract involving homonyms, a textualist might allow semantic or communicative intentions (real or hypothetical) a limited role in determining how genuinely ambiguous terms are to be disambiguated. This would not amount to wholesale capitulation to intentionalism. It is one thing to ask what the parties *said* to one another by means of the contract[29]—or more impersonally, *what the contract says*—and another to ask what the parties hoped to accomplish by means of the contract, what they intended its practical or legal consequences to be, and so on. If Jones says to Smith, 'I'll pay you $20 for the bats in your attic', we can ask: in saying this, what did Jones *offer to do*? And the answer to this question might be: Jones offered to pay Smith $20 for the *baseball bats* in Smith's attic. This might be so in virtue of some fact about Jones's intentions—his intention to use 'bat' to mean *baseball bat*, for instance. But it might also be true in virtue of certain more 'objective' facts about Jones and his circumstances. Suppose the contract also includes references to 'baseballs', 'baseball gloves', and the like. Then the moderate textualist might say: regardless of the real intentions of the parties, since any impartial spectator confronted with the contract as a whole (and perhaps with relevant extrinsic evidence) would interpret the word 'bat' in the contract to mean *baseball bat*, that is what the word as it occurs in the contract does in fact mean. In either case, the approach suggests a *moderate textualism* which sees the legal effect of a contract as grounded, not in the real or hypothetical *legal* intentions of the parties, and not simply in the impersonal semantic facts about the linguistic meanings of words, but rather in these facts together with the semantico-pragmatic facts about what the parties *said* to one another by means of the contract. In the simplest version of this approach—the one most congenial to the rhetoric of textualism—the role for intentions is restricted to the case in which the impersonal semantic meaning does not fix a determinate battery of obligations because the sentence is semantically ambiguous or non-specific. The moderate textualist allows that the legal effect of the contract is *constrained*

---

[29] Or what they *offered, accepted, agreed to, promised*, etc.

by the impersonal semantic meaning of the contract text, and (where necessary) *specified* by the semantic intentions of the parties—their intention to *say* this or that by means of the contract. To explore the consequences of this approach, let us consider a puzzling case.

7. Beyond ambiguity: Soper's Estate[30]

In 1911 Ira Collins Soper of Louisville, Kentucky, married Adeline Westphal. The couple lived together as man and wife until 1921, when Soper disappeared. A suicide note was found in his house; his car and some clothing were found on the bank of a nearby canal along with another note, etc. In reality, the suicide was a sham: Soper had abandoned his wife and skipped town to start a new life, traveling first to Canada and then to Minneapolis, where he assumed the aspirational name 'John Young' and settled down. In 1925 he married—or rather 'married'—a Minneapolis widow named Gertrude Whitby. They lived as husband and wife until 1932, at which time Soper/Young committed suicide in earnest. While 'married' to Gertrude, Soper/Young formed a fuel oil company with a man named Karstens. The two partners owned the company together, splitting the bulk of 400 shares of stock, with the understanding that the company would take out an insurance policy in the amount of $5,000 payable to the First Minneapolis Trust Company as trustee. The contract with the Trust Company contained the following provision:

Upon the decease of either John W. Young or Ferdinand J. Karstens, the Trust Company shall proceed to collect the proceeds of the Insurance Policies on the life of such deceased Depositor, and shall handle and dispose of such proceeds as follows:

The Trust shall deliver the stock certificates of the deceased Depositor to the surviving Depositor and it shall deliver the proceeds of the insurance on the life of the deceased Depositor to *the wife of the deceased Depositor* if living.

After Soper/Young's death, the Trust Company collected on the insurance policy, conveyed Soper's shares to Karstens, and paid Gertrude Whitby Young $5,000.

Several months later, Adeline Soper arrived in Minneapolis, having tracked her husband across the country, and sued Gertrude Whitby and the Trust Company for $5,000, arguing that the money had been distributed to Gertrude in error and was in fact owed to Adeline as 'the wife of the deceased Depositor'.

---

[30] *Re the Estate of Ira Collins Soper* 196 Minn 60, 264 NW 427 (1935).

The court's discussion focuses on the Plain Meaning Rule, the question being whether extrinsic evidence of the intentions and understandings of the parties is admissible for the interpretation of a contract that is not ambiguous on its face. All parties agree that a man can have only one wife at a time, and that at the time relevant to the case, Soper's wife was Adeline and not Gertrude. If the notion of 'semantic meaning' makes any sense at all, then as a matter of semantics, the phrase 'the wife of the deceased Depositor' is not ambiguous. When the depositor is Soper/Young, the semantic referent of the phrase (relative to the context) is Adeline and no one else.[31] On the other hand, extrinsic evidence adduced by the defendant, including testimony from Karstens and the Trust Company lawyer who had drafted the document, made it plain that Soper/Young had intended and expected the money to go to Gertrude in this contingency, and that the other parties to the agreement all believed that Gertrude was Soper's wife and so had similar expectations. The question is whether, and in what ways, these beliefs and intentions bear on the legal effect of the contact.

The dissenting opinion by Judge Olsen maintains that the language of the contract is not ambiguous, and hence that extrinsic evidence as to the real intentions or expectations of the parties is not germane:

I am unable to agree that a court should make a new contract for the parties and so change either the policy of the trust agreement as to substitute a new beneficiary. A man can have only one wife....The contract in this case designates the 'wife' as the one to whom the money is to be paid. I am unable to construe this word to mean anything else than the only wife of Soper then living [namely Adeline].[32]

This is an application of the Plain Meaning Rule, and both the result and the reasoning are consistent with textualism (simple or moderate), and also with a cramped version of hypothetical intentionalism that restricts the reasonable interpreter to evidence that lies within the 'four corners of the agreement' when the agreement is semantically unambiguous. Note that Holmes's trick of allowing private intentions to play a role by recasting them as lexical intentions has no application in this case. The word 'Peerless' may be two names, each with its own entry in the lexicon; but the word 'wife' as it occurs in the Soper/Karstens contract is not a homonym. Holmes's textualist principles, according to which the public language meanings of words determine their

---

[31] If descriptions are not terms but rather predicates or quantifiers, the phrase 'semantic referent' may be inapt; but this will not matter in what follows. The important point is that the semantic value of the description, relative to the context of utterance, either *is*, or *includes*, or *ranges over*, or *applies to*...Adeline and not Gertrude, and hence that a sentence of the form 'The wife of the Deceased depositor is φ' depends for its truth-value relative to this context on whether Adeline is φ.

[32] *Re Soper's Estate* at 433.

legal effect (when they are sufficient to determine such an effect), clearly require Judge Olsen's preferred result in this case.

The majority opinion by Judge Olson (with an 'o') holds that the contract exhibits 'latent ambiguity' that 'emerges' when the court seeks to apply it to the facts of the case, and that extrinsic evidence is therefore admissible for the purposes of interpretation. Taking this extrinsic evidence into account, the court finds that the phrase 'the wife of the deceased Depositor' refers to Gertrude given the background facts, and that Adeline is not entitled to the money. The detailed reasoning of the majority does not bear scrutiny. (The court seems particularly impressed by the fact that Gertrude is blameless in the matter, a fact with no bearing on the result, and which is in any case balanced by Adeline's blamelessness.) The majority opinion does however sound a note that runs through the cases and commentaries, and which has been taken to support intentionalism over textualism:

Were we to award the insurance fund to plaintiff Adeline, it is obvious that we would thereby be doing violence to the contract entered into by the decedent Young with his associate Mr. Karstens. That agreement points to no one else than Gertrude as Young's 'wife'. To hold otherwise is to give the word 'wife' 'a fixed symbol,' as 'something inherent and objective, not subjective and personal'. Dean Wigmore in his excellent work on evidence . . . has this to say:

> 'The ordinary standard or "plain meaning" is simply the meaning of people who did *not* write the document. The fallacy consists in assuming that there is or ever can be some *one re al* or absolute meaning. In truth, there can only be *some person's meaning*, and that person, whose meaning the law is seeking, is the writer of the document.'[33]

This view, widely cited in discussions of the Plain Meaning Rule and of textualism generally, amounts to a form of skepticism about semantic meaning: the sort of meaning that might attach to a token sentence independently of the speaker's intentions or beliefs. The textualist's fundamental thought is that the legal effect of a contract is determined, or at least massively constrained, by semantic meaning in this sense. If this notion makes no sense at all, or if (somewhat more plausibly) the semantic meaning in this sense is always too 'thin' to determine a concrete legal effect, then textualism as we have defined it is not a real possibility after all.

Taken at face value, this radical view amounts to the rejection of 'plain meaning' and hence of the conceptual basis for the Plain Meaning Rule. But that is not in fact the court's holding in this case. The holding is rather that, while the Plain Meaning Rule remains in force, the Soper contract exhibits a

---

[33] *Re Soper's Estate* at 431.

'latent ambiguity' that emerges when the language of the contract is applied
to the facts of the case, and that extrinsic evidence is therefore admissible for
the purposes of resolving this ambiguity. What might this mean?

Since the only pertinent bit of language is the phrase, 'the wife of the
deceased Depositor', the court's position must be that this phrase is somehow
ambiguous. We could make sense of this if we took the court to be suggesting
that the word 'wife' is ambiguous, sometimes meaning 'legal wife' and sometimes (say) 'female life partner'. As a conjecture about the meaning of the
word in twenty-first century English, this may be on its way to being true.
But writing in 1935, the court never considers this possibility and rightly so.

The court's position must therefore be that the description, 'the wife of the
deceased Depositor' is ambiguous even though the word 'wife' is not. How
could this be? It has occasionally been proposed that the English word 'the' or
the definite description construction, 'the F', is ambiguous, admitting both
an attributive sense in which 'the F' picks out the unique satisfier of the predicate 'F', whoever that may be, and a referential sense, according to which the
phrase picks out some salient individual whom the speaker and hearer typically *believe* to satisfy the predicate, but who may not actually satisfy it.[34] To
illustrate with an apt example due to Linsky as modified by Kripke:

> Someone sees a woman with a man. Taking the man to be her husband and observing
> his attitude toward her, he says, 'her husband is kind to her,' and someone else may
> nod, 'yes, he seems to be'. Suppose the man in question is not her husband. Suppose
> he is her lover, to whom she has been driven precisely by her husband's cruelty.[35]

According to the view presently under discussion, even though the word 'husband' is not ambiguous, the description 'her husband' is. When the ambiguity is resolved in one way, the sentence is true iff the woman's husband,
whoever he may be, is kind to her; when it is resolved in another way, it is true
only if a certain salient individual x (whom the speaker and hearer take to be
the woman's husband) is kind to her.

With this in mind, we might take the decision in the *Soper* case to involve
the following argument. Though a casual observer unaware of the weird facts
of the case might not realize it, the language of the contract is materially
ambiguous, since the crucial description can be understood either referentially or attributively, with the two readings yielding different results given the
facts. This is *latent* ambiguity, since in a legal context this sort of ambiguity
rarely matters. Extrinsic evidence nonetheless suggests that the ambiguity
matters in this case, and also shows us how it is to be resolved. Both Karstens
and the Trust Company lawyer testified that Soper introduced Gertrude as

---

[34] Donnelan (1966) at pp 281–304.   [35] Kripke (1977) at p 256.

'Mrs Young', and that they routinely referred to her in their conversations as Young's wife. Contemporaneous insurance contracts taken out by Soper/ Young and not at issue in the present case included a beneficiary clause designating Young's heir as 'Gertrude Young, wife'. The evidence thus suggests that the description is used referentially in the contract, in which case the legal effect of the contract is to create an obligation in the Trust Company to convey the money to Gertrude and the right in Gertrude to receive it.

This is a reading of the majority decision that is consistent with moderate textualism—the sort of textualism that allows the intentions of the parties and other extrinsic facts to resolve material semantic ambiguity. There are, however, two main difficulties with this approach. First, as Kripke has shown, it is probably a mistake to think that the so-called referential *use* of definite descriptions amounts to a genuine semantic ambiguity in descriptive phrases. It is beyond dispute that speakers who are mistaken about the facts (or whose audiences are mistaken about the facts) can use a sentence of the form 'The F is G' to express and communicate thoughts about objects that are not in fact F (much less *the F*). When the speaker in Linsky's example says, 'her husband is kind to her', one of the things he manages to do with his words is to say, of a certain man x (who is not in fact the woman's husband), that x is kind to her. But from the fact that a description can be used in this way to express a singular thought about a salient individual, it does not follow that the descriptive phrase refers to that individual as a matter of the semantic rules of the language together with pertinent facts about the circumstances of its utterance. The best way to see this is to note, as Kripke does, that something like the referential/attributive contrast arises even in the case of unambiguous proper names. If we see a man in the distance whom you and I both take to be Malcolm Fishbein of Astoria, Queens, I can say 'Malcolm Fishbein is picking daisies' to express and communicate the thought that a certain person is picking daisies. But if the man in the distance is not Malcolm Fishbein, it would be bizarre to take this to show that the name 'Malcolm Fishbein' is ambiguous. Since there is no limit as to how mistaken a speaker and his audience can be about an item glimpsed in the distance, this would entail that every name is wildly ambiguous, and that is absurd.

Second, even if we allow that definite descriptions have a referential *sense*— and hence that, as a matter of semantics, descriptions may sometimes function as name-like tags for contextually salient individuals—several difficulties arise in applying this idea to the Soper contract. Most obviously, the phrase 'the wife of the deceased Depositor' in the contract cannot possibly have been a name-like tag for *Gertrude*, since the clause must also have the consequence that if Karstens had died first, the money would have gone to *his* wife. Imagine a version of the case in which Karstens was not married when the contract was signed, but later married a woman who had been unknown to all the parties when the contract was drafted. If Karstens had died first, there would have been no doubt that the money was owed to her; so the description as it figures in the contract cannot possibly have been intended *in the referential sense*, since in that case it would have no application to these facts.

A related problem concerns the consequences of the contract for the following set of facts. Suppose that after Soper and Karstens signed the agreement, Gertrude had died and Soper had remarried before committing suicide. If the description in the contract had been intended as a referential tag for Gertrude, the clause would have no application in this case. But it is highly unlikely that the majority would have construed the contract in this way. It is much more plausible to suppose that in awarding the money to Gertrude, the court was construing the contract to have the following legal effect for the case in which Soper predeceases Karstens: if Gertrude survives Soper, the money goes to her unless they have 'divorced', in which case the money goes to her 'successor', if any, in the role or Soper's 'wife'. But if this is right then the description 'the wife of the deceased Depositor' in the contract was used neither *referentially* (as a tag for Gertrude) nor attributively (to pick out Soper's legal wife at the time of his death, whoever she may be) but in some third way. But no one has ever suggested that English definite descriptions exhibit a three-way ambiguity that would yield this hybrid meaning as one possible disambiguation of the contract language.

If all of this is sound, the upshot is that Simple Textualism and its moderate variant are both inconsistent with the majority opinion in *Soper*, and the same goes for any view that incorporates a strong Plain Meaning Rule that admits external evidence only for the purposes of resolving a genuine *semantic* ambiguity (or for identifying the value of some contextual parameter). The court did not reach for external evidence for the purpose of singling out one of the many linguistically available *meanings* associated with the words of the contract, and, if the Plain Meaning Rule admits extrinsic evidence for this purpose, the dissent is correct: the reliance on extrinsic evidence in this case was a mistake. If the court's decision was nonetheless correct in its result, this shows that textualism was not a correct account of contract law in Minnesota in 1935—which is not to say that textualism is intrinsically incoherent or otherwise objectionable.

8. Personal meaning as the ground of contractual obligation

That textualism is incoherent is the burden of the court's most interesting claim, for which it cites Wigmore:

The ordinary standard or 'plain meaning' is simply the meaning of people who did not write the document. The fallacy consists in assuming that there is or ever can be some one real or absolute meaning. In truth, there can only be *some person's meaning,* and that person, whose meaning the law is seeking, is the writer of the document.[36]

This passage involves two ideas. There is the radical claim that there is simply no such thing as impersonal, semantic meaning—the sort of meaning that is settled independently of what the speaker on some occasion has in mind. And then there is the more moderate thought that, even if there is such a thing as semantic meaning, there is also what might be called *personal meaning:* the meanings that individual speakers on particular occasions *attach* to their words. The core principle underlying the majority opinion is that the legal effect of an explicit contract provision is determined by the personal meanings of the parties, and that semantic meaning plays no constitutive role in fixing these effects. In so far as this second thought is central, the court's rejection of semantic meaning is incidental.

The idea that speakers *attach* meanings to their words is ubiquitous in modern writing about contracts, much of which seeks to repudiate the hard-core textualism of Holmes, Williston, and Hand. Consider §201 of the *Restatement (Second) of Contracts*:

§201. Whose Meaning Prevails
(1) Where the parties have attached the same meaning to a promise or agreement or a term thereof, it is interpreted in accordance with that meaning.
(2) Where the parties have attached different meanings to a promise or agreement or a term thereof, it is interpreted in accordance with the meaning attached by one of them if at the time the agreement was made
    (a) That party did not know of any different meaning attached by the other, and the other knew of the meaning attached by the first party; or
    (b) That party had no reason to know of any different meaning attached by the other, and the other had reason to know the meaning attached by the first party.

Or Corbin:

In the case of most contract transactions, there are at least two participants, each playing some part in the formation and performance of the contract, each choosing some of the symbols of expression, and each *giving them a meaning* that may differ materially from the meaning that is given to them by the other.... The result is that the

---

[36] Wigmore (1923) at §2462, p 378.

court must determine, in accordance with applicable law, whose meaning is to prevail.[37]

Or Farnsworth:

In a dispute over contract interpretation, each party claims that the language should be given the meaning that the party attaches to it at the time of the dispute. However the resolution of the dispute begins, not with these meanings, but with the meanings attached by each party at the time the contract was made.[38]

How should we understand this ubiquitous idiom?

There is no doubt that it often makes good sense to ask what a person meant by a word or phrase on some occasion of use. When a word is ambiguous, we can ask which of the semantically available senses the speaker had in mind. When a phrase has no standard meaning but has been introduced for some transitory purpose in the course of negotiations, we can ask what each of the parties intended it to mean. (When you said that you would pay $10,000 for the 'Swiss Coin Collection', did you mean the expression to apply to all the Swiss coins in the owner's possession, or only those you recently examined at the bank?) When two parties wish to speak in code, or when they simply speak an eccentric dialect in which ordinary words have special meanings, we can ask what their words meant in the language they were speaking, and so on.

In these cases, questions about what a person meant by a word on some occasion amount to questions about which language he was speaking, and which of the many meanings that language makes available he meant to employ. If we interpret talk of personal meaning in this way, then the relevant inquiry is an inquiry into the *linguistic* intentions of the parties. In many cases, this inquiry will make good sense, and when the default public language meanings diverge from the shared personal meanings of the parties, a version of intentionalism that relies on these personal meanings will yield results that are at odds with a strictly textualist analysis.

And yet it seems to me that there is good reason to resist this understanding of personal meaning in the present context. To see why, let us analyze the *Soper* case by reference to the linguistic intentions of the parties. It seems perfectly clear that both Karstens and the Trust Company lawyer who drafted the document intended to use the word 'wife' in its ordinary English sense to mean *(legal) female spouse* and to use the definite description 'the wife of the deceased Depositor' attributively, as is shown by the fact that the clause was clearly designed to cover the case in which Karstens predeceased Soper, and

---

[37] Corbin (1952) at p 496.   [38] Farnsworth (2004) at p 445.

also by the plausible conjecture that it was designed to have application in the case where Gertrude dies and Soper 'remarries' before his own death. When it comes to Soper himself, the situation is more muddled. He may well have intended to use the words in their ordinary English meaning. After all, he took himself to be communicating with Karstens and the Trust Company, and perhaps with future legal actors who might apply the contract, and, since he could be confident that they would give the words their ordinary English meanings, it would have been pointless for him to attach another 'private' meaning to them, and so to speak a language that none of his counterparties would have been speaking. In that case, the parties all 'attach' the same meanings to the words in the sense presently under discussion: they were all speaking standard English, a language in which the relevant clause is not ambiguous. When the contract is interpreted according to this shared meaning, the beneficiary of the trust is Adeline.

We might of course imagine that Soper intended to speak a variant of English in which 'wife' means *female domestic partner* or something of the sort, or to speak in standard English but to understand the description as a referential tag for Gertrude, or in some hybrid way. In that case we would have a clash of 'meanings' and the second clause of *Restatement* §201 might apply. Since Soper had reason to know about the meanings his counterparties attached to the contract, but they had no reason to know of his idiosyncratic meaning, the Restatement rule entails that *their* meaning should prevail, in which case, again, the beneficiary under the contract should be Adeline.

The upshot is that it is probably a mistake to understand the ubiquitous invocations of the 'meanings of the parties' in the law of contracts as an invocation of the linguistic meanings or intentions of the parties—their intentions to speak one language or another, or their intention to opt for one or another linguistically available disambiguation of their words. We do better justice to this (the prevailing) approach to contract interpretation if we suppose that, when courts and commentators invoke the personal meanings of the parties, they are not referring to anything specifically semantic or linguistic at all, but rather to the *legal* intentions and expectations of the parties—their intentions to change the legal score in certain ways by means of the contract in question. Without inquiring into what Soper *meant by his words*, we may say with some confidence that he intended the *legal effect* of his agreement to be that Gertrude, and not Adeline, would acquire the right to collect $5,000 on his death.

It is of course somewhat harder to say what Karstens and the Trust Company intended the effect of this provision to be. On the one hand, they clearly intended/expected that the contract would create a right in Gertrude to collect the money should Soper die while their relationship remained intact.

On the other, they also intended/expected to create such a right in *Soper's wife at the time of his death*. Since these intentions are not jointly satisfiable given the facts of the case, a court that regards the legal effect of a contract as grounded in the legal intentions of the parties would have to apply some principle for assigning a legal effect to the document in the presence of in consistent legal intentions. We have not discussed principles of this sort, but it is not hard to imagine how the inquiry might proceed. In the construal of a contract clause it often matters whether the clause was intended to benefit both parties or only one. In this case, it was presumably a matter of complete indifference to Karstens and the Trust Company who should benefit from the policy in the event of Soper's death. If that is right, the court might have grounds for resolving the inconsistency in the legal intentions of Karstens and the Trust Company in such a way as to honor Soper's unambiguous legal intention. If we understand the majority decision in this way, we may understand the court to be attempting to honor the intentions of the parties, or to apply the contract in accordance with the 'meanings' of the parties. But the relevant 'meanings' are not linguistic meanings at all; they are rather intentions to change the legal score in certain ways by means of the contract. This is a version of intentionalism that really is incompatible with textualism as we have defined it.

One important question for this reconstruction of the majority reasoning in *Soper* is how to understand the majority's application of the Plain Meaning Rule. The court does not mean to abrogate the rule, and it does not insist, at least not unequivocally, that the language of the contract is literally ambiguous as a matter of English. What then can it mean to say that the contract displays a 'latent ambiguity' when applied to the facts of the case? Perhaps the best we can do is this: in many cases in which a dispute over a contact arises, there will be only one plausible hypothesis about the legal intentions of the parties given the language of the contract and the background information that an uninvolved third party can be expected to have. To say that such a contract exhibits *latent* ambiguity is not to say that it is *semantically* ambiguous, but rather simply that, given the surprising facts as revealed by the extrinsic evidence, it might have been the vehicle of a number of distinct legal intentions which, if enacted, would entail different results in the case at hand. Now there is a longstanding debate among courts and commentators about whether, in applying the Plain Meaning Rule, extrinsic evidence is admissible for the purposes *demonstrating* an ambiguity, and not simply for the purposes of resolving an ambiguity that is clearly present in the contract. If we understand 'ambiguity' to mean uncertainty at the level of intended *legal* effects, and if we take a liberal view according to which extrinsic evidence is admissible for the purposes of demonstrating such an ambiguity, then we can make sense of the court's understanding of the Plain Meaning Rule. We can take the court to have found that extrinsic evidence is admissible in this case for the purpose of demonstrating that the language of the contract might have been the vehicle of materially different legal intentions—that is the *latent* ambiguity—and to have held that, when this evidence is taken into account, the controlling intention is one that might not have been obvious without it—ie the intention that someone who is not in fact Soper's wife, namely Gertrude, should receive the money that the contract assigns to 'the wife of the deceased Depositor'.

9. An alternative account of 'personal meaning'

I have suggested that, when courts and commentators invoke the personal meanings that parties 'attach' to the language of their contract as the ground of contractual obligation, they are best understood as invoking the legal intentions of the parties with respect to their contract. The fact that the parties intended a certain clause to impose certain legal obligations is not a distinctively *linguistic* feature of that clause, so views that ground the content of a contract in such personal meanings are best understood as forms of intentionalism where the pertinent intentions are not linguistic intentions, but rather legal intentions.

Before we settle on this view, we should consider another possibility—or at least, an apparently different possibility.[39] Return to the case in which you and I mistake a man in the distance for Malcolm Fishbein of Astoria, Queens, and I say, 'Malcolm Fishbein is picking daisies.' You may then report my remark as follows:

You said that *he* or (*that guy*) is picking daisies.

This sort of indirect report may be true even when the proposition semantically expressed by the sentence that I uttered (relative to the context of utterance) does not match the proposition semantically expressed by the embedded sentence in the report itself. This shows that *what is said* by means of an assertoric utterance may diverge from the proposition semantically encoded by the uttered sentence. (This is a familiar point, and might be made in many other ways.)

The alternative proposal identifies the 'personal meaning' of a contract provision with *what the parties said* by means of that provision. Facts of this

[39] This view was suggested by participants in the Soames–Marmor seminar in law and philosophy at USC.

sort are in some clear sense *linguistic*, even if they are not *semantic* in some narrow sense. They appear to be distinct from facts about what the speakers intended to accomplish by means of their utterance, and, in particular, from facts about the intended legal effects of the utterance. A proposal that would ground contractual obligations in *what the parties said by means of the contract* would thus appear to be an alternative to Simple Intentionalism as we have defined it (since that view grounds contractual obligation in the *legal* intentions of the parties) and to textualism as we have defined it (since that view grounds contractual obligation in impersonal semantic facts about the contract). Of course this third view might *collapse* into one of these other views if the theorist goes on to ground *what is said* by a particular contract provision either in the legal intentions of the parties or in the impersonal semantic content of the text of the provision. But it is important to distinguish the view that contractual obligation is grounded in *what the parties said* from any particular view about how facts about what the parties said are to be grounded. If the theorist does not offer a reductive account of *what is said*, his view looks to be an alternative to textualism and to intentionalism as we have understood them.

In order to explore this possibility, let us consider a version that would apply more directly to the case of contracts. Suppose that you and I mistake *X* for Malcolm Fishbein, and I say, gazing at *X*: 'I'll pay you $20 to introduce me to Malcolm Fishbein.' You might then report my remark as follows:

You said that you would pay me $20 to introduce you to *him* (or to *that guy*);

or, I think equivalently:

You offered (agreed/promised) to pay me $20 to introduce you to *him*.

Just as we use ordinary assertoric utterances to *say that p*, we use contractual utterances to *say that we will* φ, or to *agree/offer/promise to* φ. The proposal is that the legal effect of a contract is determined by the objective linguistic facts about what the parties said they would do in this sense. To ascertain the meanings that the parties 'attached' to the language of their contract is not to ascertain an impersonal semantic fact, or a fact about the legal intentions of the parties, but rather a linguistic (though not narrowly semantic) fact of this sort.

Is this view a genuine alternative to the textualist and intentionalist views we have been discussing? I have my doubts. It is completely uncontroversial that when we seek to determine the legal effect of a contract provision, we are seeking to determine what the parties agreed to do by virtue of including that provision in their contract. This is not a *theory* of the ground of law of the contract; it is simply a restatement of the fact that contractual obligations are obligations that are generated by agreements. The theories we have been discussing are attempts to specify that in virtue of which a given contract provision generates a determinate obligation, or, equivalently, to specify the facts in virtue of which the parties managed to *agree to* φ by incorporating a certain provision into their contract. The textualist says that they agreed to φ because the language of the contract semantically encodes a promise to φ; the intentionalist says that they agreed to φ because they intended their contract to impose an obligation to φ, etc. If the alternative approach included an account of that in virtue of which a speaker manages to say what he says (or to agree to what he agrees to) when he utters a sentence, it would be an answer to the question we have been discussing. But if the theorist is content to ground the legal effect of a contractual provision in *what the parties agreed to do* when they signed it, then the theorist is saying rather little, and what he is saying is not in competition with the views we have been discussing.

10. Skepticism about plain meaning

We now turn to the more radical theme in the majority opinion in the *Soper* case, namely the claim that the minority's textualist approach is untenable because the very idea of plain semantic meaning makes no sense. ('The fallacy consists in assuming that there is . . . some one real or absolute meaning.') This has been an extraordinarily influential idea in modern contract theory and in the development of contract law by the courts. The most important statement appears in Judge Traynor's famous decision in *Pacific Gas & Electric Co v Thomas Drayage and Rigging Co*:

When the court interprets a contract on this basis [the alleged plain meaning] it determines the meaning of the instrument on the basis of ' . . . extrinsic evidence of the judge's own education and experience.' . . . The exclusion of testimony that might contradict the linguistic background of the judge reflects a judicial belief in the possibility of perfect verbal expression. . . . This belief is a remnant of a primitive faith in the inherent potency and meaning of words. . . .

A rule that would limit the determination of the meaning of a written instrument to its four corners merely because it seems to the court to be clear and unambiguous would deny the relevance of the intention of the parties or presuppose a degree of verbal precision and stability our language has not attained.

Some courts have expressed the opinion that contractual obligations are created by the mere use of certain words, whether or not there was any intent to incur such obligations. Under this view, contractual obligations flow, not from the intentions of the parties, but from the mere fact that they use certain magic words. Evidence of parties' intentions therefore becomes irrelevant.

In this state, however, the intention of the parties as expressed in the contract is the source of contractual rights and duties. A court must ascertain and give effect to this intention by determining what the parties meant by the words they used. Accordingly, the exclusion of relevant extrinsic evidence to explain the meaning of a written instrument could be justified only if it were feasible to determine the meanings the parties gave to the words from the instrument alone.

If words had absolute and constant referents, it might be possible to discover the contractual intention in the words themselves and in the manner in which they were arranged. Words, however, do not have absolute and constant referents. 'A word is a symbol of thought but has no arbitrary fixed meaning like a symbol of algebra or chemistry.' . . . The meaning of particular words or groups of words varies with the '. . . verbal context and surrounding circumstances and purposes in view of the linguistic education and experience of their hearers or readers (not excluding judges). . . . A word has no meaning apart from these factors, much less does it have an objective meaning, one true meaning.'[40]

This passage, which nearly abolished the Plain Meaning Rule in California on the ground that impersonal or plain meaning is a myth, represents one of the most significant points at which the philosophy of language (or something like it) has influenced the real content of law in the United States. It is therefore worth untangling some of the threads that run through it.

(a) The proponent of plain meaning is said to hold that words have 'one true [absolute, immutable] meaning', but of course no one has ever denied that languages change or that ambiguity is commonplace. The view is simply that sometimes—in fact quite often—a contract provision will exhibit no material vagueness or ambiguity. This may be so either because the language of the contract is entirely unambiguous, or, more commonly, because the text exhibits no *material* ambiguity—no ambiguity that would matter for the purposes of the dispute at hand. Perhaps the word 'wife' is vague or ambiguous. If Soper had married a post-operative transsexual, would she have been his 'wife'? But given the real facts of the case, *this* bit of semantic indeterminacy is immaterial. The proponent of the Plain Meaning Rule holds that even if vagueness and ambiguity are everywhere, many cases are of this sort and he is surely right.

(b) The Plain Meaning Rule is said to be at odds with a standard formula according to which the obligations of the parties are determined by their *intentions as expressed in the contract*, but this is misleading. It is true, as we have seen, that proponents of the objective theory have sometimes claimed that the real intentions of the parties are utterly irrelevant. But the proponent of the Plain Meaning Rule is not committed to this view. He may say

---

[40] 442 P 2d 641 (Cal 1968), internal citations omitted.

instead, what is entirely plausible, that in normal cases of contracting the parties enter into the agreement with many intentions, one of which is the intention to be bound by its terms or, in other words, to undertake and impose the obligations that the language of the contract, interpreted according to its plain meaning, describes. The parties may also have beliefs about the meaning of the contract, and about the determinate legal obligations they undertake by signing it. And if they are mistaken or confused about what the contract says, or if they intend to use the contract language in a non-standard way, there may be a clash between their intention to be bound by the terms of the agreement and their intention to undertake specific obligations by means of it. *Everyone* needs a principle for identifying the real obligations of the parties in cases of this sort. The proponent of a strong Plain Meaning Rule offers one as his candidate (which privileges the obligations corresponding to the plain meaning of the document); Traynor offers another (which privileges the specific obligations that the parties intended to undertake by means of the contract). Traynor's rule may be better, but he should not object to the Plain Meaning Rule on the ground that it severs contractual obligation from the intent of the parties. When elaborated in these ways, the two views differ about which intentions are decisive, but they may agree (as against proponents of a radical version of the objective theory) that the ultimate ground of contractual obligation lies in the intentions of the parties.

(c) Traynor objects to the Plain Meaning Rule on the ground that since contract interpretation always requires evidence that transcends the 'four corners' of the agreement, there is no principled reason to exclude such evidence even when the contract exhibits no material ambiguity so far as the judge can tell. There is a correct philosophical point in the vicinity of this objection. When the judge determines that the contract is not materially ambiguous (and so excludes extrinsic evidence), he presumes that the contract is written in English and not in some private code composed of English words, and he brings to bear his knowledge of English and the special technical dialects associated with commercial trades. He may also bring to bear his background knowledge—eg in concluding that the reference to 'bats' in a contract that also makes referents to 'baseballs' and 'baseball gloves' refers to 'baseball bats' and not to flying rodents. And of course there is no way even in principle for a judge to glean all of *this* knowledge from the four corners of the document. There is no such thing as a 'self-interpreting text' whose semantic features are determined by intrinsic features of the text itself. Fair enough. But it does not follow that there is no significant difference between the kind of *general* knowledge that anyone must bring to bear if he is to determine the public language meaning of a text and the sort of specific knowledge that the Plain Meaning Rule sometimes excludes: knowledge of the specific intentions and expectations of the parties such as might be gleaned from testimony, contemporaneous memoranda, etc. The fact is that we frequently interpret texts—road signs, textbooks, conversations overheard on the subway—by bringing to bear only general knowledge of the language and of the circumstances under which the text was produced, without knowing anything in particular about the special circumstances of the speaker. Of course we may frequently make mistakes when we attribute intentions and expectations to speakers on the basis of the text in this way. But that does not mean, in general, that we have misunderstood *what he or she has said*, or that we have misinterpreted *the text itself*. The difficulty may lie instead in the inference from what a person says to the attitudes that led him to say it.

Nothing in Traynor's discussion casts real doubt on the idea that there is often such a thing as the plain meaning of an agreement, and that this meaning is often sufficient to determine a result without recourse to extrinsic evidence. One may of course object to the Plain Meaning Rule on other grounds. If contractual obligations are grounded in the real legal intentions of the parties, or in the intentions that a third party would impute to them if he had access to every relevant fact about them, then it may seem pointless to restrict the evidence available to courts when they seek to identify those intentions, even when the language of the agreement appears sufficient for the purpose. The proponent of the Plain Meaning Rule has an easy response—rules of evidence limit what courts may consider for all sorts of reasons: to promote efficiency, to discourage fraud, to provide incentives for careful draftsmanship, etc. The Plain Meaning Rule might be justified on these grounds even if it often serves to exclude relevant evidence. This is not a deep dispute about a matter of philosophical principle. It is a practical dispute about the costs and benefits of a rule of evidence. The novelty in Traynor's decision, which may be traced through Corbin[41] back to the remarks of Wigmore cited in the *Soper* case, is to insist that there is some theoretical difficulty with the very ideal of a plain or impersonal meaning. If there were such a difficulty, it would exclude textualism as a theory of the ground of contractual obligation, along with any form of hypothetical intentionalism that incorporates a strong version of the Plain Meaning Rule. So far as we have seen, however, there is no clear ground for skepticism of this sort.

---

[41] See especially Corbin (1965).

11. Some conclusions

We have surveyed a small number of relatively simple answers to the question: when a contract provision has legal effect, in virtue of what does it have the effect it has?

In exploring these answers, we have made the following substantive claims:

- Simple Textualism—the view that the legal effect of a provision is determined by its impersonal semantic content together with objective features of the context of utterance—is ruled out by the fact that an ambiguous contract provision can sometimes impose a determinate legal obligation. (The simplest cases are those in which the parties resolve the ambiguity in the same way.) The claim is not that a simple textualist regime would be impossible, but rather that it is wildly at odds with the contract regime we have.

- Moderate Textualism—the view that the legal effect of a provision is *constrained* by its impersonal semantic content and *specified* by the parties' intentions to resolve all pertinent ambiguities in certain ways—is a tenable view, though it appears to be incompatible with the result in the *Soper* case.

- In saying that Moderate Textualism is a tenable view, we reject the radical strand in twentieth century contract theory (deriving from Wigmore) according to which impersonal 'plain' meaning is a myth.

- Simple Intentionalism—the view that the legal effect of a contract provision is a function of the legal intentions of the parties with respect to that provision—yields no clear verdict in *Soper*, or in cases like *Raffles* or *Frigaliment*, unless it is supplemented with a rule generating determinate legal effects in the presence of inconsistent legal intentions.

- When courts invoke personal meanings for this purpose—the meanings the parties 'attach' to their words—we should understand them to be referring not to any special linguistic feature of the contractual provision, but rather to the legal intentions of the parties with respect to that provision.

- When personal meanings are understood in this way, the rule of *Restatement (Second)* §201 amounts to a rule for generating determinate legal effects for contracts when the legal intentions of the parties are inconsistent with one another. When real intentionalism is supplemented with this rule, it is at least broadly compatible with contract law as we now have it.[42]

---

[42] The *Soper* case remains a problem for real intentionalism so understood since, given the weird facts of the case, one of the parties may well have had internally inconsistent intentions with respect to a single provision. Karstens (for example) may have intended the clause in question to impose an obligation on the Trust Company to pay $5,000 to *Soper's wife* in the event of his death, but he may

• We have not discussed hypothetical intentionalism at any length, but since we never have direct access to the legal intentions of the parties to a contract, the differences between real intentionalism and hypothetical intentionalism will normally be 'metaphysical'. There will be cases in which, thanks to misleading evidence, a suitably informed third party will attribute intentions to the parties that they did not have. According to the hypothetical intentionalist, the law of the contract is grounded in these imputed legal intentions, so a court that imputes these intentions to the parties and adjudicates the case accordingly will be enforcing the obligations the parties in fact incurred. According to the real intentionalist, a court that proceeds in this way will be mistaken. But of course the result will be the same no matter which view the court adopts.[43]

The views we have discussed are all versions of *originalism*, in the sense that they all ground contractual obligation in facts that were in place when the contract was formed. These views will therefore all face real difficulties in making sense of the application of old contracts to factual situations that were not and could not have been contemplated either by the parties themselves or by their linguistic communities. In 1961 the novelist William Styron granted Random House Inc the exclusive right to publish *The Confessions of Nat Turner* 'in book form'. In 2000, Styron granted Rosetta Books LLC the right to publish the same work as an 'e-book'. Random House sought an injunction against Rosetta Books.[44] The court faced the question whether e-publication amounted to publication 'in book form', and here it is plausible that both the public linguistic meaning of these words as used in 1961 and the legal intentions of the parties at the time (real or hypothetical) simply fail to settle this question. If the contract has some determinate legal effect that covers this case (as the court concluded), then none of the theories we have considered explains the ground of that effect. Originalism in the theory of contracts thus has its limits; how it might be modified to cover cases of this sort is a question for another time.

---

simultaneously have intended the clause to impose an obligation on the Trust Company to pay $5,000 to *Gertrude*. Intentionalism yields no clear verdict in such cases in the absence of a rule for generating legal obligations in the face of internally inconsistent legal intentions on the part of one of the parties. Many such rules are possible.

[43] This raises a nice question about how to understand the notion of legal effect (and the correlative notion of a legal mistake) in contexts in which courts employ restrictive rules of evidence like a strong Plain Meaning Rule. Suppose that we in fact intended our contract to impose a certain obligation O, but that a hypothetical interpreter constrained to consult only the text of the agreement would impute to us some incompatible obligation O*. When a court construes the agreement and enforces O*, we are then obliged to perform O*. So how can the intentionalist say that our *real* obligation under the contract was O? Do considerations of this sort rule out real intentionalism in favor of hypothetical intentionalism? Not automatically. It is open to the real intentionalist to say that our real obligations under the contract were given by O, but that the court's legally correct decision (which involves a mistaken construal of the contract) replaces those obligations with O*.

[44] *Random House, Inc v Rosetta Books LLC* 150 F Supp 2d 613 (SDNY 2001).

8

Modeling Legal Rules

Richard Holton

1. Introduction

Common law rules admit of exceptions. When a court, especially a higher court, finds that the routine application of a rule would result in an injustice, it is likely to distinguish. It will concede that, yes, the case does appear to fall under the rule as it is currently understood, but will insist that there are further factors, not mentioned in the rule (though perhaps acknowledged in other rules in other parts of the law) that distinguish this case from the cases that the existing rule was meant to cover. The court will conclude that in this case the verdict that the existing rule suggests would be wrong. Nevertheless, the old rule does not die.[1] When the writers of casebooks come to accommodate the new ruling it will come in as an amendment: the old rule was correct except under these new circumstances.

So how should we understand the form of legal rules? A simple-minded approach is to see them as universally quantified claims: whenever this holds, then this is the right verdict. But exceptions make this hard to maintain. A universally quantified sentence cannot have exceptions, only counterexamples, and counterexamples show that the sentence is false. Of course, one could insist on the approach, maintaining that a simple legal rule is indeed false, and that the need to amend it shows this to be so. But since every common law rule, however amended, is very likely to admit of further amendment, this leaves us in the uncomfortable position of saying that no rule is strictly true. We might try to soften the blow by saying that, as they are amended, the rules get closer to the truth, but proposals to explain such an idea have had a very checkered history.[2]

---

[1] Or at least, hardly ever. When the Australian High Court gave the *Mabo* decision (*Mabo v Queensland (No 2)* [1992] HCA 23; (1992) 175 CLR 1 (3 June 1992)), possibly the whole set of rules based around *terra nullius* was thrown out. But that is unusual.

[2] This was part of Karl Popper's idea of verisimilitude. David Miller and Pavel Tichy raised the classic problems with it. For relevant citations and a clear review of the debate since, see Oddie (2007).

So we need an approach that allows rules to have exceptions. Elsewhere I have developed an account that sees legal rules as universals containing implicit *unless*-clauses; the idea is that the exceptions trigger the clauses.[3] The challenge comes in doing this in such a way that the rules do not become trivial. In the first part of this chapter I reformulate and extend that account. In the second part I ask how it fares against some alternatives: I see two. One treats legal rules not as universal generalizations at all, but as generics. I argue that while this has some plausibility for legal *principles*, it does not do the job for legal *rules*. The second alternative is more radical, treating legal rules as default rules within a nonmonotonic logic. Here I argue that the move to nonmonotonic logic does not bring the advantages claimed for it, and further that it fails to explain something that is handled very nicely by the approach I favor: how it is that a legal decision can be criticizable, even though the court used the legal rules that were in force at the time.

2. Particularism and rules

In *The Concept of Law*, H.L.A. Hart writes:

We promise to visit a friend the next day. When the day comes it turns out that keeping the promise would involve neglecting someone dangerously ill. The fact that this is accepted as an adequate reason for not keeping the promise surely does not mean that there is no rule requiring promises to be kept, only a certain regularity in keeping them. It does not follow from the fact that rules have exceptions incapable of exhaustive statement, that in every situation we are left to our discretion and are never bound to keep a promise. A rule that ends with the word 'unless...' is still a rule.[4]

So here Hart at least implicitly accepts that some valid rules have exceptions that cannot be exhaustively stated. The passage comes after his famous discussion of the open texture of law that results from the open texture of language—is a child's bicycle covered by a regulation that prohibits vehicles from the park?—so one might think that the ideas here can be similarly explained. But clearly they cannot. Whilst there may be vagueness in the idea of a promise—is it a promise if made under duress, or if the promisor does not understand what he is committing himself to, or if the promisee is not aware of it?—such vagueness is not what is causing the open-endedness here. There

---

[3] Holton (2010).   [4] Hart (1961) at p 136.

may be no doubt that my promise was as clear and central an example as one is ever likely to find, and yet it still be true that in the circumstances I am not bound to keep it. So we need a different explanation.[5]

Hart's example might put us in mind of recent work on ethical particularism. Those who advocate such an approach contend that any putative rule is subject to exceptions, and as a result they tend to reject any role for rules. Take any rule that links the normative to the descriptive, they say, and we can find an exception to it; amend the rule to embrace the exception and we can find an exception to the amended rule, and so on. So the rules must be false.[6]

But it does not follow from the supposition that there are no exceptionless rules, that rules are false or have no useful role to play. As we have seen, Hart suggests a model: perhaps rules end with an (often unstated) *unless*-clause; where this is not triggered, the rule applies. Hart, however, does not tell us how the *unless*-clause is to be completed. And here it might seem that he is faced with a dilemma. On one approach the *unless*-clause contains a full statement of all the factors that would defeat the rule, but that is clearly incompatible with the idea that the exceptions are incapable of exhaustive statement. On the other approach the *unless*-clause would provide no information: 'One should keep one's promises unless one shouldn't.' But that is clearly trivial. If we are to give substance to an open-ended *unless*-clause we need to find a middle way between these two approaches. This is what I aim to provide.

3. That's it

The intuitive idea that I shall work with is that a rule can be overruled if there is a justification for the exception.[7] In Hart's example there are moral grounds for tending to the seriously ill person rather than keeping my promise. But if so, then there is plausibly a moral rule that tells us that there are such grounds. So the *unless*-clause can be read as quantifying over other moral rules. It says

---

[5] One complicating factor is that Hart's discussion here concerns *moral* rules rather than the legal rules that are the main subject of the book. This is somewhat surprising, since it is not obvious that what holds for moral rules also holds for legal, especially if, like Hart, one wants to maintain a broadly positivist framework. I have discussed whether they can be treated in the same way elsewhere (Holton (2010)); here I am going to assume that they can.

[6] Dancy (1983) at pp 530–47; Dancy (2004).

[7] I here broadly follow the account that I gave in Holton (2002) at pp 191–209. Readers wanting discussion of some of the difficulties it faces should consult that article. Note that there I used the term 'principle' for what I am here calling a rule. Following Dworkin I now reserve 'principle' for something couched at a greater level of generality: see below.

that the rule will apply to the case unless there are other moral rules that apply to that case that render the verdict of the first rule wrong. That is: a rule like, 'Killing is wrong', applies to a case of killing if and only if there are no other moral rules—for instance, 'Killing in self-defense is not wrong'—that apply to the case and render the verdict of the first rule wrong.[8] But the *unless*-clause does not list all the possible further rules that would defeat the application of the initial rule. That would be impossible if they are incapable of exhaustive statement as Hart supposes. It simply quantifies over them. Likewise for legal rules: the *unless*-clause quantifies over other legal rules.

The crucial thought here is that what makes a rule apply to a case is not just what obtains: it is also what does not obtain. So as well as adding an *unless*-clause to the rules, the full form of a moral or legal argument will also require the addition of a premise to the effect that the *unless*-clause is not triggered. We can make these ideas more precise by defining a notion of what it is for one set of considerations to be *superseded* by a second; that is, for the second set to allude to some further consideration that would upset the conclusion that one would reach on the basis of the first. Then we can construct the *unless*-clause, which I call '*That's it*', in terms of that notion of supersession.

I start with a definition of supersession for sentences.[9] More precisely, the definition is for ordered pairs, the first of which consists of a set of sentences that will stand as the premises of the argument (minus the rule), the second of which consists of a single sentence that will stand as the conclusion (ie the verdict):

Supersession for sentences
A set of sentences $\{F_1a, F_2a, \ldots F_ma\}$ and a verdict F_va are superseded by another set of sentences $\{G_1a, G_2a, \ldots G_na\}$ and a verdict G_va if and only if:

(i) $(G_1a \,\&\, G_2a \,\&\ldots\&\, G_na)$ entails $(F_1a \,\&\, F_2a \,\&\ldots\&\, F_ma)$, but not vice versa;
(ii) G_va is incompatible with F_va.

The first clause here requires that the second set of sentences says everything that is said by the first *and* something more; the second clause requires that the second verdict is incompatible with the first. For instance, the singleton {'a is a killing'} and the verdict 'a is wrong' are superseded by the two-

---

[8] Phrased like this, the rules might look like generics, not properly analyzed as universally quantified generalizations at all. Below I try to say why we need more than this.
[9] Here I have somewhat revised the definitions that I gave in my earlier papers to make them more perspicuous. Those given here should be seen as replacing the earlier ones, which involved some rather awkward features such as entailment relations between predicates. But I do not think that there are radical differences.

membered set {'a is a killing', 'a was done in self-defense'} and the verdict 'a is not wrong'.

Using this we can now define supersession for legal arguments of simple *modus ponens* form:

Supersession for simple arguments
A legal argument[10] of the form

$F_1 a$
$F_2 a, \ldots$
$F_m a$
$\forall x ((F_1 x \ \& \ F_2 x \ \& \ldots \& \ F_m x) \rightarrow F_v x)$

———————————————————

$F_v a$

is superseded by a legal argument of the form

$G_1 a$
$G_2 a \ldots$
$G_n a$
$\forall x ((G_1 x \ \& \ G_2 x \ \& \ldots \& \ G_n x) \rightarrow G_v x)$

———————————————————

$G_v a$

iff

(i) the set of non-quantified premises, and the verdict, of the first argument are superseded by
(ii) the set of non-quantified premises, and the verdict, of the second argument.

We can now define the *unless*-clause making use of this idea of supersession:

That's it: There is no sound legal argument that supersedes this argument.

But things are not quite right, since to know whether an argument is sound we will need to know whether the rule it contains is true, and if what we said earlier is correct, true moral rules must contain *That's it* clauses; and that leads to trouble since we have not defined a notion of supersession for arguments containing such clauses. So let us do so:

Supersession for That's it arguments
A legal argument of the form

$F_1 a$
$F_2 a, \ldots$
$F_m a$

———————————————————

[10] ie one in which the universally quantified conditional—here $\forall x ((F_1 x \ \& \ F_2 x \ \& \ldots \& \ F_m x) \rightarrow F_v x)$—is a legal rule.

$\forall x ((F_1x \& F_2x \& \ldots \& F_mx \& \textit{That's it}) \rightarrow F_vx)$
That's it

F_va

is superseded by a legal argument of the form

G_1a
$G_2a\ldots$
G_na
$\forall x ((G_1x \& G_2x \& \ldots \& G_nx \& \textit{That's it}) \rightarrow G_vx)$
That's it

G_va

iff

(i)   the set of non-quantified premises minus the *That's it* clause, and the verdict, of the first argument are superseded by
(ii) the set of non-quantified premises minus the *That's it* clause, and the verdict, of the second argument.

This leads to something a little strange: *That's it* is defined in terms of argument supersession; but the relevant notion of argument supersession itself makes reference to *That's it*. I do not think that this is pernicious; it just means that we need to understand supersession and *That's it* together.[11]

So, for example, we get legal arguments like this:

(1)

P1	A killed another human being
P2	$\forall x$ ((x killed another human being & *That's it*) $\rightarrow$ x is guilty of murder)
P3	*That's it*
C	A is guilty of murder

Recall that Hart claimed that the *unless*-clause cannot be exhaustively stated: no matter how many exceptions are given to a rule, one can always imagine further exceptions that have not been captured. Equivalently, no matter how much is built into the content of the rule itself, one can always imagine further factors that will render the rule invalid. In our current framework, this can now be understood as the claim that any legal argument like (1) is bound to be superseded by other valid arguments: take any legal argument, we can always find another that supersedes it. So for instance, we can say that (1) is superseded by the valid argument:

---

[11] I discuss this circularity a little further in Holton (2002).

(2)

P1	A killed another human being
P2	A killed in self-defense
P2	$\forall$x ((x killed another human being & x killed in self-defense & *That's it*) $\rightarrow$ x is not guilty of murder)
P3	*That's it*
C	A is not guilty of murder

Similarly, (2) would be superseded by an argument that added the claim that the killing was not necessary for self-defense, and that in turn would be superseded by one that added that the defendant did not realize this to be so, and that would be superseded by one that added that he could have known it had he only paid due care, and so on. If Hart is right, no matter how complicated the rule gets, we will always be able to think of an argument that supersedes it. But the fact that every legal argument is superseded by some *valid* argument does not mean that it is superseded by a *sound* argument, that is by a valid argument that has *true* premises. If the killing was not done in self-defense, and there is equally no other excusing condition, then the *That's it* premise in the original argument (1) will be true, (1) will not be superseded by any sound argument, and the conclusion, that the defendant is guilty of murder, will in turn be true. Put another way: the fact that every legal argument would be superseded by a sound argument were certain facts to obtain does not show that every legal argument is in fact soundly superseded. A good legal argument is one that is not.

So the approach meets one of the desiderata with which we started: we have found a way to interpret the *unless*-clause that does not involve a simple list. The approach also meets the second, for clearly it does not lead to triviality. The *That's it* condition is a substantial one. Many real legal arguments go wrong exactly because it is not met: a court will reach a mistaken legal conclusion because there is some further relevant factor that it is overlooking.

4. Distinguishing, overturning, and other legal actions

Let us see then how this machinery works to account for how courts can distinguish a case, and how it might be extended to some other phenomena. Sometimes courts will simply overturn previous rulings. This might be an appellate court overturning a lower court's decision; or, less commonly, it might be a court overturning a whole run of precedent. In such cases the overturning court will hold that the legal rule implicit in the earlier rulings was simply mistaken. The account offered here has nothing to say about such cases.

However, as we have seen, very often a court's attitude to precedent will be more subtle. The court will distinguish the rule that is applicable to the case at hand from the established rule. It is this that the current account is meant to explain. For in judging that the new case should be handled differently, the court implicitly invokes the *That's it* clause. The court claims that there is a sound legal argument that supersedes the argument that would come from applying the existing rule. Indeed, the rule in the superseding argument—the *superseding rule*, as I shall call it—comes into existence as a result of the very judgment that the court is making. If this is a subordinate court, then the judgment, and the superseding rule itself, will be provisional, pending appeal to a higher court: the higher court could find that there is no superseding rule, a possibility that we shall discuss later. But if the decision stands, then the superseding rule will have been established by the action of the court.[12]

I have written as though there is a partition into the cases that involve overruling and the cases that involve distinguishing. In fact, though, things are often messier. For the law is often unclear, and it is often contradictory, so courts will find themselves in the business of making unclarities precise, or resolving contradictions. Nevertheless, even here we can make a distinction between, on the one hand, judgments that precisify or resolve in a way that is tantamount to overturning, and, on the other, judgments that precisify or resolve in a way that is tantamount to distinguishing. The idea is this: sometimes the precisification of a rule is designed to apply to all its applications; at other times it is limited to those cases where some further distinguishing feature is in play. Likewise for resolution. Sometimes contradictory rules can be resolved so that one of them holds across the board; at other times they can be resolved only for cases that have some further distinguishing feature.

We can accommodate these further cases by extending our definition of supersession. So far we have required superseding sentences to involve a verdict that is straightforwardly incompatible with the verdict of the sentences they supersede. But the incompatibility might be less absolute than that. We can think of an unclear or a contradictory legal argument as containing not a single conclusion but a class of conclusions. An argument can then supersede it so long as its conclusion contradicts at least one member of that class. So

---

[12] This means, I think, that the account is compatible with positivism: we do not need to assume that the superseding rules exist independently of the actions of the courts. I discuss this further in Holton (2010). In effect we have here a process of accommodation. For an overview of the process, see Lewis (1983) at pp 233–49. Note though that since a higher court can find that the lower court made a mistake about what the relevant rules are, the lower court must be implicitly quantifying over the set of rules that the higher court will recognize. I discuss this below.

thinking in terms of a verdict set rather than a single verdict, we can redefine supersession for sentences as follows:

Supersession for sentences

A set of sentences $\{F_1a, F_2a, \ldots F_ma\}$ and a verdict set $\{F_{v1}a, F_{v2}a, \ldots\}$ are *superseded* by another set of sentences $\{G_1a, G_2a, \ldots G_na\}$ and a verdict G_va if and only if:

(i) $(G_1a \ \& \ G_2a \ \& \ldots \& \ G_na)$ entails $(F_1a \ \& \ F_2a \ \& \ldots \& \ F_ma)$, but not vice versa;

(ii) G_va is incompatible with one member of $\{F_{v1}a, F_{v2}a, \ldots\}$

The original definition is the special case where the verdict class contains a single verdict.

So much for my presentation of the account. I now want to turn to compare it with some alternatives.

5. Alternative I: Could legal rules be generics?

English contains a generic construction, or, rather, a family of related generic constructions. If someone says:

Chimpanzees have ten toes; or
The chimpanzee has ten toes; or
A chimpanzee has ten toes.

the claim (assuming that the same claim is made by all these sentences) is true, and it is not made untrue by the rare cases of chimpanzees born with more, or fewer, than ten toes, or by those who have lost them in accidents. So generic sentences are sentences that admit of exceptions.

There is still much debate over how the semantics of generics work. But there is now a large body of evidence that generics should not be seen as universal quantifications at all, but rather as involving some innate faculty of generalization: children understand them long before they understand universally quantified sentences that apply to whole kinds.[13] Could legal rules be examples of generics?

Let us start, once again, by considering moral sentences. It would be odd to use the bare plural, as in the first of the chimpanzee sentences, and say:

Killings are wrong.

But we might naturally use the singular:

---

[13] That is, they understand sentences like, 'Chimpanzees are fierce', before they understand sentences like, 'All chimpanzees are fierce'. For review, see Leslie (2008) at pp 1–47. The restriction to whole kinds is important since the understanding of generics does not seem to precede understanding of sentences like, 'All the chimpanzees in this cage are fierce'. I'm grateful to Leslie for discussion here.

Killing is wrong.

'Killing' in that case though looks to be a verb and not a noun, since we can modify it by adding a noun:

Killing people is wrong.

But take a case like:

Murder is wrong.

'Murder' here is clearly an abstract noun. We cannot add a further noun as we could with 'killing':

*Murder people is wrong.

So we plausibly have a generic: not a count-term generic as illustrated by the chimpanzee sentences, but a mass-term generic, like:

Water is liquid at room temperature.

Note that 'murder' is already a moralized term: to count something as a murder is already to count it as at least prima facie wrong. It is, in other words, a thick moral (and legal) term, one containing both normative and descriptive information. And once we think of thick moral (and legal) terms we find that examples are legion, whether critical (theft/coercion/bribery is wrong) or complimentary (loyalty/bravery/kindness is good).[14]

We might well appeal to such sentences in justifying legal rules, but I want to argue that they are not themselves legal rules of the kind in which we are interested. Many of what Dworkin terms 'principles' look as though they might have this form.[15] One of his examples can be formulated as what looks like a generic, here with a bare plural:

Wrongdoers should not benefit from their own wrongdoing.[16]

Similarly, the principle that is often said to underpin contract law is put very naturally in bare plural form:

Agreements are to be kept.[17]

---

[14] Interestingly, it is harder to find purely descriptive non-count terms that work in this way. It looks as though we may be readier to use abstract non-count terms for virtues and vices than for actions in general; but if this is so, I do not know why.

[15] Dworkin (1977) at pp 22 ff.

[16] Though he actually formulates it as a universally quantified claim: no man may profit from his own wrong (ibid at p 26).

[17] *Pacta sunt servanda*; here again, at least in its use in international relations, the principle is usually qualified with an open-ended *unless*-clause: *clausula rebus sic stantibus* (things remaining as they are).

As I say, these look rather like generics; I am not sure that is right, but let us assume that they are. Still, these are not yet the kinds of rules that we find in the details of common law texts; they are too general and open-ended. As Dworkin stresses, principles can clash. An argument that contained only principles would not culminate in a conclusion for how to decide a particular case: we would need to know whether the principles applied in this case, and that requires something more specific than a principle.

Let us look further at the case of contract law. When we move beyond the general principles to something more specific we find things like this:

A contract is only valid if it is accepted;
but its acceptance does not count if it is not heard by the offerer (for instance, if it is drowned out by an airplane);
but it does count if the offerer did not hear it, but it was clearly made;
but it does not count if it was clearly made but the offerer made it known to the acceptor that he did not hear it.[18]

And this is just one of the necessary conditions for a contract to be valid; stating the necessary and sufficient conditions requires a hefty textbook, which even then will leave a great deal out. These are the materials from which legal arguments are actually made. Now they do culminate in a binding conclusion, and they do so because they plausibly have the form, not of generics, but of universally quantified sentences, along the lines of:

$\forall x$ (If x is a valid contract $\rightarrow$ (x is accepted & (the acceptance is heard by the offerer v (the acceptance is clearly made & the offerer does not make it clear that he does not hear the acceptance))))

Nevertheless, despite the complexity of the condition, we can easily imagine circumstances in which the very considerations that prompt the complexity require further complexity: what if the offerer's statement that he did not hear the acceptance was itself drowned out by an airplane, and so on. So even here we need *That's it* clauses once we try to define necessary and sufficient conditions for being a valid contract.

We can think of the development of the common law as the process of arriving at rules from a set of principles—that, I think, is a plausible account of at least one aspect of its history. If we understand principles as generics, we can therefore think of it as a move from generics to universally quantified sentences. If, in a parallel way, we think of moral principles as generics, there is a question of whether we have need of the move to moral rules at all, and therefore of whether a *That's it* account for moral rules (something that I have

---

[18] Denning LJ in [1955] 2 QB 327.

advocated elsewhere) has any role to play. On the one hand, we do not have need of rules to play the roles of public justification and of guidance that they play in the common law. On the other, if we stop just with principles then we do not get moral arguments that entail their conclusions. I leave the question open.

6. Alternative II: Are legal rules governed by nonmonotonic logic?

The proposal developed so far uses classical logic; indeed, it does not even involve any new connectives. An alternative, proposed in a set of important articles by John Horty, seeks to achieve a similar end by very different means: a similar end, in that Horty too wants to develop a framework in which legal rules play an important role but can be superseded; different means, in that he proposes a logical framework that moves a long way from classical logic.[19]

Classical logic is monotonic: adding new premises to a valid argument cannot result in the argument becoming invalid. In contrast, a nonmonotonic logic does allow for this possibility. So let me start by spelling out the logic that Horty wants to use, before asking what benefit is gained.

Horty suggests using a logic modeled on Reiter's default logic. Typically this is presented as an interpretation of generic sentences, but here I will consider the idea that it can serve to provide a logical interpretation for legal rules. Reiter's logic was developed as a logic for drawing consequences from a set of premises, given that further premises might serve to undermine those consequences.[20] In classical first-order logic understood proof-theoretically, the consequences of a set of sentences are simply the sentences that follow from that set, given the rules of inference, rules that operate on the original sentences in virtue of their logical form. Thus if the premise set contains P and $(P \rightarrow Q)$, and *modus ponens* is one of the rules of inference, then Q will follow from the original set. We can think of the *conclusion set* as being the set of sentences that is obtained by collecting all the logical consequences so understood.[21]

But classical logic is monotonic: adding extra sentences to the premise set cannot result in sentences being deleted from the conclusion set. In moving

---

[19] Horty (2007a) at p 3; Horty (2008). For discussion of the nonmonotonic logic that lies behind his discussion see Horty (2001).

[20] Reiter (1980).

[21] More standardly in classical logic we would simply call a set closed under logical entailment a *theory*. But I will try to keep the discussion parallel to Reiter's.

to a nonmonotonic logic, Reiter takes the premise set to consist not just of the set of sentences as classically conceived, but in addition a set of *default rules*. Although these are often referred to as rules of inference, they are not akin to classical rules of inference like *modus ponens*. Rather they are more like additional premises. Reiter introduces them as something like a three-place conditional, roughly of the form: if A, then B, provided that C is compatible with the conclusion set. He symbolizes this as

(A: C / B).[22]

There is a special case of the default rule—the so-called 'normal rule'—where the role of C is taken by B itself:

(A: B / B).

We can read this as: if A, then B provided that B is compatible with the conclusion set. Let us write it in abbreviated form, using a special arrow to distinguish it from the material conditional, as

A ↦ B

Following most writers on the topic, from now on we shall just work with normal rules of this form.

We can see now why the approach is nonmonotonic. If our initial set contained just A and A ↦ B, then we would be entitled to add B to the conclusion set. But if we were to add ~B to the initial set, thus making it inconsistent with B, we should no longer be entitled to add B. How do we construct the conclusion set given this approach? The idea, of course is that, given both A and A ↦ B in our initial set, B should end up in the conclusion set just in case ~B is not in the conclusion set. But it turns out that constructing that set is no simple matter, since, even if ~B is absent from the initial set, it might arrive in the conclusion set as a result of other inferences. In consequence there is no simple iterative procedure that will take us from the initial set to the conclusion set. We need instead to determine the conclusion set as a kind of equilibrium set that accommodates all the information in the initial set.

---

[22] In Horty's discussion the default rules are presented in ways that make them seem more like classical inference rules—the idea being that given A, one is committed to inferring B provided that C is compatible with the conclusion set. But they are not logical rules; they are not supposed to apply to a sentence just in virtue of that sentence's logical form. Their application crucially depends upon the interpretation of the non-logical vocabulary. For some discussion of the issues here, and of whether some presentations of nonmonotonic logic muddle the idea of the frame and the interpretation function, see Stalnaker (1994) at pp 7–21. In general Stalnaker argues that it might be helpful to recast nonmonotonic logic, understood in terms of the consequence relation, as a theory of nonmonotonic operators—ie operators that do not obey the rule of inference (if $p \models q$ then $Op \models Oq$)—within a monotonic logic.

Reiter suggests doing this using a fixed-point approach: posit a conclusion set, and then show that it stands as a limit of operations performed on the initial set.[23] However, even on this approach, a given initial set will sometimes enable us to arrive at different putative conclusion sets—or *extensions* as he calls them. So how should we determine *the* conclusion set given different consistent extensions? One approach is to simply pick an arbitrary extension as the conclusion set. Another is to say that a sentence will go in the conclusion set just in case it is in *any* extension (though such a set may not be consistent). A third is to say that the conclusion set contains only those sentences that appear in *every* extension (though such a set may be empty).

Deciding which of these approaches is right is beyond the scope of our enquiry here; I will assume that the issues can be resolved satisfactorily.[24] Let us instead focus on how the default rule approach, with its new nonmonotonic logic, gives us any advantages over the *unless*-clause approach that I have been advocating. Horty argues that the default logic has two things in its favor.[25] However, what he has in mind as the alternative is not the *That's it* proposal, but a rather more simple-minded theory that uses a material conditional and then simply lists the possible *unless*-conditions as conditions on the antecedent. So instead of the simple conditional

$A \rightarrow B$

it will have the qualified conditional

$(A \ \& \ {\sim}C_1 \ \& \ {\sim}C_2 \ \& \ {\sim}C_3 \ldots) \rightarrow B$

where C_n is the nth *unless*-condition. Call this the *list account*. The differences between the list account and the quantified approach involved in the *That's it* account are important, and we shall return to them shortly. But it will help fix the issues if we first consider this simpler list account, since I am not convinced that the default rule approach brings a real advantage even over it.

The first problem that Horty identifies with the list account is that 'the list of circumstances that might interfere... is open-ended. No conceivable list of possible interfering circumstances could be complete'.[26] That is a legitimate worry, and it is the reason that I tried to capture the defeating conditions using quantifiers rather than a list. But does the default rule account escape the worry? Defeating conditions only get into the default approach once they

---

[23] For a summary of the fixed-point approach, see Horty (2001).
[24] In recent work, Horty has greatly reduced the indeterminacy here by introducing an ordering on default rules: see Horty (2007b). But since he only requires it to be partial, indeterminacy will remain.
[25] Horty (2001) at p 7.
[26] ibid.

are incorporated into the default theory. One obvious way of incorporating them is to add to the simple default rule A ↦ B a set of further default rules that capture the unless clauses

$C_1 \mapsto {\sim}B$
$C_2 \mapsto {\sim}B$
$C_3 \mapsto {\sim}B\ldots$

If the worry is that no finite list account could list all the possible defeating conditions, then it is equally true that no finite set of default rules could capture them either. In both cases the theory that we have will only accommodate some of the defeating conditions. We can always extend it by adding more—more clauses in the antecedent for the list account, more default rules for the default account—but the two are on a par.

Let us turn then to the second advantage that Horty claims for the default account. He writes:

> The second problem is more subtle, and would arise even if we did have a relatively exhaustive list of qualifications. The point of placing preconditions in the antecedent of a [principle] is that we must verify that the preconditions are satisfied before concluding that the [principle applies].... But it seems less reasonable to suppose that we must actually have to verify that all of the various weird circumstances that might interfere with this [principle] do not occur.... It would be better to be able simply to assume that weird circumstances like these do not occur unless there is information to the contrary.[27]

This was an important consideration in the development of default logic—it is the initial motivation in Reiter's original article for instance—so we should spend some time on it. Part of the reason for providing default logics was to provide a logic that enabled one to move forward—to draw conclusions, or to perform actions—in the absence of information. Default logic does not give us a decision procedure for determining membership of the conclusion set.[28] But the idea was that, to take the standard example, on learning that Tweety is a bird, we should be able to defeasibly conclude that Tweety can fly. We do not want to have to hold off from drawing that conclusion while we make sure that Tweety is not a penguin, or an emu, or an ostrich, or has had his wings clipped, or was born deformed, or whatever. But clearly if we had built these conditions into the antecedent of the conditional

---

[27] ibid.
[28] Indeed, Reiter's default logic is even worse off than first-order predicate calculus, in that it is not even semi-decidable, ie not only is there no procedure for demonstrating that a sentence is not in the set, there is also no procedure for showing that a sentence is: see Reiter (1980) at pp 104 ff.

If Tweety is a bird & Tweety is not a penguin & Tweety is not an emu . . . then Tweety can fly

we would need to establish each of the conjuncts of the antecedent before we could detach the consequent.

In contrast, in the absence of defeating conditions, the default approach will enable us to move forward. We do not need to establish that Tweety is not a penguin, not an emu, and so on. Provided that we do not have evidence that he is, the instantiation of the default rule

(x is a bird $\mapsto$ x can fly)

will enable us to (defeasibly) conclude, from the information that Tweety is a bird, that Tweety can fly.

Call this the *no stalling* feature of the default account. Sometimes no stalling will indeed be a feature we want. Typically, whether we do so will depend on the number of exceptions that there are to the rule, the benefits of moving on, and the costs of the occasional mistake. In making rough and ready predictions about a creature's flying capacity a no stalling feature might be very useful. Is it something we want in moral and legal reasoning though?

This is a difficult question. In moral reasoning I think that it generally is not. We put high store on getting the conclusion right. By and large, if there are known defeating conditions, we want people to ensure that they are not met before moving to a moral judgment. In the terms of default approach, we ask that they check that none of the known defeating conditions obtain; and that involves adding to the initial evidence set information on whether they do or do not. So it seems to me that the no stalling feature is not much of an advantage in moral reasoning. In fact, it can look to be something of a liability.

In legal reasoning the situation is rather different. Courts and jurisdictions differ, but in the adversarial Anglo-American system, it is not normally the role of the judge and jury to seek out new information: decisions are made on the basis of the (admissible) evidence presented. To that extent, then, the default account might look to give a good basis for legal reasoning. For the court needs to not stall: it needs to make a decision on the basis of the evidence it has.

Even here though the advantages of the default account over the list account should not be overplayed. Courts have a complex set of default assumptions stemming from the idea of the burden of proof. They are allowed to *assume* many things unless proved otherwise, and perhaps this would allow them to complete the list: items in the list could be assumed to hold unless they were shown not to. But I shall not pursue the question of whether this will work.

For it strikes me that both the list approach and the default approach share a fundamental flaw, a flaw that can only be avoided by moving to a quantified approach like the one embodied in the *That's it* account.

So far we have been concerned with *recognized* defeating conditions: with clauses that are contained in the list or embedded in the default rules. When it comes to moral and legal reasoning, though, we ask for more than that. We ask that agents be sensitive to considerations that are relevant to the judgments they make but that have not been previously recognized. Admittedly, when it comes to moral reasoning, this is to place the bar very high: it is only a somewhat idealized moral judge who will recognize the significance of factors that have not been recognized before. But in the case of legal reasoning the requirement is far more realistic. It is quite common for a case to come before a court that involves factors that have not previously been dealt with by the law. And in such a case, as we said before, the court will have either to reaffirm the existing rule, thereby in effect judging that the new factors are not sufficient to warrant a different verdict; or it will have to distinguish.

Let us take the case where the court reaffirms the existing rule. It is important to note that here, just as much as in the cases where they distinguish, courts are open to criticism. Most obviously, if the case goes to appeal, the decision may be rightly overturned.[29] What are we to make of such a happening? On either the list approach or the default approach, it looks as if the court did nothing wrong: it applied the existing rules, and arrived at the conclusion. The obvious response is that applying such rules is not good enough. But if that is so, in virtue of what is it not good enough? It seems that the flaw must stem from some further feature. Neither the list account nor the default account has the resources to account for it.

In contrast, on the account I am offering, it is clear where the mistake lies. In endorsing a legal argument, the court is implicitly endorsing the *That's it* condition. It is committed to the claim that the argument is not superseded, and so that there are no further relevant facts and rules. And in the circumstances imagined, where the verdict is subsequently overturned, that was not true.

I say that this is clear, but if it is right it does bring out a further feature of the account. For if the lower court is making a mistake in not distinguishing, then the class of rules over which it quantifies cannot just consist in the previously acknowledged rules and whatever further rule it recognizes. By

---

[29] I leave open the question of whether the lower court can be wrong in its decision even if it is not overturned. Obviously we might think that the court can be morally wrong, but can it be legally wrong? This opens difficult questions about the strength of positivism on which the present approach can remain neutral.

hypothesis, there is no superseding rule there. We have to say that the domain of quantification includes the previously acknowledged rules and the rules that the court should have recognized. I do not think that this requires us to give up positivism, but it does mean that the court sees itself as bound by requirements that go beyond those of the extant rules.

A parallel issue arises when the court does distinguish, and where on appeal the move is rejected. Here again, we want to know what it was that the court did wrong. And again neither the list account nor the default approach has anything to say on the matter, whereas the approach that I have offered does: the court held that the *That's it* clause in the argument using the original rule was false, whereas it was not.

How might the proponent of the default account respond? One way is just to reject the idea that the lower court has made a mistake; one might say instead that it has simply lost out to a more powerful player. But short of embracing legal realism, it is hard to maintain that that is true in all such cases. Another response is to say that the mistake is a mistake of prediction: the lower court predicted that the appellate court would support its judgment. But that does not seem right either: the lower court is making a ruling of law, not trying to second-guess what the appellate court will say. More plausibly, the proponent of the default account might insist that all this can be explained by a further requirement to which they are perfectly well entitled: a requirement on courts to come up with the right default rules. Courts make mistakes when they fail to conform to that requirement. I shall not try to guess exactly what such a proposal would look like, but a natural idea would be that the court will be committed to the claim that there is no further default rule that, added to the existing rules, would overturn the verdict that it reached. But what we have now is looking very much like the *That's it* clause. And if we add it to the default account, we have to ask whether it cannot do the work that the default rules are doing. The default account is in danger of collapsing into the *That's it* account, in which case the use of non-monotonic logic looks redundant.

The proponent of the default account might take another tack, denying that we can ever know whether the *That's it* condition is met. The issue would gain importance if we agreed with Horty's implicit requirement that we must *verify* the premises in an argument. The *That's it* condition is equivalent to a universally quantified sentence, and Karl Popper built a hugely influential theory on the idea that such sentences can *never* be verified. We need not follow him in that to think that we are in no position to verify that the *That's it* condition is met. But what I think we should conclude is that verification is far too high a standard for the premises in legal argument. As with much else in law, we might want them to be beyond reasonable doubt. However, we want to concede that judges need to act in the awareness that they might be making mistakes; and this strikes me as placing the fallibility in just the right place.

In responding to Horty's arguments I have made no use of the familiar idea that classical logic is well behaved and well understood, whereas non-monotonic logic is not. I do think that that is true, and so if two theories did the job equally well, I think that we would still have grounds to prefer a theory that used classical logic over one that did not. But if I am right that the default theory does not do the job equally well, I have had no need of the argument.

7. Conclusion

In relation to its rivals, the *That's it* approach stands up surprisingly well. It does require us to posit implicit claims, but they are far from outlandish. Perhaps it has little role to play in moral argument: that will depend how well a generic account can be developed. But in law, where we do have need of tight, precedence-justifying arguments that nonetheless admit of exceptions, I know of no better approach.[30]

---

[30] Thanks to Irene Heim, Jeff Horty, and Sarah-Jane Leslie, and Steve Yablo for discussion of some of these issues; and to the participants at the USC law and language seminar where the paper was presented, especially Andrei Marmor and Scott Soames.

9

Trying to Kill the Dead: *De Dicto* and *De Re* Intention in Attempted Crimes

Gideon Yaffe

1. Introduction

Melvin Dlugash, Joe Bush, and Michael Geller went drinking together one night. Geller repeatedly demanded that Bush give him $100 toward the rent of Geller's apartment, where Bush was staying. Bush repeatedly refused. When Geller pressed the point one last time, Bush, angry with him, shot him three times. Geller lay motionless for several minutes, and showed no signs of life. At that point, Dlugash fired five bullets into Geller's head. It is not clear why Dlugash did this, although one possibility is that he did it to demonstrate to Bush that he was in league with him and not an innocent witness whom Bush would have a motive to kill. But whatever his motive, did Dlugash murder Geller? If Geller was dead when Dlugash shot him, then Dlugash did not commit murder, but merely mutilated a corpse—a crime, perhaps, but a far lesser crime than murder. And since the prosecution cannot prove beyond a reasonable doubt that Geller was alive, they choose to charge Dlugash with *attempted* murder.[1] A question one needs to answer to resolve the case is whether an attempted murder requires that the victim is alive at the time of the attempt; if so, then the prosecution's inability to establish that fact undermines its case against Dlugash not just for completed murder, but also for attempted murder. We also need to know what *attitude* Dlugash needs to have had toward the question of whether the victim was alive or dead to be guilty of an attempted murder. If Dlugash was intending to finish Geller off, then he would not have fired had he been certain that Geller was already dead. Is *that* the attitude he needs to have had to have attempted murder? Or is it enough for the attempt that Dlugash

[1] *People v Dlugash* 41 NY2d 725 (1977).

believed that Geller was alive? Or is uncertainty about the question—together with a willingness to go ahead whatever the facts—enough for attempted murder? It is quite possible, that is, that Dlugash was at the time no more certain than we can be in retrospect whether Geller was alive. If that is right, did Dlugash attempt murder?

As it is in *Dlugash*, so it often is: where the question of the defendant's mental state with respect to his circumstances arises in an attempt case, there is often a question also about whether the relevant feature of the circumstances needs to be in place. This chapter offers an account of how to answer both questions. It offers principled grounds for deciding what attitude an attempter must have toward what are called 'the circumstantial elements of the completed crime': roughly, those standing conditions that must be present for guilt.[2] And the chapter provides principled grounds for deciding when the circumstantial elements of the completed crime need to be in place for the attempt.[3] As we will see, the solutions offered here require appreciation of a key concept from the philosophy of language—namely the distinction between *de dicto* (or attributive) and *de re* (or referential) uses of descriptions. Some implications of this distinction allow us to see what facts do and do not contribute—and under what conditions—to the content of a person's intention, and that turns out to be the crucial issue here.

Issues of this sort are not at all uncommon in the law of criminal attempts. In another well-known example of such a case, which has occupied the imagination of many a criminal law theorist, *People v Jaffe*,[4] the defendant, a suspected 'fence,' was charged with an attempt to receive stolen property after he purchased some fabric that he believed to be stolen but which was in fact

---

[2] More carefully, the circumstantial elements of the completed crime are those facts that must be proven beyond a reasonable doubt by the prosecution but which need not be shown to have been caused by the defendant. Murder requires a showing that the victim was alive prior to the defendant's act, but does not require any showing to the effect that the defendant *caused* the victim to be alive (what would that even amount to?). Similarly, theft requires a showing to the effect that the defendant did not have permission to take the property he took—a fact that the defendant need not have caused in order to be guilty. Or, to give one final example, various sex crimes with child victims require a showing that the victim was under a certain age, but do not require even a showing to the effect that the defendant would have selected a different victim had he believed the victim not to be a child. The defendant need not have caused his particular victim to be underage, nor to have caused it to be the case that his victim was a child by selecting a victim on the basis of age.

[3] The task undertaken here has been undertaken by many others. I discuss many such efforts, and contrast them with the approach taken here, in Yaffe (2010), ch 5, section 1. See, for instance, Stannard (1987), Duff (1996), Fletcher (1986), and Williams (1991).

[4] 185 NY 497, 78 NE 169 (1906).

falsely represented to him as stolen as part of a sting operation.[5] Since the fabric Jaffe received was not stolen, Jaffe did not succeed in receiving stolen property; but did he attempt the crime? Or consider *United States v Crow*.[6] Crow had multiple conversations in an Internet chat room with someone going by the name of 'StephieFL'. During the course of their conversations, StephieFL claimed to be a 13-year-old girl. In fact, the messages were written by an undercover (adult) police officer. Crow tried to convince StephieFL to send him sexually explicit photographs of herself and was charged with attempting sexual exploitation of a minor. The completed offense requires a showing to the effect that the person exploited is indeed a minor. Did Crow attempt sexual exploitation of a minor, or does the fact that it was an adult he was actually in contact with show that he did not?

The position to be defended here does not imply that it is always relevant what the circumstances of the defendant charged with an attempt were like; it does not always matter whether the victim was alive, or underage, or whether the property was stolen. The fact that the defendant believed these things, even falsely, is sufficient for criminal liability for attempt. But nor does the position defended here imply that it is always irrelevant how things actually were. Under the view to be defended here, if the defendant has a particular sort of intention, a sort to be identified with some precision and which is consistent with uncertainty about how things are, then whether or not he has committed an attempt turns on how things actually are. As we will see, the position allows us to identify the crucial features of particular cases

---

[5] The court in *Jaffe* conceptualizes the case as one in which the defendant tried to receive stolen property but could not possibly have succeeded, since the property was not stolen, and then struggles with the question of whether success was impossible in the right sense of 'impossible' for acquittal. The literature that cases like *Jaffe* have spawned is very large and most of it engages directly with the question that the court in *Jaffe* takes to be crucial: the question of the sense, if any, in which it must be possible to succeed if one is to be guilty of an attempt. (There is too much literature on this topic to list it all. Some of the best-known early discussions include Strahorn (1930); Skilton (1937); Keedy (1954); Smith (1957); Hall (1960), pp 586–99; Williams (1961), pp 633–53; Smith (1962); and Hart (1981). Helpful recent discussions include Duff (1996), pp 76–115, 378–85; and Hasnas (2002).) There is a very thin sense in which attempt requires the possibility of success: so-called 'inherent impossibility', when properly specified, does indeed provide a sound basis for acquittal; consider the person who attempts murder by incantation. (For a defense of this claim, see Yaffe (2010), ch 9.) But there is no need to tackle the issue of impossibility's relevance to attempt in connection with cases like *Jaffe*. If it was possible, in some given sense, for the fabric that Jaffe bought to have been stolen, then it was possible, in that sense, for Jaffe to have successfully received stolen property. But the *Jaffe* court does not inquire whether it was possible, contrary to fact, for that property to have been stolen; that is not what concerns the court. What concerns the court, whether it knows it or not, is not the *possibility* that the fabric was stolen but *the simple fact* that it was not. But if that is the court's concern, then the question of the possibility of success just is not the crucial question even by its own standards.

[6] 164 F3d 229 (5th Cir 1999).

that determine whether the facts about the circumstances matter, and what mental attitude the defendant needs to have had with respect to them to attempt the crime. One lesson of the application of the *de re–de dicto* distinction to these questions is that the two issues are not entirely separable.

2. Background: attempt, intention, and *mens rea* standards

What we are seeking here is what is referred to in the criminal law as a *mens rea* standard. Crimes consist of various components that need to be shown beyond a reasonable doubt by the prosecution to establish the case against the defendant. These are divided, typically, into those that constitute the *actus reus* of the crime, and those that constitute *mens rea*. For our purposes, the *actus reus* consists of anything that needs to be shown *other than the mental states of the defendant*, while the *mens rea* of the crime consists of all and only those mental states the defendant needs to be shown beyond a reasonable doubt to have had for guilt. Often a crime's *mens rea* consists of several distinct mental states. Say the *actus reus* of arson, for instance, involves the lighting of a fire that causes damage to some property. The *mens rea* of the crime might include an intention to light the fire, a belief that damage to someone else's particular object is a likely, although not certain, result (assuming some other conditions are met, the legal term for such a mental state is 'recklessness') and certainty that the object in question is not one's own (what the law typically calls 'knowledge,' or 'belief to a practical certainty'). Typically, where there are separable components of a crime's *actus reus*, there are separable and corresponding components also of the crime's *mens rea*.

Typically, a variety of possible mental states will serve as components of the crime's *mens rea*. In arson, as imagined above, for instance, either intent or foresight or recklessness that damage will result from the fire will suffice for *mens rea* with respect to that component of the completed crime. The idea of a *mens rea* standard is the idea of the *minimal* mental state with respect to a particular component of the crime that is required for guilt for that crime. From the criminal law's point of view, mental states stand in a hierarchy based on how bad the behavior is of someone who has them. It is worse to cause damage to something with intention than it is to cause it with foresight and without intent. Hence foresight is the lesser mental state. Similarly, it is worse to cause such damage while foreseeing it than it is to do so while merely thinking that it is likely to happen, but might not. Hence recklessness is the lesser mental state. Negligence—absence of awareness of a substantial risk of which one should be aware—is lesser still. Thus, recklessness constitutes the *mens rea* standard for arson, as defined above; that mental state, or any worse mental state, will suffice for guilt of the crime when all the other components of the crime are also shown beyond a reasonable doubt (and the defendant lacks an affirmative defense).

So, when we seek, as we do here, a *mens rea* standard for attempt with respect to circumstances involved in completion—circumstances like the victim's being alive or underage, or the property's being stolen—what we are after is a description of the least-bad mental state that a person can be in with respect to that circumstance while still having attempted the crime. It seems clear that were it merely true that a reasonable person in the defendant's shoes would have thought it likely that the victim was alive, in a case like Dlugash's, even though the defendant himself positively believed the victim to be dead, the defendant falls short of attempting murder. Firing a gun into what one flat-out believes to be a dead body is not an attempted murder, even if one is wrong. But, on the flip side, to require that the defendant is positively certain that the victim is alive is to require too much; a person who fires bullets into another's head with less confidence than this that he is thereby injuring someone living, but with intent to kill, nonetheless attempts murder. The question is what the nature is of the crucial mental state in the middle—the mental state that both qualifies the act of the person who has it as an attempt, and, at the same time, is less bad than all other mental states that would so qualify his act.

The solution to this problem offered in the next section builds on a particular view of what it is to try to act in the sense of 'trying' that is relevant to the criminal law, a view that I have defended elsewhere.[7] Under what I call the Guiding Commitment View, *to try to do something is to be committed by one's intention to each of the components of success and to be guided in one's behavior by each of these commitments.* Say that a completed fraud involves (a) an act of deceiving someone which (b) thereby injures him.[8] Fraud, on this view, is harmful lying. A person who attempts fraud, but fails, might fail to deceive, or might fail to injure, or both. A person who attempts fraud, under the Guiding Commitment View, has an intention that commits him to (a) and commits him to (b). In addition, he is moved by these commitments. He might, for instance, be moved to say something false to a potential victim.

The word 'try' can be used in a variety of ways and the Guiding Commitment View only aligns with one of them. For instance, consider someone who intends to kill his dying parent out of mercy while believing falsely that euthanasia is legal. Is this person trying to commit murder? Or to put the same question

---

[7] See Yaffe (2010), ch 3.

[8] Fraud is, in fact, more complicated than this. To note just one complexity, the victim must be injured because he relies on the truth of the perpetrator's deceptive statements, and not for other reasons. To note another, typically the lie must not be so outrageous that only an unreasonable person would believe it.

another way, does the phrase 'to commit murder' correctly describe what this person is trying to do? The answer is that, in some senses of the term 'try', it does and in others it does not. Under one narrow conception of trying to act, what a person is trying to do is determined entirely by the content of his intention in acting. Thus, the narrow conception implies that the mercy killer is not trying to commit *murder* since part of what it is for a killing to be murder is that it is *illegal*, and the mercy killer does not intend to commit an *illegal* killing since, after all, he does not even believe that the killing he will commit, if he does as he intends, is illegal. By contrast, a very broad conception of trying to act allows that anything that is true of the act that the agent would perform, were he to do as he intends, can be appealed to in describing what he is trying to do. In this sense, the mercy killer is trying to commit murder. In this sense, he is also trying to empty a hospital bed, for were he to do as he intends, a hospital bed would be emptied. The Guiding Commitment View aligns with neither the narrow nor the broad sense, and there are other senses of trying still with which it does not align. Under the Guiding Commitment View, the mercy killer is trying to commit murder. The reason is that he is committed by his intention to each and every component of the completed crime of murder. The illegality of the killing is not one of the components of murder since the prosecution need not show beyond a reasonable doubt that the killing was illegal to show that a murder has taken place. It is enough, instead, that the killing *is* illegal, quite independently of the prosecution's ability to convince a jury of that. (This is why questions of law of this kind are to be decided by judges *before* trial.) Any qualities of the completed act that are not components of it—things that the prosecution must show beyond a reasonable doubt—can be appealed to, under the Guiding Commitment View, in a description of what the agent is trying to do. By contrast, the Guiding Commitment View implies that the mercy killer is *not* trying to empty a hospital bed. A component of that act is that a hospital bed is emptied and nothing about the mercy killer's intention commits him to that; he would not have fallen short of doing as he intends if his parent is buried with the bed in which he is killed. Qualities of the completed act that are components of it cannot be appealed to in an account of what an agent is trying to do unless he is committed to them by his intention, while qualities of the completed act—such as its being illegal—that are nonetheless not components of it can be.

That the Guiding Commitment View aligns with *one* ordinary sense of trying is, I believe, indisputable. That it aligns with *the* ordinary sense that is of relevance to the criminal law is much harder to show. Showing it requires showing that the Guiding Commitment View provides the right resolution of a wide variety of very different sorts of cases in which defendants are charged with attempted crimes. Notice that the Guiding Commitment View provides precisely the correct resolution of the euthanasia case just described. After all, the would-be mercy killer who falsely believes that the killing he intends is legal is attempting murder in the sense that matters to the criminal law and is not attempting to empty a hospital bed. If the latter were a crime, he would not have committed an attempt of it. So, in this one hypothetical case, the Guiding Commitment View yields the correct result and neither the narrow nor the wide views described briefly above do. Still, to fully defend the Guiding Commitment View we would need to show that it yields the correct resolution of many more kinds of cases than this. I have tried to show this elsewhere and cannot do so here.[9] Instead, I will take the Guiding Commitment View as a fixed point in what follows.

A full defense of the Guiding Commitment View requires elaboration on many different aspects of it. Notably, for instance, such a defense requires an account of 'guidance'. What, exactly, is it to be guided by a commitment? Does that which one is committed to play a role in determining what it is to be guided by the commitment? For instance, is it different to be guided by one's commitment to *acting* a particular way than it is to be guided by one's commitment to a particular *result* of one's action coming to pass? As it turns out, the issue that we are concerned with here does not require an account of the guidance involved in trying, and so does not require an answer to these questions. The problem to be solved here requires only consideration of the intention involved in trying under the Guiding Commitment View.

The Guiding Commitment View implies that trying always involves intending. One cannot try to act unless one has an intention that commits one to each of the components of success. This claim requires some unpacking. First, what one's intention commits one to must be distinguished from what one intends. Our intentions have a particular, primary function. Their primary function is to make the world match their content—to make the world as intended—as a result of their playing their proper causal role in our psychology. The function of a person's intention to deceive another into handing over his money is to make it the case that both the person deceives the victim and that the victim hands over his money. In the ordinary case, the intention serves its function by motivating the agent, in the normal way, to behave in ways that will succeed in making the world as intended. The intention, for instance, motivates the agent to think up a story about how it came to pass that he is in possession of the Brooklyn Bridge and must sell it immediately for a song. Concocting such a story is believed by the agent to

---

[9] Yaffe (2010), ch 3.

bring him closer to the world's coming to match his intention's content, and so the intention motivates him to concoct it.

What one is committed to by one's intention is the conjunction of what would necessarily be true were the world to match the intention's content and what would necessarily be true were the intention to play its proper causal role in making it the case that the world matches the intention's content. It is common, then, for one to be committed to something by one's intention even though one does not intend it. This happens whenever the condition is one that would necessarily come to pass were the intention to play its proper causal role, but is not represented in the intention's content. Consider some-one who intends that his neighbor's house burn to the ground. In having this intention, he is thinking only about the event of his neighbor's house burning down. He is not thinking about *how it comes to pass* that his neighbor's house burns down. He may be thinking about that, but *his intention* is not, itself, a thought about that. In particular, he is not thinking about whether he, or someone else instead, *causes* the neighbor's house to burn down. His inten-tion will come to match the world even if someone else burns the house down, without any encouragement, even, from him. Is this person commit-ted by his intention to *causing* the house to burn? Yes, for although his caus-ing it is not in the content of his intention, he would cause the house to burn *were his intention to play its proper causal role.* If it were to play its proper causal role, it would motivate him to burn the house down, and, in that case, he would be the cause of the house's burning. Hence his intention commits him to something that is not represented in its content—namely his causing his neighbor's house to burn. As will become important later, it is not gener-ally the case that we are committed to causing all those conditions that are represented by our intentions. But it is more common to be so committed than not to be. For now what matters is only that such a commitment need not derive from explicit representation in one's intention of oneself as cause; the commitment can derive, instead, from the proper causal role of an inten-tion lacking any causal content.

Now, the Guiding Commitment View implies that the commitment to each of the components of success of a person who attempts derives *from his intention.* A person who is committed to some component of success by his desires, his hopes, his beliefs, or any other aspects of his psychology distin-guishable from his intentions, is not thereby committed to that component in the way that is required to try to act. Since, as just noted, we are typically committed by our intentions to causing those conditions that are represented by them, it can seem that the advocate of the Guiding Commitment View is committed to an implausible position with regard to the *mens rea* standard of attempt with respect to the circumstances of the completed crime. After all, the completed crime of sexual exploitation of a minor, for instance, does not require that the defendant *caused his victim to be a minor*. This is something that a person *could* cause, not (ordinarily) by causing someone to have a particular age but, instead, by choosing someone to be the victim who is believed to be a minor while ready to switch victims should it turn out that the victim is not a minor after all. But a person who knows that his victim is a minor, but would not have switched victims had he been an adult, is nonetheless guilty of sexual exploitation of a minor. However, if intentions that represent conditions, such as the victim's being a minor, typically constitute a commitment to causing those conditions, then it would seem that to require for an attempt of the crime an *intention-based* commitment to the victim's being a minor is to require a commitment to causing that. Why should an attempt require a commitment to something—namely causing the victim to be a minor—that is not required for completion? In short, the Guiding Commitment View *seems* to impose too lenient a *mens rea* standard when it comes to the attitude of the attempter to the circumstances involved in the completed crime. One important aim of this chapter is to show that this is merely an appearance. The reason, as we will see, is that it is possible for a person's intention to commit him to a condition without committing him to causing that condition. Such an intention is all that is required to meet the *mens rea* standard with respect to circumstances in attempt. Hence the Guiding Commitment View does not imply too lenient a *mens rea* standard in the relevant respect.

Given this background, we can narrow our discussion here to the following questions: under what conditions is a person committed by his intention to his circumstances being a certain way without thereby being committed to causing his circumstances to be that way? And, is it ever the case that how the world actually is determines whether or not his intention commits him to the world's being a certain way? Or, put in the context of our lead example, what do we need to know about what was in Dlugash's mind, and what if anything do we need to know about the state of Geller's health, to know whether Dlugash was committed by his intention *to killing* Geller? This is the crucial question, since without an intention that constitutes such a commitment, Dlugash did not attempt murder.

3. The solution

The strategy undertaken in this section can be summarized, schematically, like so: the section identifies two different things that someone might be asserting when he says of himself that he has a particular intention, as when he says 'I intend to A the thing that is P'. For now, call one of these 'the *de dicto* interpretation' and the other 'the *de re* interpretation' saving for later the description of what these interpretations involve and why they are labeled as such. Correlatively, the intention the agent has, when such an assertion is true, is to be called 'a *de dicto* intention' or 'a *de re* intention', depending on how the assertion is to be interpreted. It is then argued that a *de re* intention to A the thing that is P commits the agent who has that intention *to the thing he A's being P*. It is further argued that this is the minimal commitment to that which is needed for the *mens rea* of attempt, assuming that a circumstantial element of the completed crime is the thing's being P. If the thing's being P is one of the circumstantial elements of the completed crime, then it suffices for the *mens rea* of attempt with respect to that circumstantial element that the defendant has a *de re* intention to A the thing that is P. Thus, the *de re* interpretation of assertions of sentences in which people attribute intentions to themselves gives us what we need to construct the *mens rea* standard that we seek. The rest of the section considers the implications. It is argued that, given the *mens rea* standard identified, belief that the circumstance obtains frequently suffices for attempt. And it is further argued that, given the *mens rea* standard identified, there are conditions under which a defendant meets the *mens rea* standard for the attempt only if the circumstance actually obtains.

3.1 The *de dicto* and the *de re*

Sentences attributing mental states, including intentions, to people are frequently ambiguous in a way that requires note so as to avoid confusion later.

(*) He intends to enter the house on the corner

is ambiguous between

(**) He intends to enter the house, and intends that the house that he enters is on the corner

and

(***) He intends to enter the house, and the house he intends to enter is on the corner.

The person described in (**) intends to enter a house, but the world would not come to match his intention if it turned out that the house he enters is not (perhaps as he thought) on the corner. (Perhaps if he does not enter the house *on the corner*, he fails to signal his confederates as he plans to.) By contrast, the man described in (***) will succeed in doing what he intends even if the house that he enters is not on the corner. He is aiming to enter a house which is, in fact, on the corner but that fact is not part of what he aims to realize in having the intention that he has. To avoid this ambiguity, it is helpful when writing of intention to place the content of an intention in square brackets so that (**) and (***) can be represented, respectively, like so:[10]

(**') He intends [to enter the house on the corner].
(***') He intends [to enter the house] on the corner.

This convention serves merely as a shorthand way of indicating which of the two relevant meanings of the sentence—in our example, (**) or (***)—is intended. I will use this shorthand in what follows.

However, even after we have eliminated this ambiguity, other ambiguities remain. This is best illustrated by a somewhat complicated analogy. To see this, consider, first, the following sentence:

(a) The governor of California makes more than $1,000,000 a year.

Under one interpretation, the sentence expresses the same proposition as that expressed by one of the following two sentences:

(b1) Anyone who is governor of California makes more than $1,000,000 a year.
(b2) Someone who is governor of California makes more than $1,000,000 a year.

Someone who asserts (a) and expresses the same proposition as that expressed by (b1) is making a claim to the effect that two properties—namely being governor of California and making more than $1,000,000 a year—are always found together. This is the kind of thing that someone might say who believes (falsely, as it turns out) that the state of California pays the governor more than $1,000,000 each year to do the job. Someone, by contrast, who asserts (a) to express the same proposition as that expressed by (b2), makes an existence claim. Say that I have not yet heard the outcome of the election and you assert (a) to give me a clue about who won. I learn from your assertion that there is a person who has the two properties in question and so, if I know that only one of the candidates makes more than $1,000,000 a year, I am able to determine who won. However, your assertion will be false if the person who is governor does not make more than $1,000,000 a year. Therefore, if (a) is to be interpreted as expressing the same proposition as either (b1) or (b2), it is true only if at least one person who makes $1,000,000 a year is also the governor of California.

---

[10] This notation is used, also, by R.A. Duff (1996), p 6.

However, these are not the only ways of interpreting (a), nor are they the most important for our purposes. If, for instance, we assume that the speaker of (a) is using the phrase 'the governor of California' in just the way in which he uses the proper name 'Sylvester Stallone'—he mistakenly thinks Stallone is governor—then (a) expresses the same proposition as the following sentence:

(c) Sylvester Stallone makes more than $1,000,000 a year.

When so interpreted, (a) asserts something about the income of the person referred to by the speaker with the phrase 'the governor of California'. When (a) is understood in such a way that it expresses the same proposition as (c), the properties referred to in the description 'the governor of California' are not used to determine whether or not the sentence is true. After all, (c)'s truth value does not turn on whether or not Sylvester Stallone is governor; so if (a) is interpreted as expressing the same proposition as (c), then neither does (a)'s truth value turn on that. What this implies is that when a person asserts (a) and is rightly taken to express the proposition that (c) expresses, he can be mistaken in his belief that the description he uses applies to the object he refers to with it and still assert something true. The person who asserts (a) while falsely believing that Sylvester Stallone is governor of California might be asserting no more than that Sylvester Stallone makes more than $1,000,000 a year, which is perfectly true, although he is not governor of California.

Philosophers of language frequently draw the distinction between *de dicto* interpretations of referential descriptions, like 'the governor of California', and *de re* interpretations. Although there is controversy about how, exactly, that distinction is drawn, for our purposes, to interpret (a) as expressing the same proposition as either (b1) or (b2) is to interpret the description as it appears in (a) *de dicto*, while to interpret (a) as expressing the same proposition as (c) is to interpret that description *de re*. When a descriptive phrase is interpreted *de re*, it contributes only its referent to the truth conditions of the use of the sentence. When it is interpreted *de dicto*, by contrast, the properties referred to in the description contribute to the sentence's truth conditions independently.

A sentence like (a) is, when asserted, usually correctly construed as an expression of a belief that the speaker holds. How we characterize what the speaker believes will depend at least on whether we interpret the phrase 'the governor of California' *de dicto* or *de re*. Let us say, however, that we interpret the description *de re*. Further, let us imagine that the speaker, as in the case just mentioned, falsely believes that Sylvester Stallone is governor of California and uses the phrase 'the governor of California' to refer to Stallone. By asserting (a), he expresses the belief that Stallone makes more than $1,000,000 a year, and this belief has a particular kind of primacy: the question of whether what he said is true or false turns only on the question of whether this belief is true or false. However, typically we learn more about his psychology from his assertion of (a) than merely that he believes that Stallone makes more than $1,000,000 a year. If the circumstances cooperate—say he is watching Stallone give an interview on television and pointing at the screen when he utters (a) and circumstances are otherwise normal—we also learn, perhaps among other things still, that he believes that Stallone is governor of California.

Is there a psychological difference between the person who asserts (a), understood *de re*, and the person who asserts (c), assuming that both falsely believe that Stallone is governor of California? There are, to be sure, differences between what we would need to do to reconstruct each one's beliefs. In order to reach the conclusion that the person who asserts (a) believes that Stallone makes more than $1,000,000 a year we need to learn, somehow, that he uses the description 'the governor of California' in the same way that he uses the name 'Stallone'. No such step is required to determine that the person who asserts (c) believes that Stallone makes more than $1,000,000 a year. But does a difference of this sort speak to a difference in the psychology of these two people, or only a difference in what we need to do to reconstruct their psychologies? Happily, we do not need to answer this very difficult question. As stated, this question concerns *de re belief* while our ultimate concern here will be with *de re intention*. Further, as we are about to see, the question is easier in the case of *de re* intention.

To see this, consider what is involved in intending [to A the thing that is P], where A is an act and P is a property. Imagine that the person who has an intention of this sort asserts the following sentence:

(d) I intend [to pay the governor of California $1,000,000].

Like (a), (d) admits of a *de dicto* or *de re* interpretation. Under its *de dicto* interpretation (and assuming that the speaker envisions a one-time payment, rather than a payment to all who will ever be governor of California) it expresses the same proposition as the following sentence:

(e) I intend [that someone is both the governor of California and paid $1,000,000 by me].

However, if (d) is interpreted *de re*, it expresses the same proposition as the following sentence, assuming that the speaker falsely believes Stallone to be governor and so is using 'the governor of California' in the same way in which he uses 'Stallone':

(f) I intend [to pay Stallone $1,000,000].

The parallel question to the one asked above is this: is there a psychological difference between the person who asserts (d), understood *de re*, and the person who asserts (f), assuming that both falsely believe that Stallone is governor of California? There must be. The reason is that the world does not match the intention of the person who asserts (d) unless Stallone is governor of California, while that is irrelevant to the question of whether the intention of the person who asserts (f) matches the world. Notice, and this is important, for this to make sense there must be a difference between the world matching an intention, on the one hand, and the person doing as intended, on the other. Both the person who asserts (d), *de re*, and the person who asserts (f) *do as intended* when each gives the money to Stallone. But only the latter's intention matches the world. Thus, the person who asserts (d) is *not* characterized as having a belief that Stallone is governor and an intention to give Stallone $1,000,000. If that were correct, then his *intention* would match the world in all respects when he gives the money to Stallone (although his belief would not). So whatever we ought to say about the belief case—perhaps there is no psychological difference there—we must not say that there is no psychological difference between the person who asserts (d), *de re*, and the person who asserts (f). The psychological difference consists in the fact that a role is played by the description in the first's intention but that description plays no role in the intention of the second. Put, perhaps, more intuitively, the person who asserts (d) can point to the fact that Stallone, to whom the money is given, is not governor and say, 'In this respect, things have not turned out as I intended.' The person who asserts (f) can only say, 'That's not what I believed' for there is no sense in which the fact that Stallone is not governor indicates a failure of his intention to match the world.

As Scott Soames has helped me see, behind the view just summarized lies a particular way of understanding the referential use of descriptions, like 'the governor of California', at least in intention-contexts. In particular, on the view being assumed here, 'the governor of California', when used *de re*, contributes two things to what the sentence is used to assert. It contributes both *the x: x is the governor of California* (as in the standard Russellian view) *and x = o*, where o is the person referred to by the speaker when the descriptive phrase is used in the same way that a proper name for o would be used. The gap, then, between (d) and (f) is in the first of these elements: (d) asserts the same proposition that (f) asserts, but it asserts another in addition—namely that the speaker's intention commits him to the person to whom the money is given being the governor of California. As Soames has suggested in considering this approach to referential descriptions as they appear in belief contexts, this view is not obviously incorrect and captures something right.[11] In the case of intention, what it captures is the intuitive sense that the person of whom the following three

[11] See Soames (2008b) and (2008c).

things are true *has ended up in a world that fails to match his intention in all respects*: (1) he has the intention he attributes to himself by uttering (d) *de re*, (2) he uses the phrase 'the governor of California' to refer to Stallone, and (3) he gives the money to Stallone. It is further true that the world may match his intention in the *crucial* respect, the respect that he cares most about—it is Stallone to whom he gives the money and that might be what matters most to him—but this does not weaken the point. There remains a sense in which the world is not as his intention committed him to its being since Stallone is not governor.

Intentions set two different standards of success by which the future world can be judged. They set a standard for the agent's act, and they set a standard for the world as a whole, including, but not limited to, the act. In the typical case, if the world lives up to the first standard, it also lives up to the second. This is the case when the person asserts (d), *de re* believes Schwarzenegger to be the governor of California, and gives $1,000,000 to Schwarzenegger, who is, indeed, the governor of California. His act has succeeded to meet the standard set by his intention since he gave the money to the person he had in mind—namely Schwarzenegger. And the world has lived up to his intention as a whole because the person to whom he gave the money met the description that he used, in his intention, for thinking of that person—namely, 'the governor of California'. In the case, however, in which the person asserts (d), *de re*, but falsely believes Stallone to be governor, and gives the money to Stallone, the world has lived up to the first standard set by his intention, but not the second. He has given the money to the person he had in mind, but in doing so he has not given the money to someone who meets the description included in his intention. And there is a third case to consider, too—namely, the case in which the person asserts (d), *de dicto* falsely believes that Stallone is governor, and gives the money to Stallone. In that case, the world has fallen short of both of his intention's standards because, in essence, the standards collapse into one another. In such a case, his act succeeds only if the person to whom he gives the money is, in fact, the governor of California, and the second standard is met only if this same thing is true.

3.2 The commitments constituted by *de dicto* and *de re* intentions

As indicated earlier, for convenience, the term '*de dicto* intention' will be used to refer to the intention of the person who asserts a sentence like (d) *de dicto*, and the term '*de re* intention' to refer to the intention of the person who asserts a sentence like (d) *de re*. The difference between *de dicto* and *de re* intentions marks a difference in the commitments of the people who have those intentions. To see this, consider the difference between an event's occurring, on the one hand, and the defendant being the cause of the event's occurring, on the other. The latter includes the former plus more. Typically, as mentioned earlier, including a reference to an event in the content of one's intention is sufficient for generating two commitments: a commitment to the event's occurring, and a commitment to being the cause of the event's occurring (since one would be the cause were the intention to play its proper causal role). In a large class of cases, we are to interpret *de dicto* the description of the relevant event employed in a sentence stating that the defendant includes the event in the content of his intention. In fact, it is so natural to give the *de dicto* interpretation of the descriptions of acts and results that appear in the contents of intentions that it sometimes takes some mental gymnastics to even see what it would be to interpret them *de re*. What this indicates is that, when a description appearing in the content of an intention is to be interpreted *de dicto*, the agent has two commitments: (1) a commitment to its being the case that the object with respect to which he acts falls under the description, and, also, (2) a commitment *to causing* this to be the case. For instance, when (d) is interpreted *de dicto*, the intention that it asserts the speaker, D, to have brings with it two commitments: a commitment to its being the case that the person who receives $1,000,000 from D is the governor of California, and a commitment to causing this to be the case. In this example, D can cause this to be the case in one of two ways. He could, in theory, cause a particular person to be the governor of California—perhaps by fixing the election—and then give that person $1,000,000; or, what is far more likely, he could see to it that he only gives $1,000,000 to the person who is, in fact, the governor of California when the money is given. If he follows the latter strategy, then he would switch the target of his money when he learns that the person at whom it is aimed is not, in fact, the governor of California. If (d) is true, then, and the description is interpreted *de dicto*, the person who asserts it has an intention that commits him to doing one of these two things.

By contrast, the agent with the *de re* intention has merely the first of the two commitments. The *de re* intention, that is, commits the agent to its being the case that the object with respect to which he acts falls under the description, but does not commit the agent to causing this to be the case. This is why, when (d) is to be interpreted *de re*, and the person who has the relevant intention gives $1,000,000 to Stallone falsely believing him to be the governor of California, the right way to diagnose the failure of the intention to match the world is to say that, although the act succeeded, the intention misrepresented the world in which that success was to take place. The intention represented the world in which success of the act takes place as a world in which the governor of California is given $1,000,000, when, in fact, in one such world someone, namely Stallone, who is not the governor of California, is given the money.

The very idea of being committed to a condition's obtaining, without being committed to causing that condition, can seem quite puzzling. You are not really committed to it, we might say, if you are not willing to take steps to see to it that it obtains. You need to at least *be ready* to cause it should that be needed, and so you need to be committed to causing it. The very idea of *commitment to the condition*, the thought is, brings with it the idea of commitment *to causing* the condition. But the puzzlement is dissolved when we recognize the range of ways in which a person can be committed to a condition by his intention. Although there may be further senses yet, consider two different ways in which one can be committed by one's intention to the world being a certain way without being committed thereby to causing it to be that way:

Commitment to Non-Reconsideration: The commitment to not reconsider one's intention on the grounds that one believes the condition to hold.
Commitment to Not Complaining: The commitment to not complaining that the world fails to be as intended in light of the fact that the condition holds.

In both of these cases, to fail to live up to what one is committed to is to be in violation of a norm of rationality to which one is subject thanks to the fact that one has the intention. (As we will see later, a person can have a commitment to not complaining with respect to a condition while lacking a commitment to non-reconsideration with respect to that same condition.) Commitments to non-reconsideration involve norms of rationality that apply to agents after intention formation and before what we might call 'plan's end'—the moment at which the world has come to match their intentions in all respects. Commitments to not complaining, by contrast, involve norms of rationality that apply to agents at and after plan's end. Consider a person, for instance, who has the *de re* intention [to receive stolen cloth] but reconsiders that intention. When asked why he reconsiders, he says, 'Well, I think the cloth I intended to receive is stolen!' This explanation falls flat because the fact that the agent cites in explanation was already represented by his intention. He can no more cite the fact that he thinks the cloth is cloth in explanation of his decision to reconsider than he can cite the fact that the cloth is stolen. He is equally irrational to reconsider *for that reason* in both cases. He might rationally decide to reconsider on the grounds that the cloth's being stolen is a weightier consideration than he thought at the time of intention formation; or he might rationally decide to reconsider on the grounds that he just learned that it is illegal to receive stolen cloth. But what he cannot do in full rationality is to reconsider merely on the grounds that he believes the cloth is stolen. Similarly, if he succeeds in receiving the cloth, he cannot without irrationality complain that the world is not as he intended it to be in light of the fact that the cloth he received is stolen: that is part of what he intends and so the world has not fallen short of being as he intended it to be in light of that fact.

A person with a *de re* intention [to A the thing that is P] has both a commitment of non-reconsideration with respect to the thing he A's being P and a commitment not to complain with respect to that same condition. Since one can have either or both of these commitments without being committed to causing the thing to be P, or to selecting a thing to A that is P, these commitments are independent of any commitment to cause the thing one A's to be P.

3.3 The *mens rea* standard and beliefs about circumstances

Circumstantial elements of crimes are conditions that must be shown to have held at the time of the crime. But they are different from other elements of crimes in that the prosecution need not show either that the defendant caused the condition to obtain or that he selected a time to act, or an object with respect to which to act, in part because the condition held at that time or with respect to that object. It can be an accident, caused by no one at all, that the condition holds, or it can be caused in one or the other sense, or both, by some third party. Recall that, under the Guiding Commitment View, to try to do something is to be committed by one's intention to each of the components of success and to be moved by those commitments. Circumstantial elements of crimes are components of success. But since success does not require that the defendant cause them, an attempt requires no more than an intention-based commitment to their occurrence that falls short of commitment to causing their occurrence. When we put this together with the view of *de re* intention just offered, we reach the following result: *to have the commitment to the circumstantial elements involved in an attempted crime, it is sufficient for the defendant to include the circumstantial elements of the completed crime in the content of his intention as part of a* de re *description. De dicto* descriptions will do, but since such intentions constitute a commitment to causing the circumstances to obtain, they are more than is required for attempt. We, therefore, have identified the *mens rea* standard that we sought.

When we add to this the idea that an intention that includes a *de re* description (such as the intention [to pay the governor of California $1,000,000]) involves a commitment of non-reconsideration and a commitment to not complaining, we are tempted to hold that a person who merely believes a circumstantial element of the completed crime to be in place, and has the relevant accompanying intention, is sufficiently committed to that circumstance for attempt. This is not quite true, although there is a live possibility, to be discussed shortly, that it is close enough to being true for the government's work of assessing the *mens rea* of attempt. To see why it is not strictly true, consider (d) again, together with the following two sentences:

(g) Arnold Schwarzenegger is the star of *The Terminator*.
(h) I intend [to pay the star of *The Terminator* $1,000,000].

Now imagine that (d) is true when 'the governor of California' is interpreted *de re*, and that the person who asserts it, D, uses the phrase 'the governor of California' as a proper name for Schwarzenegger. He would point to the man at the podium, who is Schwarzenegger, and say things like, 'There's the governor of California!' And imagine that (g) could be asserted by this same person to express his belief. The question is whether, in such a case, we can, without exception, conclude that (h) is true (or, rather, would be if uttered by D). Given the conception of the *de re* interpretation of (d) described above, we cannot.

There are at least three kinds of cases in which (d) and (g) are true and (h) is false. First, there are so called 'Frege Puzzles':[12] imagine that D believes that Arnold Schwarzenegger and the governor of California are different people. In that case, (h) does not follow from (d) and (g), even though (d) and (g), both of which are to be interpreted *de re*, concern the very same person, namely Arnold Schwarzenegger. The fact that he thinks they are different people prevents his intention-based commitment to the person who receives the money being the governor of California from becoming an intention-based commitment to that person being the star of *The Terminator*. Second, there are failures 'to put two and two together': imagine that D's belief that Arnold Schwarzenegger starred in *The Terminator* is entirely dispositional. He pays little attention to the movies and a great deal of attention to politics, and just never has occurrent thoughts about movies except in special circumstances. Were you to ask him if Schwarzenegger starred in that film he would assert (g), but he would not have an occurrent thought that it would be proper for him to express by uttering (g) in the absence of prompting. In having the intention [to pay the governor of California $1,000,000], D simply is not thinking about the movies that the governor of California starred in. But if he is not thinking about that, then he very well may not have the intention [to pay the star of *The Terminator* $1,000,000]. Perhaps he has it in some purely

[12] The term refers to Gottlob Frege, who introduced puzzles of this sort in his famous Frege (1948).

dispositional sense, but he does not have it occurrently. Such an intention includes an occurrent thought about the movies that a particular person has starred in and we are stipulating that D just is not thinking about that when he has the intention he attributes to himself with (d). But on the assumption that it is occurrent intentions, and not dispositional ones, that actually motivate token actions, it follows that (h) is not true in the sense of relevance to the criminal law.

There is a third category of cases in which sentences like (d) and (g) are true and a sentence like (h) is false, and it is in some ways the most important of the three for legal purposes.[13] For reasons that will become clear, call these cases 'insalience cases'. To appreciate this category, consider someone who has the *de re* intention [to pay the governor of California $1,000,000], who also has the occurrent belief that the governor of California has an Austrian accent, and who believes, truly, that the person whom he intends to give the money and the person he believes to have an Austrian accent are one and the same person, namely Arnold Schwarzenegger. His is neither a Frege puzzle case, nor a failure to put two and two together. Now let us further imagine that this person could not care less that Arnold Schwarzenegger has an Austrian accent. He takes this fact to give him no reason whatsoever to refrain from giving him the money, nor a reason to give him the money, nor does he see it as in any way a salient fact about Arnold Schwarzenegger in any other respect pertaining to the act he intends to perform. Does this person have the *de re* intention [to pay the Austrian-accented person $1,000,000]? He does not. In asking about the *de re* intention, we are assuming that a person who has this intention uses the description 'the Austrian-accented person' analogously to a proper name to refer to Arnold Schwarzenegger. The man in the example very well might be willing to use that phrase in that way. But even if he is, that does not mean that he has the relevant *de re* intention. In having the intention that he attributes to himself in asserting (d), he is not thereby thinking of Arnold Schwarzenegger *as* an Austrian-accented person, although at that very moment he has another thought—namely his occurrent belief that Arnold Schwarzenegger has an Austrian accent, that does involve thinking of Schwarzenegger in that way. The intention and the belief remain distinct thoughts that represent the same object in different ways. Only the belief, in this case, represents Schwarzenegger as having an Austrian accent. In this case the insalience of the fact that Schwarzenegger has an Austrian accent blocks the inference from the intention and belief to the further intention [to pay the Austrian-accented person $1,000,000].

---

[13] Robin Jeshion helped me recognize this third category and its importance. Many of the examples that I use to illustrate it are thanks to her, as well.

The results just reached depend crucially on the construal of referential descriptions in intention contexts described above. It is because in uttering, *de re*, a sentence like (d), a speaker ascribes to himself an intention that commits him to the object on which he acts meeting the description he uses to refer to it that we are blocked from inferring a sentence like (h) from sentences like (d) and (g). A belief that an object meets a particular description does not all by itself provide an intention-based commitment to act on an object that meets the description. Nor does it provide such a commitment without exception when the agent has an intention-based commitment to act on that very object. An intention-based commitment to the object on which one acts meeting a description requires an *intention* that so describes the object. In Frege puzzle cases, failures to put two and two together, and insalience cases, this further intention is absent.

Frege puzzle cases, failures to put two and two together, and insalience cases are cases in which the agent falls short of a commitment to not reconsider the intention in the face of the belief that the relevant condition holds. In Frege puzzle cases, the agent could without irrationality reconsider his intention at the moment that he discovers that the object of his intention and the object of his belief are one and the same. D might without any form of irrationality give up his intention [to pay the governor of California $1,000,000] when he realizes that the person he has in mind is the very one who is drawing large sums every year from the residual income that he gains thanks to having been the star of *The Terminator*. Because he would not be irrational in any sense in such a case, he does not have the intention he would ascribe to himself with (h). The same is true if the case is a failure 'to put two and two together'. The agent in such a case lacks the commitment to non-reconsideration constituted by the *de re* intention [to pay the star of *The Terminator* $1,000,000]. At the point that he puts two and two together and comes to have an occurrent belief that the man whom he intends to pay the money is the star of *The Terminator*, he can without irrationality reconsider his intention [to pay the governor of California $1,000,000]. And, similarly, the person for whom the movies the governor has starred in is completely insalient can, nonetheless, reconsider an intention [to pay the governor of California $1,000,000] on the grounds that Schwarzenegger starred in *The Terminator*. In some such cases, the person will have come to recognize this fact as providing him with reason not to pay Schwarzenegger the money. But even if he does not change his mind about that, *his intention* is not rationally stable in the face of the relevant belief. It might be *factually* stable in the face of that belief—perhaps he will not, in fact, reconsider his intention in the face of the belief—but he would not be in violation of a commitment constituted by his intention were he to do so. This is the sense in which *his intention* does not place him under any rational pressure to not reconsider in the face of the belief and hence he does not have a commitment of non-reconsideration with respect to the condition that the person he gives the money to starred in *The Terminator*.

Still, although sentences like (d) and (g) do not entail sentences like (h), it is also the case that the truth of sentences like (d) and (g) can provide powerful evidence in favor of the truth of a sentence like (h), especially when conjoined with other evidence to the effect that the case is not a Frege puzzle case, a failure to put two and two together, or an insalience case. To see this, consider again *United States v Crow*, in which the defendant falsely believed himself to be chatting with a 13-year-old girl whom he asked to send him sexually explicit photographs of herself; he was actually chatting with a detective. Crow has the *de re* belief that the person he is chatting with is a minor. He also appears to have the intention [to sexually exploit the person he is chatting with]. It is a bit unclear whether this intention is *de dicto* or *de re*—does it matter to Crow whether the person he sexually exploits actually chats with him, or not? Is it part of what he is after that he *convinced* the minor whose photos he enjoys to send them, or would it be enough for success merely that, at the end of the day, he has her photo? We do not know enough about Crow to know the answers to these questions. But let us assume that the relevant intention is *de re*. The question is whether we can infer that Crow intends [to sexually exploit a minor]. If he does have that intention, then he is sufficiently committed to his target's being a minor for an attempt to sexually exploit a minor.

We cannot *deduce* that Crow has the intention [to sexually exploit a minor]. It is possible that his is a Frege puzzle case: perhaps he falsely believes that the person he intends to sexually exploit and the person he believes to be a minor are different people. We would need a complicated story to make this plausible, but imagine that we have it; perhaps he mistakenly thinks that he is chatting with two different people, one of whom is a minor and one of whom is not, who happen to be using the same screen name. Or perhaps he is like the person whose relevant belief is dispositional. Perhaps, that is, although he believes that the person he is chatting with is a minor, he does not have an occurrent thought to that effect and so cannot have formed the intention [to sexually exploit a minor]. These things are *possible*, but they are highly unlikely. They are so unlikely, in fact, that the doubt that their possibility supplies could hardly be thought reasonable in the absence of compelling evidence in their favor. It seems much more likely that Crow believes that the person he intends to sexually exploit and the person that he believes to be a minor are one and the same. And, given that the detective explicitly claimed to be a minor, it is hard to imagine that Crow did not have the occurrent belief that the person he was chatting with was a minor. Further, there is little reason to think that the person's status as a minor was not extremely salient to Crow.

He knows, for instance, that there are criminal penalties for the sexual exploitation of minors that do not apply to the sexual exploitation of adults. And there may be reason to think that he is positively in search of sexually explicit photographs of minors, and so, assuming that he has reason to believe that the pictures he hopes to receive are of the person he is chatting with, that person's minor status is extremely important to Crow. Given all of this, chances are that he intends [to sexually exploit a minor]. At the least, it seems that if the prosecution has proven beyond a reasonable doubt that the defendant has a *de re* intention [to A a thing] and a *de re* belief that the thing he intends to A is P, then the burden switches. At this point, it seems, we are justified in assuming that the defendant has a *de re* intention [to A the thing that is P], and is thus committed by his intention to its being P, unless the defendant is able to provide us with a compelling reason for thinking that we ought not to reach this conclusion. What this implies is that we ought to hold that *proof beyond a reasonable doubt that the defendant had the* de re *belief that the circumstantial element of the crime is in place, together with a relevant intention, creates a rebuttable presumption that he has an intention that commits him to the circumstantial element of the completed crime.*

Although it is an empirical question, it seems that insalience cases are likely to be far more commonly found in courtrooms than are the other sorts of conditions that block the inference from the belief to the intention that commits the defendant to the circumstantial element of the completed crime. For instance, imagine an 18-year-old defendant who tries and fails to have sex with a 15-year-old in a jurisdiction in which the age of consent is 16. Let us imagine that the defendant has a *de re* intention [to have sex with Victim], and an occurrent *de re* belief that Victim is 15. And let us further imagine that the two are of comparable emotional maturity when it comes to sex. If this is an attempted statutory rape, the defendant must, at least, have a *de re* intention [to have sex with a minor]. But does the defendant have this intention? We need to know much more about him to answer this question. The question is whether he takes the minor status of his would-be partner to be at all salient. Given the small age difference between them, the stipulated small difference in emotional maturity, and, even, perhaps, some rather foggy-headed ideas on his part about what his legal obligations are, it is perfectly possible to imagine that the victim's age just is not salient at all and so prevents the content of his belief from making its way into the content of his intention. This is why, when he says, on the stand, 'But I really love her!', what he says is of relevance to his case. What he is saying is that her age was not relevant to him. It was as irrelevant to him as was Schwarzenegger's accent in our example earlier. But irrelevant facts, even those that one believes to be present, often do not make their way into the contents of our intentions, even in the face of occurrent belief that they are present. By contrast, if the facts are the same except that the defendant is 50 years old, then our perception of the case changes radically. Here we are much more likely to see him as having intended, *de re*, [to have sex with a minor]. The reason is that it is hard for us to imagine that the minor status of one's partner would be entirely insalient to a person of that age. It *could* be so; the conceptual possibility remains. But it seems extremely unlikely given a few basic assumptions about human psychology.

There is a fourth way in which a defendant could rebut a presumption to the effect that he has the intention needed for attempt given that he has a relevant belief and a *de re* intention. He could show that his belief is *de dicto*. In the case in which Crow's belief is *de dicto*, he might not intend [to sexually exploit a minor]. The *de dicto* belief that the person he is chatting with is a minor amounts to the belief that two properties co-occur—the property of being the person he is chatting with and the property of being a minor. It is awkward, although possible, to try to imagine having this belief. Other similar beliefs are more familiar. Consider, for instance, a woman who has the *de dicto* belief that the man she is dating resembles her father. She may not see the resemblance herself. She may, in fact, have the *de re* belief that the man she is dating does not resemble her father. But she also might know herself well enough to know that she always ends up dating men who resemble her father. She believes that two properties co-occur: the property of being dated by her, and the property of resembling her father. Imagine that Crow's belief is like that. He believes that it so happens that he always finds himself chatting with minors. There is little reason to think that Crow, in such a case, intends [to sexually exploit a minor]. Note that it is clear that even if the woman in our example intends [to marry the man she is dating], she does not intend [to marry a man who resembles her father]. How could she intend that given that she has the *de re* belief that the man she is dating does not resemble her father, and it is *he* that she intends to marry? Similarly, there are reasonable grounds for doubting that Crow, when he has the *de dicto* belief, intends [to sexually exploit a minor]. Of course, given that StephieFL *told* Crow she was a minor, it seems very unlikely that his actual belief is *de dicto*.

What we have shown, then, is that the position enshrined in Model Penal Code §5.01(1), and accepted in many jurisdictions, is too strong. Under that section, belief that a circumstantial element of a crime is present suffices for the *mens rea* of the attempt with respect to that element. Under such a position, the relevant *mens rea* is present even in cases in which the defendant lacks an intention that commits him to the circumstantial element of the completed crime because of one of the conditions that would block the relevant inference. The correct policy is that such a belief creates a rebuttal presumption that there is *mens rea*, provided that the defendant has been shown to have an appropriate intention. The defendant can rebut this presumption by showing that his case is a Frege puzzle case, a failure to put two and two together, an insalience case, or, even, by showing that his relevant belief is *de dicto*. These are all hard roads for any defendant to follow, and so typically all the prosecution will need to show is that the defendant had a relevant belief. But law should not close possible roads to a showing of innocence, no matter how unlikely they are to be open to any given defendant.

3.4 Disjunctive descriptions of circumstances

So far we have no reason to think that the circumstantial elements of the completed crime need actually to be in place for the attempted. We have identified a minimal condition for the commitment to circumstances involved in attempt: the defendant has a *de re* intention that includes the circumstantial element. We have also identified a distinct condition that creates a rebuttable presumption that this is the case: the defendant has a *de re* belief that the circumstance obtains, together with an intention that serves for commitment to performing the act involved in the completed crime. But, in fact, there is one class of cases in which a defendant charged with attempt probably has an intention that incorporates a circumstantial element of the completed crime only if that circumstance is actually present. These are cases in which the property included in the *de re* description in his intention is a disjunctive property, one of the disjuncts of which includes the circumstantial element. I will explain.

Say that I am offered a choice between two boxes. One of the boxes contains $5; the other contains either $100 or a small amount of marijuana with equal probability, although I am not certain which it contains. I see no attraction to possessing marijuana and recognize that, were I to possess it, I would incur, let us say with certainty, a fine of $50. Assuming my only motive is profit, I calculate the expected value and act accordingly, thereby forming the intention to take the box containing either $100 or marijuana: that box has an expected value of $25. So, were I to utter the following sentence it would be true:

(i) I intend [to take the $100-or-marijuana box].

Let us assume that 'the $100-or-marijuana box' is to be interpreted *de re*: I have in mind a particular box—the very one that I occurrently believe contains either $100 or marijuana—and I intend to take it. Imagine that I act on this intention although I fall short of taking the box I have in mind because I am arrested and charged with an attempt to possess marijuana. Whether I have committed this crime turns on whether or not the intention I report with (i) committed me to the following condition: the box I intended to take contains marijuana. Did my intention commit me to that?

The first thing to see is that I do not have a commitment of non-reconsideration with respect to the box's containing marijuana. After all, imagine that before I can take the box I come to believe that it contains marijuana. At this point, I know that the box I intend to take promises nothing but a $50 fine, while the other box promises me $5. There is no irrationality in reconsidering my intention in the face of this belief. In fact, rationality may even require reconsideration in this case. Hence, I am not committed *in the sense involved in a commitment of non-reconsideration* to the box containing marijuana.

But this does not show all by itself that I am not sufficiently committed to the box's containing marijuana for the attempt to possess it. Recall that an intention might also constitute a commitment to not complain about a particular condition; one might be irrational, that is, were one to cite the fact that a condition is met to support a complaint to the effect that the world is not as intended. I would be sufficiently committed to the box containing marijuana if my intention constitutes a commitment to not complain with respect to that condition. As I will now argue, I do have this commitment *if the box contains marijuana*. Appreciating this requires further reflection on the nature of commitments not to complain about conditions.

Start with the following observation: a reasonable complaint is, by its nature, about some actual fact. A person's complaint can always be neutralized by noting that the world is not actually the way that the person is complaining about its being. If I complain that I repeatedly am given the short end of the stick, my complaint has no bite in the face of the fact that I am not, in fact, repeatedly given the short end of the stick. What this implies is that each and every one of us is committed to not complaining about unactualized conditions. We all have that commitment simply because of what complaints are. Any complaint about an unactualized condition is, by its nature, misplaced, and therefore we are all committed to not offering such complaints. But it is possible for people to have commitments to not complaining that go beyond this. People can have commitments to not complaining that are special to them, and, in particular, that are special to them thanks to their intentions. It is natural to characterize their situation as involving some kind of conditional commitment. A person who is committed to not complaining about condition K, in the sense of interest, is someone who is committed to not complaining *if K*.

The claim that D is committed to not complaining if K admits of scope ambiguity. Is that to which D is committed conditional in its nature, or is the presence of D's commitment conditional? We find, that is, that there are two kinds of conditional commitments, which the recent philosophical literature has labeled 'wide scope' and 'narrow scope'.[14]

Wide Scope Commitment to Not Complaining: the commitment to not complaining that the following conditional is true: if K, then the world fails to be as intended.

Narrow Scope Commitment to Not Complaining: if K, then one is committed to not complaining that, in light of K, the world fails to be as intended.

The first thing to see is that a Wide Scope Commitment to Not Complaining with respect to condition K does not amount to any kind of commitment *to K*. The commitment involved there is a commitment to the conditional of which K is the antecedent, but it is not a commitment to K itself. However, those who have Wide Scope Commitment to Not Complaining with respect to a particular condition also, typically, have Narrow Scope Commitment to Not Complaining with respect to that very condition. However, Narrow Scope Commitments to Not Complaining also fall short of commitment to K all by themselves. To say that a person *would* be committed to something *if* a particular condition were met is not to say, *ipso facto*, that he is committed to anything at all given the way things actually are. After all, the condition might not be met. But those who have the Narrow Scope Commitment are committed by their intentions *to K itself* under one particularly important circumstance: the circumstance in which K is realized.

So, this is what we have learned: a person who has the *de re* intention [to A the thing that is P] has, at least, a Narrow Scope Commitment to Not Complaining with respect to the following condition: the thing he A's is P. He may also have the Wide Scope Commitment to Not Complaining. In fact, that he has that Wide Scope Commitment might be why he has the Narrow. But, whatever the reason he has the Narrow Commitment to Not Complaining, nothing of interest yet follows about his commitment to the thing he A's being P. However, if the thing he A's *is* P, then he is committed by his intention to not complaining about that. Hence, his intention commits him to that condition *when the thing he A's is P*, and it does not commit him to that if that is not so.

Now return to our example involving the *de re* intention [to take the $100-or-marijuana box]. In having this intention, I am not committed to not reconsidering with respect to the condition that the box I take contains marijuana. But I do have the Narrow Commitment of Not Complaining with

---

[14] The terminology appears to have been introduced in Schroeder (2004). The concept of wide and narrow scope was present in the philosophical literature far before the introduction of those terms. Sometimes, for instance, philosophers would refer to the wide scope cases as 'internally conditional' and the narrow scope as 'externally conditional'.

respect to that condition. Thus, if the box contains marijuana, I am committed by my intention to not complaining that the world has, on those grounds, fallen short of being as intended. Whether I am committed by my intention to that condition, then, turns on whether or not that condition is actually in place. Notice that if the box turns out to contain methamphetamine, I am not committed by my intention to its containing methamphetamine. In that case, I can without irrationality complain that the world has failed to be as intended since my intention did not represent the box, even disjunctively, as containing methamphetamine.

Notice—and this will turn out to be of some importance when applying what we have learned to cases like *Dlugash*—it is perfectly possible for the disjuncts involved in the disjunctive representation of the object on which one intends to act to fill logical space. A person can intend [to receive the stolen or unstolen cloth], for instance. To have such an intention is to represent the cloth one intends to receive as having some relevant legal status or other, without representing it as being stolen, and without representing it as being unstolen. The property of being stolen or unstolen, despite being possessed by every object, might or might not be included in the representation of the object in one's intention. Every object is made in China, or not made in China; every object has that disjunctive property. But for someone for whom the belief that the object is or is not made in China is entirely dispositional, or for someone for whom the fact that the object possesses that property is entirely insalient, this property is unlikely to be included in the intention to receive the object, or to steal it, or to act in some other way with respect to it. That is, everything that we learned above about the ways in which the properties of an object are and are not found in an agent's intention when he has the belief that the object possesses that property apply to disjunctive properties in which the disjuncts fill logical space.

As we saw, the fact that a person's case is a Frege puzzle case, a failure to put two and two together, or an insalience case defeats the otherwise safe inference from the fact that he believes *de re* that a thing is P and has a *de re* intention [to act on it] to the conclusion that he has a *de re* intention [to act on a thing that is P]. Similarly, in the absence of one of these same defeaters, a person who believes *de re* that a thing *might* have a property and has a *de re* intention [to act on that thing] has a disjunctive *de re* intention [to act on a thing that has or lacks the property]. For instance, if a defendant has a *de re* belief that the cloth might be stolen and might not be, and intends [to buy the cloth], then chances are that he intends [to buy the stolen or unstolen cloth]. This further intention is not *entailed* by the relevant intention and belief: the case might be a Frege puzzle case, a failure to put two and two together, or an insalience case. But we are nonetheless safe in assuming that the person has the relevant disjunctive intention in the absence of evidence supportive of the claim that his case is of one of these three sorts. As before, the intention and belief support a rebuttable presumption that the agent has the relevant further intention.

3.5 The position in action

It is worth summarizing the position offered here. In the preceding parts of this section, we have reached the following four, interconnected results. Here A is an act involved in crime C, P is a property such that some thing's being P is a circumstantial element of C, and Q is an alternative property that is incompatible with P. So, for instance, A might be the act of receiving goods, while P might be the property of being stolen, and Q the property of not being stolen. In that example, the circumstantial element of C is that the goods received are stolen.

(1) If D intends [to A the thing that is P], then D has the *mens rea* with respect to the thing being P needed for an attempt to C, whether his intention is *de re* or *de dicto*.

(2) If D has the *de re* intention [to A] and the *de re* belief [that the thing that he intends to A is P], then there is very good evidence that D intends [to A the thing that is P]. There is, therefore, very good evidence, given (1), that D has the *mens rea* with respect to the thing being P needed for an attempt to C.

(3) If D has the *de re* intention [to A the thing that is P or Q] and the thing is P, then D is committed by his intention to the thing's being P. Therefore, given (1), in such cases D has the *mens rea* with respect to the thing's being P needed for an attempt to C.

(4) If D has the *de re* intention [to A] and the occurrent *de re* belief [that it is at least likely that the thing is either P or Q], then there is very good evidence that D has the *de re* intention [to A the thing that is P or Q]. Therefore, given (3), if the thing is P there is very good evidence that D has the *mens rea* with respect to the thing's being P needed for an attempt to C.

These results provide us with sufficient resources to resolve both the *Jaffe* case and the *Dlugash* case, and others like them. Jaffe has a *de re* belief that the cloth that he is buying is stolen. And he intends [to buy the cloth]. His is not a Frege puzzle case. He does not falsely believe that the cloth he intends to buy and the cloth that he believes to be stolen are distinct. Nor is his likely to be a case of failure 'to put two and two together'. Further, given the salience of the status of the cloth as stolen or unstolen, it seems very likely that he has its status in mind when he buys it. Further evidence, such as evidence that he took precautions to avoid detection, would support this contention. His case, in other words, is to be handled exactly the same way as the *Crow* case discussed above. In both, the defendant has a *de re* belief (that the cloth is stolen, that the person he is chatting with is a minor) and a relevant intention (an intention [to buy the cloth], an intention [to sexually exploit the person he is chatting with]). And in both there is no reason to think that the special conditions that defeat an inference to the conclusion that the defendant has the intention needed for attempt (the intention [to buy stolen cloth], the intention [to sexually exploit a minor]) are present. Because of these defendants' *de re* beliefs about the presence of the circumstantial element, we are in a position to say that they are sufficiently committed to those elements for attempt *without any inquiry into the question of whether those elements are in fact present.*

To resolve the *Dlugash* case we must draw on the lesson provided by reflection on the hypothetical involving the box containing either $100 or marijuana. Start with a prior question: what, exactly, did Dlugash intend? Given what little we know of the case, the answer to this question is surely indeterminate. But the answer to a closely related question might not be: consistent with what we do know, what characterization of Dlugash's intention will paint him in the best possible light? It is tempting to characterize Dlugash's intention as conditional. Perhaps he intended [to kill Geller, if Geller was alive, and to mutilate Geller's corpse, if Geller was already dead]. If this was Dlugash's intention, then the case is a relatively easy one to resolve, although not through appeal to the principles presented here but, instead, through principles for determining the conditions under which a conditional intention serves to meet an unconditional intention *mens rea* standard. That is, if this is Dlugash's intention, then the question is just whether an intention [to kill if Geller was alive] should serve to meet the *mens rea* standard for a crime that requires intent to kill. I have developed an account of how to answer such questions elsewhere.[15] Under both the account that I advocate, and under the rival account to be found in the *Model Penal Code*,[16] the conditional intention under consideration would suffice for *mens rea* for attempted murder. So if that was Dlugash's intention, he is guilty of attempted murder. This is why a showing to the effect that Dlugash was firing insurance shots—a showing to the effect that he was seeing to it that Geller was dead while recognizing that he might be wasting ammunition—would be enough to show that he had the intention needed for attempted murder.

So the characterization of Dlugash as possessing the conditional intention [to kill if ...] does not paint him in the best possible light. There is, in

---

[15] Yaffe (2004).   [16] §2.02(6).

other words, a characterization of his intention that is less bad and is consistent with what we know of Dlugash. To see this, let us assume that Dlugash takes shooting Geller to be a necessary means to some end of his, and let us further assume that the end is not, itself, killing Geller. For instance, perhaps Dlugash believes that shooting Geller is the necessary means to impressing Bush. Let us further assume, as seems plausible, that Dlugash occurrently believes Geller to be alive or dead and his is not a Frege puzzle case, a failure to put two and two together, or an insalience case. Assume, yet further, that Dlugash intends the consequences of his act. He does not merely foresee, for instance, that Geller will be in some condition following the shooting; he positively intends that Geller be in that condition. So understood, it seems that Dlugash intends [to put the person who is dead or alive into the condition that results from his shooting him several times in the head]. This is different from the conditional intention discussed above since Dlugash is not under pressure from his intention to do one thing if Geller is alive and another if Geller is dead. There is just one thing that Dlugash's intention commits him to doing: bring about a further condition in Geller by shooting him in the head. What he does not know is *what* condition that will be; but he intends it either way. So characterized, Dlugash's intention is similar to that of the person who intends [to take the $100-or-marijuana box]. Both such a person and Dlugash intend an act (shooting, taking) and intend a result of that act (putting Geller into the resulting condition, placing oneself in possession of the box's contents). But both think of the result under a disjunctive description. In Dlugash's case, and not in the other case, the disjuncts fill logical space, since Geller is either alive or dead. But that difference need not detain us.

So, for our purposes, Dlugash intends [to put the person who is dead or alive into the condition that results from his shooting him several times in the head]. But it follows, then, for the reasons discussed above, that Dlugash's intention commits him to Geller's being alive at the time he is shot only if Geller *is* alive at the time he is shot. In representing Geller as dead or alive in his intention, Dlugash has a narrow scope commitment to not complain with respect to Geller's being alive; he is thus committed to not complaining that Geller is alive *if he is alive*. Thus, whether or not Dlugash is committed to Geller's being alive at the time of the shooting—whether he is committed by his intention *to shooting someone living*—turns on whether or not Geller was, in fact, alive when Dlugash shot him. Thus, the question of what Dlugash's intention commits him to turns on the facts. It follows, then, that Dlugash attempted murder only if Geller was alive. Since the prosecution cannot show this beyond a reasonable doubt, they cannot show beyond a reasonable doubt that Dlugash attempted murder. In this case, because Dlugash's intention is disjunctive and only some of the disjuncts represent the property (being alive) that figures in the circumstantial element, the actual presence or absence of that element is crucial for determining whether or not Dlugash had the intention required for the attempted crime. At least, so it is provided that we are willing to ascribe Dlugash with the disjunctive intention and not a conditional intention that would inculpate him for the crime.[17,18]

---

[17] Notice that for parallel reasons the prosecution cannot show that Dlugash attempted to mutilate a corpse without showing beyond a reasonable doubt that Geller was dead when Dlugash shot him. Does this imply that Dlugash is guilty of no crime? No. The reason is that, when a person can be shown beyond a reasonable doubt to have committed either crime 1 or crime 2, he has been shown to be guilty of the lesser crime. This is a principle governing guilt attribution independently of proof of commission of a crime. For further discussion of such principles, see Yaffe (2010), especially ch 4.

[18] Another kind of case which is often raised in discussion of these issues is that in which some object that would have to exist for the completed crime to take place does not exist at all. What should we say, to use the standard example, of the person who, intending [to pick a pocket], reaches into a pocket and finds it empty? Here the relevant circumstantial element of the crime is that there is something in the pocket. This is a circumstantial element of the crime, since to show that the completed crime took place, the prosecution must show beyond a reasonable doubt that something was stolen from the pocket, and so must show beyond a reasonable doubt that the pocket held something, but the prosecution need not show that the defendant caused the pocket to hold something, or would have selected a different pocket to put his hand into had he known the one he did choose was empty. This last is quite likely to be true. But the prosecution need not show it to be true in order to establish that the crime was completed: it is not a component of the completed crime. The consensus view is that the mere fact that the pocket is empty is irrelevant to the question of whether there was an attempt. The view offered here has that same implication in the standard case. In the standard case, the defendant has an intention [to take something from the pocket]. If the description 'something' is interpreted *de re*, then such an intention constitutes commitments of both non-reconsideration and non-complaint with respect to the condition that there is something in the pocket. Whether the intention is *de re* or *de dicto*, that there is something in the pocket is in the content of the intention. The defendant thus has an intention-based commitment to that, and so the fact that the pocket is empty is no obstacle to his commission of an attempted theft.

However, not all missing-object cases are like the standard ones in this respect. Imagine, for instance, that the defendant has the *de re* intention [to take the contents of an empty or not-empty pocket]. Such a person is intent on taking the contents of this very pocket, the one he reaches into, and he thinks of it through the disjunction 'empty or not empty'. This might be the mental state of the person who, for instance, is just as interested in the thrill of 'taking' the contents of an empty pocket as he is in taking something of value from someone else's pocket. For him, knowing that he would have taken something of value, had there been anything of value in the pocket, is good enough for success. If, in such a case, the pocket is empty, there is no attempted theft because the person is then committed by his intention to the pocket's being empty and so does not intend to take anything of value at all. Notice, however, how very peculiar such cases are. To be convinced that a particular defendant met this description, one would have to be convinced that the defendant's act would have succeeded even if the pocket were empty. To learn, for instance, that the person would not have reached into the pocket had he known that it was empty would support the claim that he had, instead, the intention [to take something from the pocket], which is sufficient for an attempt even if the pocket is empty.

4. Conclusion

The sense that inclusion of a circumstance in the content of one's intention is more than is required for attempt arises from a failure to recognize that there are intentions, namely *de re* intentions, that include circumstances in their content without thereby constituting a commitment to causing them. When we overlook that fact we are likely to be moved by our recognition that attempters need not be committed to causing circumstances to think that they need not include circumstances in the contents of their intentions at all. This would, in turn, contradict the implication of the Guiding Commitment View that all the commitments needed for an attempt must spring from the attempter's intention. Once we avoid the error, however, the dominoes fall and we are able to identify the minimum intention-based commitment to circumstances that is required for attempt: inclusion of the circumstance in a *de re* description appearing in the content of one's intention. Add to this that on rare occasions the facts determine the content of our *de re* intentions, and we are able to identify those rare occasions in which the circumstantial elements of the completed crime must be in place for the attempted. At least, so it has been argued in this chapter.

When one thinks of the ways in which philosophy of language might be relevant to the law, one is naturally drawn to the guidance that the discipline might give to those in the law tasked with interpreting words, whether spoken in courtrooms, hearings, or on the floor of the Senate, or written in judicial opinions, statutes, contracts, or constitutions. And, to be sure, this is one very important way in which philosophy of language promises to be of relevance to the law. However, this is not the only way, as I hope to have demonstrated here. Philosophers of language have developed powerful conceptual tools, of which the *de re–de dicto* distinction is one, for systematically thinking about a particular class of content-bearing entities, namely linguistic entities like words, sentences, and utterances. But these are not the only content-bearing entities with which the law is concerned. In virtually every area of law, but particularly in criminal law, the contents of our thoughts are of crucial importance. Just as tools from philosophy of language have been used with great effect in the philosophy of mind, such tools can be used with great effect in systematizing territory where the law has been working with the blurriest of maps. This is true, as shown here, in at least one area of criminal law in which the precise contents of a defendant's thoughts can make the difference between guilt and innocence—namely in the law governing attempted crimes.

10

Legislation as Communication? Legal Interpretation and the Study of Linguistic Communication

Mark Greenberg[1]

1. Introduction

According to a view—really a family of related views—that has considerable currency at the moment, philosophy of language and linguistics have a direct bearing on the content of the law. The general outlook of this view—the *communicative-content theory of law*, or, for short, the *communication theory*—can be captured in the following way. Legal texts are linguistic texts, so the meaning or content of a legal text is an instance of linguistic meaning generally. It therefore stands to reason that, in order to understand the meaning of an authoritative legal text or utterance, such as a statute or regulation, we should look to our best theories about language and communication. Those theories tell us that a text or utterance has linguistic content—call it *communicative content*—that may go well beyond the semantic content of the text. Communicative content depends on certain communicative intentions of the speaker.[2] Communication is successful to the extent that the hearer succeeds in recognizing what the speaker intends to communicate. From this understanding of language and

[1] I would like to thank participants in a UCLA summer faculty workshop for very helpful comments. In addition, I am grateful to my colleagues for an extraordinary outpouring of suggestions in response to an e-mail request for examples. I would also like to thank Andrea Ashworth, Mitch Berman, Sam Cumming, Jon Michaels, Eliot Michaelson, David Plunkett, Nicos Stavropoulos, Stephen Yeazell, and Eugene Volokh for extremely helpful comments. I am especially grateful to Scott Shapiro and Seana Shiffrin for invaluable discussions and to Stephen Munzer for detailed written comments. The editors of this volume, Andrei Marmor and Scott Soames, very generously made extensive comments that greatly improved the chapter. I want to acknowledge the superb research assistance of Shannon Foreman and of Amy Atchison and others at the UCLA Law Library. Finally, I thank UCLA for support from a summer research stipend.
[2] I elaborate on the notion of communicative content toward the end of section 2.

communication, the communication theorists conclude that a statute's contribution to the content of the law is its communicative content.[3]

Recognizing that a statute's contribution to the content of the law is its communicative content will, communication theorists believe, solve or eliminate many problems that bedevil legal interpreters. As Stephen Neale puts it:[4]

a great deal of time and ink have been wasted in legal theory... on debates that are, at bottom, either fruitless or incoherent. The good news is that the confusions and conflations that have given rise to spurious debates or produced the illusion of intelligible arguments are readily dispelled by doing some patient philosophy of language.

For example, philosophy of language will for the most part dissolve the long-running debate between textualists and intentionalists about statutory and constitutional interpretation.[5] Similarly, philosophy of language will reveal that the law is more determinate—there are fewer cases in which there is no applicable legal standard—than it is often thought to be.[6] Moreover, these happy results can be reached without moral argument, since they are straightforward deliverances of the study of language. In fact, the main theses seem to be regarded by their advocates as obvious or even trivial in the light of developments in philosophy of language.

I often hear the communication theory offered in conversation, especially by philosophers of language, and it has recently been advocated in print by Larry Alexander (1995), Larry Alexander and Saikrishna Prakash (2004), Cheryl Boudreau et al (2007), Paul Campos (1992, 1993a, 1993b), Stanley Fish (2005, 2008), Steven Knapp and Walter Benn Michaels (1982, 1983, 2005), Andrei Marmor (2008, 2011), Stephen Neale (2009), and Scott

---

[3] The enactment of a given statute would make it the case, other things being equal, that certain legal obligations (powers, privileges, and so on) obtain. Roughly, the statute's *contribution to the content of the law* consists of these legal obligations. I define the term more carefully at the beginning of section 2. The communication theorists focus on statutes, which, apart from administrative regulations, are the most promising case for them, and I will follow this focus here for convenience. My main arguments apply with the same force, however, with respect to other authoritative legal texts, such as constitutions, regulations, and appellate decisions. In my 2011, section III.1, I sketch reasons why appellate decisions are especially unpromising for any theory according to which a law-making act's contribution to the content of the law is the meaning of its text.

[4] (2009) at pp 3–4. For similar claims, see, eg Alexander (1995), Campos (1993) and Soames (2009a).

[5] Neale (2009) at p 4, Fish (2005) at pp 645–6. For similar claims, see, eg Alexander and Prakash (2004), Boudreau et al (2007) and Knapp and Michaels (2005).

[6] Soames (2009b) at p 404. Some communication theorists would not make this claim, recognizing that communicative content may well be less determinate—and more difficult to ascertain—than other candidates for a statute's contribution to the content of the law. See, eg Alexander (1995).

Soames (2009a).[7] Of course, other positions include some but not all of the theses of the communication theory.[8]

There is something very appealing about the communication theory. If one relies on analogies between legislation and personal communication, especially commands, it may seem obvious that the goal of statutory interpretation is to figure out what the legislature communicated. The communication theory draws on up-to-date philosophy of language to show us how to understand what the legislature communicated.

But the communication theory moves from an understanding of what the legislature communicated to a thesis about a statute's contribution to the content of the law. The content of the law consists of the legal obligations (powers, privileges, and the like) that obtain in a legal system at a given time. So a thesis about a statute's contribution to the law is a thesis about legal obligations. A move from a text's *meaning* to the existence of certain legal *obligations* requires argument. It is uncontroversial that, on any plausible view, the meaning of a statute's text is highly relevant to the statute's contribution to the content of the law. But it is highly controversial what role the meaning of the text plays in explaining a statute's contribution to the content of the law.

On my view, which I do not argue for directly in this chapter,[9] enacting a statute is a way of changing our obligations, rather than a way of communicating them, and moral or other normative considerations determine what difference to our obligations the enactment of a statute makes. To take a very simple example, there are reasons of democracy and fairness why aspects of the meaning of a statute that are not publicly available should not play a role in determining our legal obligations. Such considerations support the proposition that the content of the law does not (constitutively)

---

[7] Other writers take a similar position with a focus on constitutional interpretation. eg Lino Graglia (1992) and Richard Kay (1988, 1989). The communication theorists fall into two groups—those working in or strongly influenced by contemporary philosophy of language and linguistics, and those defending similar positions without that influence. (Of the writers cited in the text, Marmor, Neale, and Soames are in the first group; their predecessors include Sinclair (1985) and Miller (1990).) Both groups think that their shared position about the meaning of texts and utterances follows from obvious facts about the nature of language and communication. My arguments apply to both groups' positions, but I will for the most part focus on the work of the first group because of its use of philosophy of language. For an important difference in the way in which the two groups frame their main arguments, see note 22.

[8] Larry Solum (2008) shares the methodological theses of the communication theory, but, in his view, what philosophy of language reveals is that, with certain qualifications, the content of the law is what the semantic content of the relevant texts would reasonably be taken to be. On this 'public meaning' notion, see note 48 and accompanying text. Solum's discussion is limited to constitutional law, but his reasoning applies to statutes and regulations.

[9] See Greenberg (2004, 2006, 2011, forthcoming). I sketch the view briefly in section 3.

depend on the intentions of legislators to the extent that they are not publicly available.[10]

On this kind of view, philosophy of language is far from irrelevant. It can, among other things, help us to an improved understanding of some of the likely candidates for determinants of the content of the law. Without such an understanding, we cannot work out what relevance to the content of the law such candidates have.

Elsewhere, I argue for my positive view and raise problems for the thesis that the meaning of a statute constitutes its contribution to the content of the law.[11] In this chapter, however, I pursue a different, more concessive argumentative strategy. I grant many of the assumptions of the communication theorists and then argue that there are many candidates for a statute's contribution to the content of the law, including different linguistic and mental contents. For example, we have what the legislature said, what it communicated, what it meant, the 'public meaning' of the statutory text,[12] and in what way the legislature intended to modify the content of the law.[13] And there are many finer distinctions. We can distinguish content the legislature intended to communicate, content the audience reasonably would have taken the legislature to have intended, content the legislature reasonably could have expected the audience to recognize that the legislature intended to communicate, etc. Differently, we can distinguish content the legislature intended to communicate but intended not to affect the content of the law, content the legislature implicated but avoided stating in order to avoid political responsibility, and so on.

The study of language can be important in helping us to make and clarify such distinctions, but beyond this information-providing role, it has nothing to say about which, if any, of these candidates constitutes a statute's contribution to the law. The communication theory therefore lacks the resources to say what any statute's contribution is.[14]

---

[10] I discuss other examples in sections 3 and 6. Dependence should be understood throughout as constitutive dependence, unless I specify otherwise.

[11] See citations in note 9.

[12] See note 48 and accompanying text.

[13] On such intentions, see section 5.

[14] Earlier incarnations of the communication theory have been powerfully attacked on a combination of related grounds concerning the nature, existence, and ascertainment of the relevant intentions of the legislature—most importantly that it is highly problematic what constitutes the relevant collective intentions. See especially Dworkin (1985) and Moore (1981). For recent discussions, see Waldron (1995) and Solum (2008). Hurd (1990) makes an impressive case that legislation does not satisfy the conditions for Gricean communication. Those attacks are compelling, and I will not repeat them. My challenge to the communication theory is, in a way, more fundamental than the earlier attacks because I argue that the theory fails even if we assume that the relevant legislative intentions are unproblematic and grant the communication theory's claims about language. It is worth noting that these claims about language are controversial within philosophy of language and linguistics.

I will defend several main theses:

- Granting the communication theorists' main conclusions from philosophy of language, it is far from obvious that the contribution to the law of a statute must be its communicative content, or indeed any ordinary linguistic or mental content associated with the statute.

- There are candidates for a statute's contribution to the content of the law other than communicative content, such as the content of the legislature's legal intentions.

- Beyond clarifying the nature of such candidates, the considerations offered by the communication theorists—and linguistic considerations generally—do not help to support one candidate for a statute's contribution to the content of the law over others.

- There are different aspects or components of communicative content that plausibly are differently situated with respect to whether they form part of a statute's contribution to the content of the law.

- Beyond clarifying the nature of the different aspects of communicative content, the considerations offered by the communication theorists—and linguistic considerations generally—do not help to explain the relevance of different aspects of communicative content to a statute's contribution to the content of the law.

- There are different legitimate notions or types of communicative content. Different notions are more fruitful for different theoretical purposes.

- The considerations offered by the communication theorists—and linguistic considerations generally—do not explain why one notion of communicative content rather than another is the appropriate one in the legislative context.

- Trying to understand legislation on the model of communication is misguided because legislation and legislative systems have purposes that have no parallel in the case of communication and that may be better served if a statute's contribution to the content of the law is not constituted by what is communicated by the legislature.

2. Motivating the communication theory

In this section, I clarify the motivation for, and the appeal of, the communication theory.

Let me start with a note about terminology. The communication theorists sometimes write of, for example, what a statute 'says', 'states', or 'asserts', or of a statute's 'content' or 'legal content'. Such terms are ambiguous between, on the one hand, aspects of the linguistic meaning of the statutory text and, on the other hand, the relevant difference that the statute makes to legal obligations, powers, and the like. Because the communication theory draws a conclusion about the latter from the former, it will be important to have terminology that is unambiguous. Otherwise, one can easily slide from, for example, 'what the legislature says'—a linguistic content—to 'what the law says'—legal obligations. For aspects of the meaning of a statutory text or utterance, we can use the same terms as for other kinds of texts, eg *semantic content, conversational implicature*. For the (relevant) difference that the enactment of a statute or other law-making action makes to legal obligations, I will use the term *contribution to the content of the law—contribution*, for short.

Which difference is the relevant one? On standard views, the enactment of particular statutory language would make it the case, other things being equal, that certain legal obligations (powers, privileges, and so on) obtain (or do not obtain). That is, it would do so constitutively, not by causally influencing further events. The 'other things being equal' qualification is needed because other factors, such as another statute, may interfere, defeating or modifying the statute's contribution.[15] The intuitive idea is that the legal obligations that would obtain in virtue of the statute's enactment are the statute's contribution. A little more precisely: for a law-making action, such as the enactment of a statute, to be successful qua law-making action is for it to make the case that certain legal obligations obtain. The enactment of a statute may also incidentally bring about other changes in the law, for example by persuading someone to bring a court action that changes the law. But a statute's causing such changes is neither necessary nor sufficient for it to be a successful law-making action. A statute's contribution is the effect on legal obligations that would constitute it as a successful law-making action.[16]

With this terminology, we can spell out the appeal of the communication theory. It is obvious that the meaning of statutory and other authoritative legal texts is intimately connected to the contribution that they make to the

---

[15] For example, the communication theory has to allow that a statute's communicative content may be inconsistent with the communicative content of an authoritative legal text that has priority over the statute. The communication theory requires an account of how the contributions of different authoritative texts are to be reconciled and amalgamated. See my 2011, section 3. For convenience, I will generally omit the 'other things being equal' qualification, but it should be understood throughout. Also, for simplicity, I will hereafter ignore the fact that statutes may change the law in ways other than by creating obligations, including by eliminating obligations.

[16] The notion of a statute's contribution could be developed more fully. And the 'other things being equal' qualification may present difficulties. But we need not do more because the notion is needed in order to formulate the communication theory. Its central thesis concerns a statute's contribution. By contrast, Dworkin's position and my own do not require such a notion because they are holistic in the sense explicated in my 2011 at pp 49–51, 59–60.

content of the law. Lawyers and judges spend a lot of time interpreting such texts. And there is often an obvious correlation between what is legally required and what authoritative legal texts say. So it is natural to assimilate the meaning of the text to what the law requires.

Moreover, despite famous attacks on a command model of law, it is natural and common to think of the law on the model of personal commands.[17] The command model vindicates and gives specific form to the idea that linguistic meaning is closely related to what is required. For it is plausible to think that what a command requires one to do is what the commander said or meant or communicated.

I have argued elsewhere that there is a picture of the relation between authoritative legal texts and the content of the law that is widely taken for granted. This *Standard Picture—SP*, for short—derives from the command model of law, while dispensing with certain aspects of that model that are obviously out of place in a contemporary legal system. In particular, SP retains from the command model the idea, very roughly, that what is authoritatively pronounced becomes a legal norm *simply because it was authoritatively pronounced*. In another paper (2011), I explicate in detail the intuitive idea. The main point, for our purposes, is that, according to SP, a legally authoritative utterance explains the validity of a legal norm *without explanatory intermediaries*—that is, not by explaining something else, which then explains the norm's legal validity.[18] For example, it is not that the making of the pronouncement changes people's expectations or moral obligations in a way that creates a legal obligation to act in the way that the pronouncement specifies. Crucially, the content of the legal norm that is explained by the authoritative pronouncement is simply what was pronounced. Thus, on SP, a statute's contribution (other things being equal) is the ordinary linguistic content of the statutory text or utterance.

The communication theorists typically proceed as if SP needs no defense, perhaps on the ground that it is obvious or trivial. Soames[19] begins his discussion by asserting: 'Progress can...be made on [the question of how the content of the law is related to authoritative legal sources] by seeing it as an instance of a more general question of what determines the contents of ordinary linguistic texts.' From that point on, he assumes that the content of the law is 'the linguistically-based content of the relevant legal texts—including

---

[17] Analogies to commands are ubiquitous in the statutory interpretation literature. See, eg Posner (1993), p 265, and Manning (2001).

[18] The idea is more fully explicated in my 2011 at pp 44–47. As I explain there, the thesis is consistent with the proposition that the making of an authoritative pronouncement is not sufficient for the corresponding norm's being legally valid. See also note 30 and accompanying text.

[19] (2009b) at p 403.

everything asserted and conveyed therein'.[20] Similarly, Alexander and Prakash (2004), Boudreau et al (2007), and Fish (2005) simply take for granted that the content of the law is the meaning of the authoritative legal texts.

It is easy to see how SP leads to the communication theory. According to SP, the content of the law is the meaning of the relevant legal texts or utterances. If we want to know how to work out the meaning or content of a text or utterance, we should look to our best theories about language and communication. So, the first point is that, given SP, it seems uncontroversial that philosophy of language can be straightforwardly called upon to tell us how to determine the content of the law.

Next, with qualifications not relevant here, it is uncontroversial in contemporary philosophy of language and linguistics that the linguistic content of a text or utterance does not depend on moral facts.[21] I believe that this position is correct, and I will assume it throughout.

Given SP and the fact that linguistic content does not depend on moral facts, we can see why the communication theorists think that the content of the law does not depend on moral facts: if the content of the law consists of certain ordinary contents, and those ordinary contents are determined entirely without appeal to moral facts, then, it may seem, the content of the law is determined without appeal to moral facts.

The main point lies in what we find when we turn to contemporary philosophy of language and linguistics.[22] In order to understand the point, we

---

[20] Soames (2009b) at p 403, *passim*.

[21] On some views, the meaning of, say, a botanical term may depend in part on the botanical facts. In the same kind of way, the meaning of moral terms may depend in part on moral reality. This kind of dependence is not relevant to the argument. Thanks to Seana Shiffrin for pressing the need for this qualification. There is also a well-known view according to which the 'principle of charity' is partly constitutive of meaning and mental content. According to one version of this kind of view, suggested by the work of Donald Davidson, charity involves maximizing the extent to which the subject prefers the good, as well as the extent to which the subject believes the truth. Even if meaning depends on facts about value in the way that such a view maintains, the kind of global dependence at issue would not affect the present argument. Throughout the paper, I set aside both qualifications mentioned in this footnote.

In addition, the point in the text about moral facts applies also to other facts. There are difficult and interesting issues about whether mental or linguistic content depends on normative facts other than moral (or other practical normative) facts, such as epistemic or intellectual normative facts. I am concerned here with practical normativity, such as moral or legal normativity, only. In this chapter, the points I make about morality typically apply to practical normativity generally.

[22] As noted above, the communication theorists' claims about language are controversial within philosophy of language. The account outlined in the text applies to the first group of communication theorists mentioned in note 7 above. Members of the second group reason in essentially the same way, except that—because they do not recognize the existence of other aspects of linguistic meaning, such as semantic content—they take the simpler position that the meaning of any text is what its author intended to communicate: eg Alexander and Prakash (2004), Fish (2005), and Knapp and Michaels (2005).

need a distinction between two fundamental kinds of linguistic meaning. First, there is semantic content—roughly speaking, that aspect of linguistic content that is conventionally encoded in a text.[23] In non-technical terms, the semantic content of a sentence is approximately its literal meaning.

Second, there is pragmatically communicated content—roughly speaking, linguistic content conveyed by an utterance that goes beyond what is conventionally encoded in the linguistic expressions. For example, the semantic content of the sentence 'John drank five beers and drove home' plausibly contains no information about the order in which John performed these two deeds. In many contexts, however, a speaker may utter the sentence in order to communicate that John first drank five beers *and then* drove home. Similarly, the semantic content of the sentence 'Abigail has two children' may well be simply that Abigail has at least two children. However, in some contexts, a speaker may utter the sentence in order to communicate that Abigail has exactly two children.

Philosophy of language and linguistics have, according to the communication theorists, taught us that the full linguistic content of a text is what is communicated by its utterance, including by pragmatic means. In general, the linguistic content of a text—whether in conversation, in an instruction manual, in a formal letter, or in a statute or judicial opinion—may go beyond its semantic content. Even what is said or asserted, let alone what is implicated, may go well beyond semantic content and, on some views, may not even include semantic content. Semantic content is merely a tool that we use to convey and ascertain communicative content.

The communication theorists conclude that an authoritative legal text's contribution is the content that is communicated by the enactment of the text. The communication theorists take this conclusion to be obvious in the light of basic facts about how language works.[24]

The imprimatur of philosophy of language and linguistics is an additional source of appeal for the communication theory (beyond the appeal of SP generally). The theory purports to offer a hygienic and scientific way of resolving messy debates that have long persisted in legal theory. An important part of this appeal is the way in which philosophy of language seems to show

---

[23] There are at least two levels of semantic content, but we can ignore the distinction for present purposes. Also, there are competing accounts of the nature of semantic content, but the differences will not matter for our purposes. For recent discussion of how to draw the semantics/pragmatics distinction, see the papers in Szabo (2005).

[24] eg Soames (2009b) at p 16, says: 'Thus, to interpret the law one must consult not just linguistic meaning, but also communicative intent. This point, though obvious from a correct understanding of the relationship between meaning and assertion, has proven too difficult for some of our highest courts.'

that the content of the law does not depend on moral facts, thus making it unnecessary to engage in moral reasoning to ascertain the law. A theory that excludes moral reasoning from the ascertainment of legal obligations has the advantage of avoiding a source of complexity and controversy. In addition, there is a familiar political reason for wanting to keep morality out—a role for moral reasoning is often thought to allow judges to substitute their own views for those of the legislature. Finally, legal positivist sympathies are common and grounded in an intuitive idea of the law.

The appeal of the communication theory, and in particular the way in which it draws plausibility from analogies with personal communication, can be usefully demonstrated with an example. In the notorious *Smith v United States*,[25] the central issue concerns the interpretation of a federal statute that provides an additional penalty for a defendant who 'uses or carries a firearm' 'during and in relation to' a drug trafficking crime. Several judges struggled with the question whether the meaning of 'uses a firearm' encompasses trading a firearm for drugs. The problem, the communication theorists believe, is that the judges were focused on the meaning of the statutory language—that is, on semantic content—rather than on what Congress meant or intended to communicate. If, in a typical morning exchange, my wife asks me 'Have you had breakfast?', it would be silly to waste effort parsing the semantic content, which arguably concerns whether I have *ever* had breakfast. Rather, I would take her to be asking whether I have had breakfast *today* because that is what she intends. Similarly, the judges in *Smith* should not have wasted time on the semantic content of the text, which is plausibly silent with respect to how the weapon is used. If Congress intended to communicate that only uses of firearms as weapons were to receive an increased penalty, then that is the statute's contribution.[26] Given the commonsense appeal of this line of reasoning, as well as its backing in philosophy of language, one can see how the communication theorists have been led to take it as a general prescription for statutory interpretation.

3. Refining the communication theory

In order to get clearer about the communication theory's claims, it will be helpful to distinguish it carefully from four other superficially similar positions.

First, the communication theory's claim about a statute's *contribution* must be distinguished from the thesis that the *meaning* or linguistic content of a

---

[25] 508 US 223 (1993).   [26] See Soames (2009b) at pp 412–15.

statute is its communicative content. If the communication theory took a position merely on what a statute's meaning is, it would yield no conclusions about the content of the law—nor, therefore, about the correct resolution of any legal cases. In fact, the communication theorists regularly draw conclusions about statutes' contribution to the law. They make general claims about the way in which statutes contribute to the law, claims about the resolution of debates in legal theory that turn on the way in which statutes contribute to the law, and claims about the resolution of specific cases.[27]

Second, the communication theory's claim about a statute's contribution must be distinguished from the claim that the meaning—or, in particular, the communicative content—of a statute is *highly relevant* to its contribution. As I have emphasized, on any plausible view, the meaning of a statutory text is highly relevant to the statute's contribution.

To get clearer about the communication theorists' claim about the role of the meaning of statutory language in explaining a statute's contribution, it will be useful to compare the communication theory with alternative views on this issue. Consider Ronald Dworkin's (1986) position: the content of the law is the set of principles that best justify the past legal and political decisions or practices. On this position, a statute's contribution to the law is, other things being equal, the set of principles that would justify the enactment of the statute alone. That set of principles is not the meaning of the statutory text or utterance, nor the content of any mental state of the legislature, and need not coincide with any such meaning or content. Indeed, on the Dworkinian picture, a statute is not best thought of as carrying a particular meaning or content that its enactment adds, other things being equal, to the overall content of the law. Rather, a statute's enactment changes the law by changing the set of past legal and political decisions—the data—thereby changing which set of principles best justifies the data. The content of legal texts or utterances is just one aspect of the data among others.[28]

To take a very different example, on Scott Shapiro's (2010) planning theory of law, a statute's enactment creates or modifies a plan, and the statute's contribution is the content of the plan. That content, however, is not constituted

---

[27] I offer one qualification with respect to Neale (2009). Near the beginning of his rich paper, he says that what a statute states 'leaves wide open the question of the contribution it makes to the law', and avows that the latter question goes 'well beyond the philosophy of language': (2009) at p 5. Except for the official disclaimer just quoted, however, Neale seems to assume throughout that what a statute states is its contribution to the law. Indeed, if a statute's linguistic content left 'wide open' its contribution to the law, and the nature of that contribution could not be answered by philosophy of language, Neale's paper could not do what it purports to do. For example, his paper claims, on exclusively linguistic grounds, to dissolve the debate between textualists and intentionalists. But that debate concerns a statute's contribution.

[28] For clarification and elaboration of this understanding of Dworkin, see my 2011, section II.2.

by the meaning of any text or utterance or the content of any mental state. The meaning of the statutory text is of course a relevant factor, but the content of the plan depends in important ways on the goals of the legal system.

My view, very roughly, is that a statute's contribution to the law, other things being equal, is the general and enduring effect on our moral obligations that the enactment of the statute brings about in certain characteristic ways.[29] On this *Dependence View—DV*, for short—the contribution of statutes to our legal obligations is, with important qualifications, determined by moral considerations, such as considerations of democracy and fairness. The meaning or content of a statutory text is merely one factor that may be relevant to the statute's contribution, and what relevance, if any, a particular factor has depends on what relevance moral considerations give it.

In general, enacting a statute changes our obligations by changing the morally relevant circumstances. More concretely, enacting a statute could create an obligation by making a particular solution to a coordination problem salient, by making it more likely that others will comply with a particular scheme, by making it the case that democratic considerations support the obligation, by getting officials to take actions that generate the obligation, or in diverse other ways. Some of these ways of changing our obligations rely on communication, and others do not. When they do rely on communication, what is communicated need not be the statute's contribution. For example, in the case of a coordination problem, the fact that the legislature voted for a particular bill can make a particular solution salient without the legislature intending to communicate that solution and without the audience recognizing such an intention. The legislature may even have intended to communicate a different solution. Members of the audience may have a 'public-meaning' theory of statutory interpretation; they may misrecognize what the legislature intended to communicate, and so on.

On the three positions just sketched, the meaning or content of a statutory text is relevant to the statute's contribution, but there are important differences between the role of meaning on such positions and the role of meaning on the communication theory. I believe that the most important difference is best understood in terms of the notion of explanatory directness introduced in the previous section. On the communication theory, the legally authoritative utterance of a text with a certain communicative content explains the obtaining of a legal norm with corresponding content *without explanatory*

---

[29] See my 2011, forthcoming, and also 2004, 2006. In order to understand this view, it is important to see that our moral obligations may include obligations that are not imposed by *ex ante* moral norms. For example, participation in a morally flawed scheme can become morally required if many others are participating or are likely to do so.

intermediaries.[30] By contrast, on the three positions just sketched, this proposition is not true. For example, on Dworkin's theory, the meaning of a statutory text will be importantly relevant to the statute's contribution. But the explanation runs through considerations of justice: the enactment of the statute—with its various features, including the meaning of its text—adds to the existing legal practices, thereby affecting which set of principles best justifies the practices. For convenience, I often express the distinction by saying that, on the communication theory, a statute's contribution is *constituted* by its communicative content (or *is* its communicative content, or the like), while on the contrasting views, a statute's contribution is not so constituted.[31]

Another difference between the communication theory and the three contrasting positions is that the communication theorists seem to hold that a statute's contribution (other things being equal) is fully constituted by its communicative content, though they of course accept that a statute's all-things-considered contribution may depend on factors other than its communicative content. On the contrasting positions, even a statute's other-things-being-equal contribution may depend on factors other than the meaning of the statutory text.[32]

We now come to the *third* of the types of positions from which the communication theory must be distinguished—positions that rest on normative considerations, such as considerations of democracy and fairness. In defending different positions on a statute's contribution, judges and other legal interpreters commonly appeal to political morality. For example, Justice Scalia and other textualists appeal to democratic and rule-of-law values to support textualism over intentionalism.[33]

There are familiar normative considerations that might be thought to support the communication theory's thesis about a statute's contribution. For

[30] For much fuller development of the notion of explanatory directness, see my 2011. As I emphasize there, the absence of explanatory intermediaries is consistent with (1) the existence of an explanation of what makes an utterance authoritative and (2) the possibility that the making of an authoritative pronouncement is not sufficient for the corresponding legal norm's obtaining.

[31] Someone might take issue with this characterization along the following lines. On Dworkin's view, a statute's contribution is constituted by the set of principles that best justifies the statute's enactment. Because the best justification of a statute's enactment depends constitutively on the meaning of the statutory text (among other things), Dworkin's view has the consequence, the argument continues, that a statute's contribution *is* partially constituted by the meaning of the statutory text. I think that this way of talking would be misleading, but 'constitute' and its cognates are used variously and sometimes loosely in philosophical writing. I stipulate the usage in the text as an abbreviation for the point about explanatory directness. In my 2005, I discuss the loss of explanatory power that can result from collapsing levels of constitutive explanation.

[32] On the notion of a statute's other-things-being-equal contribution, see notes 15–16.

[33] See, eg Scalia (1997) at pp 17–18. For another example of a normative defense of textualism, see Manning (2006).

example, some conceptions of democracy might support the idea that the law must be what the legislature intended to communicate. Differently, there are democratic considerations that support the idea that the content of the law must be publicly available, which may seem to resonate with the notion of what is communicated, as opposed, for example, to what the legislature wanted the law to be, but failed to communicate.

Given their overall theory, however, the communication theorists cannot rely on democratic or other normative considerations to support their position on a statute's contribution, nor would they wish to appeal to such considerations. A central theme of the communication theorists is that the philosophy of language can cut through the confused debates of legal theorists and tell us what constitutes the content of the law. By contrast, on a normative approach, normative considerations determine the relevance of different candidate contents (and other factors) to the content of the law. Philosophy of language helps to clarify what the candidates are. A normative approach thus gives philosophy of language a very different role from the dominant role that the communication theory assigns to it.

A closely related point is that the communication theorists take their position to rest exclusively on linguistic grounds. They also take it to be obviously true once one recognizes that the goal of linguistic interpretation is to discover the communicative content of the target text. It is difficult to see how the communication theory could be obviously true if it rested on considerations of political morality, given how thoroughly controversial political morality is.

More fundamentally, although some normative considerations may cut in favour of the thesis that a statute's contribution is its communicative content, it would be, to say the least, a daunting and obstacle-ridden project to defend the thesis on normative grounds. In order to do so, communication theorists would have to engage in a full-blown normative argument about what constitutes the content of the law—a debate they have not even entered.

So, an approach that appeals to moral argument to support a particular candidate for a statute's contribution would lack the features of the communication theory that give it its distinctive appeal. The approach could not claim its candidate was obvious in the light of up-to-date science. Rather, it would have an uphill struggle to defend a moral thesis that is, on its face, unpromising. Philosophy of language would take a back seat to moral argument.

Fourth, and finally, we need to get clear about the notion of communicative content deployed by the communication theory. There are different notions of communicative content. One notion of communicative content— the *neo-Gricean* one, as I will call it—derives from the seminal work of Paul Grice. According to the neo-Gricean notion, the communicative content of an utterance is the content of a certain kind of complex intention. Roughly speaking, for a speaker's utterance of a sentence to have the communicative content that P is for the speaker to utter the sentence intending his or her hearers to come to recognize that the speaker is communicating P, in part by their recognition of this very intention.[34] Following a relatively common terminology, I will sometimes call such intentions *communicative intentions*. The point I want to highlight is that, on the neo-Gricean notion, communicative content is constituted by the content of the speaker's communicative intentions.

By contrast, according to what I will call an *objective* notion of communicative content, the communicative content of an utterance is what a member of the audience would reasonably take a speaker who had uttered the relevant sentence under specified conditions to have intended to communicate—in other words, what the neo-Gricean communicative content would reasonably be taken to be. This notion is really a family of related notions that differ with respect to, for example, how the relevant member of the audience is understood, whether the speaker is idealized, and so on.[35] (I use the term *objective* because, on such notions, what is communicated by a given utterance does not depend constitutively on the speaker's—or anyone's—actual mental state.) Approaches that impute communicative intentions to speakers (that they do not in fact have) can be understood as attributing objective communicative content.

There are also hybrid notions. For example, according to one notion, the communicative content of an utterance is that part of what the speaker intended to communicate for which uptake by the audience could reasonably be expected. Again, one could understand what is communicated as that part of what the speaker intended to communicate that the audience in fact recognizes.

Some of the communication theorists leave no doubt that they understand communicative content to be constituted by the legislature's communicative

---

[34] Grice himself analyzed what a speaker *means* in terms of the speaker's communicative intentions: (1989) at pp 92–116, 219–21. Some have pointed out that such an analysis may provide a better account of what a speaker communicates than what a speaker means. eg Davis (2003) at chs 2–5. The term 'communicative content' avoids the issue.

Terms such as 'means', 'says', 'states', and 'communicates' are used in various ways in ordinary English. There is obviously something stipulative about calling the content of the speaker's communicative intentions 'what is communicated'. Among other things, we ordinarily do not consider information to have been communicated unless successful uptake occurs. See the discussion of objective notions of communicative content in the text immediately below and in my unpublished paper 'The Communication Theory of Legal Interpretation and Objective Notions of Communicative Content' (hereafter referred to as MS).

[35] cf Saul (2002), Davis (1998) and Gazdar (1979).

intentions.[36] In the case of other communication theorists, the evidence is more equivocal, though the neo-Gricean position is on balance probably the better interpretation of all the theorists.[37] Fortunately, we need not engage in extensive exegetical discussion.

First, although I will assume the neo-Gricean understanding of communicative content for concreteness, my main arguments (sections 4–6) apply, *mutatis mutandis*, to versions of the communication theory that employ an objective or hybrid notion of communicative content. (Indeed, the arguments apply to any approach that attempts to ground claims about authoritative legal texts' contribution to the content of the law on exclusively linguistic considerations.) My arguments do not depend on which notion of communicative content is in play because my basic strategy is to show that the communication theory, relying as it does on linguistic considerations, lacks the resources to favor one content over others as a candidate for the content of the law.[38]

Second, to the extent that the communication theory adopts an objective notion of communicative content, the particular choice of objective notion will have to be defended on normative grounds. As we just saw, however, an appeal to normative grounds gives up the distinctive features of the communication theory. I argue elsewhere that there are many different possible objective notions; which one is relevant for legal purposes depends on normative considerations.[39] In brief, once we are not ascertaining the speaker's actual communicative intentions, but imputing communicative content, which content is to be imputed depends in part on what assumptions we make about the speaker. For example, is the question what the legislature is reasonably taken to have intended to communicate, given what we know about the actual way in which legislatures operate? Or is the question what a single speaker who uttered the statutory text in some specified context would reasonably be taken to have intended? To take another example, as I elaborate in section 5, the Gricean conversational maxims provide a natural way of constructing objective communicative content to the extent that the speaker may

---

[36] eg Alexander (2004) especially at pp 994–5 and Neale (2009) and see also (1992). The theorists in the group not working in the philosophy of language tradition are extremely clear that they take the relevant content to be the content of the legislature's intentions, but they are not always clear about the distinction between communicative intentions and other intentions.

[37] Boudreau et al (2007) hold that the relevant content is the content of the legislature's communicative intentions, but also suggest that the intentions are 'as-if' or imputed, rather than actual, intentions.

[38] The exception is my use of examples of unpalatable contents in section 4. Different examples of unpalatable contents can be found for objective notions of communicative content.

[39] I argue this point more fully in MS. See also section 6.

be presumed to be complying with the principles. In the legislative context, however, which principles have a parallel role plausibly depends on political morality or the goals of the legal system. Philosophy of language and Gricean theory have nothing to say about what we should *deem* to be the content of the legislature's intentions—nor about looking to contents that, because of the goals of the legal system or because of political morality, are deemed to be what the legislature intended.

To save words, I will generally drop the 'neo-Gricean' qualification and use simply 'communicative content' for the neo-Gricean notion and 'communication theory' for the position that the neo-Gricean notion yields. I want to emphasize this terminological point because I have found that legal audiences tend to assume something like the objective notion of communicative content and are then surprised and puzzled to learn that the communication theorists would think that the communicative content of an utterance, especially of a statute, depends on the content of the speaker's communicative intentions.

4. Raising doubts about the communication theory

In this section, I will use two kinds of examples to raise doubts about the idea that a statute's contribution is its communicative content. Examples of the first kind show that, in general, the relevant contribution of a legally effective action may be different from its communicative content. Examples of the second sort illustrate some unattractive and counterintuitive consequences of the communication theory. The point of this section is not to refute the communication theory by counterexample; rather, the examples are meant to be suggestive, raising doubts about the underlying assumptions of the communication theory. The main burden of argument is carried by sections 5 and 6.

Anyone who thinks it is obvious that a statute's contribution is its communicative content should consider actions, such as voting for a candidate for public office and entering a verdict, that are not law-making actions but have as their primary goal the changing of legal statuses. A bit of terminology will be helpful. Just as the success condition of the enactment of a statute is its contribution to the content of the law, the success condition of the casting of votes by the electorate is a candidate's election to office. The term 'contribution to the content of the law' is inapt for the election of a candidate, however. We can use the term 'legal impact' as a more general term to encompass both a law-making action's contribution and the change in legal status effected by non-law-making actions.

Consider swearing to uphold the Constitution, announcing 'we, the jury, find the defendant not guilty on all counts', signing consent forms, and uttering marriage vows. In all these cases, the primary purpose of the speech act is to effect a change in legal status, and the utterances often have communicative content. But the legal impact of such an action standardly does not include its total communicative content, and may even be inconsistent with its communicative content.[40]

In the right context, one might intend to communicate any of a wide variety of messages by the above utterances—and, for that matter, might succeed in one's intention. Brides and grooms who use the traditional formulation 'for as long as we both shall live' may standardly mean and communicate that each one takes the other person as his or her spouse until one of them dies. That the wording is a conventional formula need not prevent the bride and groom from intending to communicate its literal content. But, of course, the legal impact in most jurisdictions is nevertheless that the couple is married only until annulment, divorce, or death, whichever comes first.

Similarly, a jury, in entering a verdict, may communicate messages that differ from the legal impact of the verdict. Consider, for example, a tort verdict that awards one dollar to the plaintiff or a criminal verdict that convicts a defendant charged with extremely serious crimes only of a trivial included offense. Signs and forms that state that one waives legal rights often communicate messages that are not the legal impact of the utterance.

The case of voting is especially relevant to legislation because legislating (in contemporary multimember legislative bodies) is simply a special case of voting. Voters often intentionally communicate messages by casting their votes for particular candidates.[41] Such communicative voting is perhaps especially common in elections that are not by secret ballot, such as in meetings of small organizations. Even in secret-ballot elections, people communicate messages by their votes. In the 2000 presidential election, many people successfully communicated how they felt about the two main parties—for example, that those parties were not worthy of governing—by voting instead for Ralph Nader. When voting on substantive proposals as well as on the election of candidates for office, people often cast votes intending to communicate messages only tangentially related to the issue officially being voted on. Philosophy department members might vote against a particular proposal to change the

---

[40] Speech act theory has sometimes distinguished such speech acts from communicative ones. See, eg Bach and Harnish (1979) at pp 108–25; (1992) at pp 105–6; and see also Searle (1976) (maintaining that a 'declaration' (Searle's term) does not express a psychological attitude and brings about the relevant change in status solely in virtue of the fact that the speech act has successfully been performed).

[41] Such intentions may satisfy standard conditions on communicative intentions. For example, a voter may intend that members of the audience come to understand what the voter is communicating by virtue of their recognizing this very intention.

curriculum, communicating by that vote that, say, the department should not bend to pressure from a powerful member. Of course, whether one can successfully communicate a particular message by a vote depends on the circumstances.

In standard electoral systems, the legal impact of a vote for a candidate—the way in which it counts toward the legal outcome of the election—is specified by the electoral system in a way that is entirely (constitutively) independent of the *communicative* intentions of the voter, and, for that matter, of what those intentions would reasonably be taken to be. Indeed, no communicative intention is needed in order for one's action to count as a valid vote. The legal impact of a vote for Ralph Nader did not depend on its communicative content.

As we are interested in the enactment of legislation by a legislature, the appropriate analogue is not the vote of an individual voter, but the election of a candidate by the electorate. I therefore want to develop an example in which the majority of the electorate votes for a particular candidate with a specified communicative intention. Suppose that a third-party candidate for a US state governorship is closely associated with a single issue—the legalization of marijuana, say. The candidate is widely assumed to have no chance of winning the election. Those who vote for the candidate intend, by casting that vote, to communicate that marijuana should be legalized. Those who vote for the candidate do not intend that the candidate become governor—they do not think that is possible, and they do not want him to be governor. Further, these facts are known to nearly everyone in the state.

In addition, as in many states, voters in the state have the power to enact legislation by direct ballot. (Also, to keep the example clean, let us ignore the relevance of federal law here and assume that the state has the power to legalize marijuana.)

To everyone's surprise, the third-party candidate receives an overwhelming majority of the votes. Because most or all of the voters in the majority have the communicative intention to communicate that marijuana should be legalized, the electorate has that intention (on any account of group intentions that would give the communication theorists what they need). Presumably, no one would maintain that the election has the legal impact of legalizing marijuana: the legal impact of the election is to elect the candidate to the governorship, despite the electorate's communicative intention.

Notice that the fact that the legal impact of the electorate's vote can only be to elect a candidate to the governorship does not prevent the vote from being successfully used to make a statement, assertion, or other communication whose content does not correspond to the vote's legal impact. In the example, the public successfully and reasonably recognizes that the electorate's vote is intended to communicate that marijuana should be legalized.

One might object that the intention to communicate that marijuana should be legalized is not the relevant intention. The objection cannot be that the intention to legalize marijuana is merely a motive for voting for the governor, not a communicative intention. It is stipulated that the voters, in casting votes for the third-party candidate, do not intend to elect him governor (eg in order that he can enact legislation legalizing marijuana). In fact, we can suppose that they believe that he would be such a poor governor that his election would doom the chances of enacting such legislation.

Also, it is stipulated that the voters' intentions satisfy the standard Gricean conditions on communicative intentions. For example, each voter intends that members of the audience—the public—come to understand what he or she is communicating by virtue of their recognizing that very intention. Moreover, the voters have no other intentions that satisfy those conditions. For example, they have no intention of communicating that the candidate should be governor. (An intention to cast the vote, even if required for the vote to be valid, is not a communicative intention.) In addition, the intention to communicate that marijuana should be legalized is the voters' primary aim in casting the votes.

A more interesting objection is that the legal impact of the electorate's vote is determined by the communicative content of a different legal utterance— for example, a statute that specifies the legal impact of an election. In the case of the enactment of a statute, the parallel move would be to maintain that a statute's contribution is not its communicative content because another statute, an appellate decision, or a constitution specifies otherwise. For example, an appellate decision or statute might specify that statutes are to be interpreted in accordance with their 'public meaning' rather than their communicative content.

In the first place, this position would represent a major retreat for the communication theory. It would be consistent with the possibility that no statute's contribution is its communicative content, as long as there is one authoritative text that so specifies.

More importantly, once it is conceded that a statute's contribution need not be its communicative content, it would be hard to avoid the conclusion that a source of law other than an authoritative legal text could determine a statute's contribution. For example, in a legal system in which practice is a source of law, a practice of interpreting statutes in a way that diverges from their communicative content could make it the case that statutes' contributions are not their communicative contents. For, if the contribution of statutes to the content of the law can be specified by the law, and practice is a source of law, what could be the reason that practice could not do so? Presumably, then, practice could make it the case, in a particular legal system, that a statute's contribution is, say, its 'public meaning' or the principles that best justify the statute's enactment.

At this point, we start to lose our grip on what the communication theory claims concerning a statute's contribution. Is the claim merely that it is the *default* that a statute's contribution is its communicative content? If so, why think that our own legal system is in the default position—after all, there is a great deal of case law and practice concerning the interpretation of statutes, much of it in tension with the claim that a statute's contribution is its communicative content. And, for that matter, why could a legal system not have a different default? At any rate, such a default thesis is much weaker than what the communication theorists want to defend.

It might be objected that votes for candidates for the governorship were not authoritative on the question of the legalization of marijuana.[42] But it is part of my point that the legal impact of an action can be determined in a way that is independent of its communicative content. To concede that the legal impact of a particular election can only be the election of a candidate to a certain office, regardless of the communicative intentions of the voters and regardless of what the audience reasonably takes to be communicated, is to concede this point. Once it is established that the legal impact of a vote can be determined in a way that is independent of its communicative content, communication theorists need to show that the legal impact of a vote by a legislature on proposed legislation is not so determined. Thus, an opponent of the communication theory could put her point in the terms employed by the objection: she could claim that the proper understanding of a vote by a legislature on proposed legislation is that the sole issue at stake—the sole issue on which the vote is authoritative—is whether, say, the semantic content of the bill should become law. What issue a legislature is addressing—that is, what impact its vote can have—when it votes on a bill is the very question at the center of the debate between the communication theorists and their opponents.

A different objection might begin by noting that, in my examples, the legal impact of the relevant action is uncontroversially specified by a legal standard or conventionally determined. For example, legal systems attempt to specify exhaustively the way in which votes in elections for public office count toward the outcome. Similarly, legal standards spell out the legal impact of going through the marriage ceremony. By contrast, the legal impact of legislation is highly controversial. It is true that the legal impact of legislation is more

---

[42] A closely related objection is that, in an election for a particular office, voters' intentions to communicate messages other than a preference for the chosen candidate are not authoritative. The objection is subject to a reply parallel to that developed in the text.

controversial than the legal impact of votes for candidates for public office or marriage ceremonies. The point of the examples, however, is that the legal impact of an action need not be the action's communicative content. And from the fact that the legal impact of an action is not uncontroversially determined by a legal standard or convention, it does not follow that the legal impact is the action's communicative content. There are many other possibilities. In section 3, I sketched three accounts on which the legal impact of a statute (or other authoritative legal action) is not constituted by the statute's communicative content or, indeed, by any linguistic content of the statute. One important possibility, illustrated by Dworkin's position and my own account, is that the legal impact of an action may be determined in part by normative facts, such as facts about what democracy and fairness require.

Promises provide a useful comparison. The analogue of a statute's contribution is the promise's 'normative impact'—the promissory obligations that it generates that constitute it as a successful promise. (Just as a law-making act's success consists in its generating legal obligations, a promissory act's success consists in its generating promissory obligations.) According to some influential accounts, a promise's normative impact is not the promise's communicative content nor is it conventionally specified. For example, on one account, the utterance of the promise generates expectations in the promisee. Because it would be unfair to disappoint these expectations, the promisor acquires a moral obligation. On a very different account, the making of a promise is a kind of action that effects a transfer of a right from the promisor to the promisee. For example, very roughly, on such an account, before I promise you that I will help you move house next Monday afternoon, I have the right to decide whether to help you move on Monday afternoon. By making the promise, I transfer that right to you, much as I might transfer ownership of a book to you by making it a gift to you.[43]

For present purposes, the point is that, on these accounts, the content of the promissory obligation is not constituted by the communicative content of the promissory utterance. Moreover, the promissory obligation need not have the same content as the communicative content. On the expectation account, obligations may diverge from the communicative content (in the neo-Gricean sense explained above) of the promise because, for example, what the promisee reasonably comes to expect may be quite different from the communicative content. On the transfer-of-right account, moral reasons

---

[43] For expectation accounts, see Fried (1981) and Scanlon (1999). For a transfer of right account, see Shiffrin (2008). On a third kind of account, promises generate obligations in virtue of a convention, but I will set this account aside, as I want to illustrate the possibility that the normative impact of an utterance may diverge from its communicative content for reasons other than a convention.

plausibly can make it the case that a promise has a different effect on the distribution of rights than what is communicated. On both accounts, the fact that a promise has a particular communicative content has no special status with respect to the content of the promissory obligation, but is just one possibly relevant fact among many, and its precise relevance depends on normative facts. And, on both accounts, it would be misleading to say that the promissory utterance's communicative content is even partially constitutive of the content of the promissory obligation.[44] Thus, the promissory analogy suggests that, even in cases in which no uncontroversial standard specifies the normative impact of an utterance, the utterance's communicative content may be just one factor potentially relevant to the utterance's normative impact, and its relevance may depend on normative facts.

The examples so far show that it cannot be taken for granted that the legal impact—or, more generally, the normative impact—of an action is its communicative content. I now turn to examples that illustrate unpalatable consequences of the thesis that the legal impact of a specifically legislative act is its communicative content.

In what is probably the typical case, the legislators have *no* communicative intention associated with the relevant clause of the statutory text. It is uncontroversial that most legislators do not read most of the text of the statutes on which they vote. The vast volume of legislation ensures this. Just to give a sense of the problem, in 2005–6, the most recent year for which statistics are available, Congress passed more than 7,000 pages of statutes.[45]

On any tenable account of collective intentions that would serve the communication theory's purposes, if most legislators have no communicative intentions associated with a particular passage, the legislature has no actual communicative intention with respect to that passage. In that case, the passage has no (neo-Gricean) communicative content, and, according to the communication theory, it makes no contribution.

In another kind of case, the legislature's communicative intentions are very different from what they are reasonably taken to be. One way in which this can happen is that the legislature can fail to understand the applicable rules of statutory drafting and interpretation. In section 5, I develop an example in which the legislature enacts a provision with the form 'A or B', intending to communicate a content involving an inclusive *or*, though the audience would reasonably understand the legislature to intend to convey a content with an exclusive

---

[44] See note 31 and accompanying text.

[45] Ornstein et al (2008) at p 127. The corresponding figures (from the state session laws) for a few important state legislatures: California 8,525 pages (1996); New York 3,734 pages (2008); and Texas 5,909 pages (2007).

or. The communication theory implies that the statute's contribution is determined by what the legislature intended, even if members of the audience—for example, skilled lawyers—would not generally recognize the legislature's intention, and even if the legislature would not reasonably be understood as having that intention. This implication is highly counterintuitive to skilled lawyers.[46]

Finally, in another type of case, which is probably very common, in order to perform a delicate political balancing act, the legislature enacts statutory language intending to communicate a particular message but not intending that that communicative content become part of the law. In one version of this type of example, the legislature implicates a particular content, but deliberately avoids stating it, with the intention that the implicated content not become part of the law. Suppose that in a health care bill, it is provided that 'federally funded facilities [as defined elsewhere] may provide abortions if necessary to save the mother's life'. The literal meaning of this clause leaves open whether federally funded facilities may provide abortions in other circumstances, but a speaker might well utter the words of the clause in order to implicate that abortions may be provided if, but only if, necessary to save the mother's life. The law-makers have the following combination of intentions. They intend to communicate that they are opposed to abortion and that non-life-saving abortions are not to be funded. The law-makers do *not*, however, intend that this aspect of the statute's communicative content form part of the statute's contribution. Rather, the legislators deliberately choose not to state the restriction on funding explicitly because they intend that the provision's contribution be entirely permissive—that abortions may be provided by federally funded facilities if necessary to save the mother's life. They intend the provision to leave open the possibility that non-life-saving abortions may be provided by federally funded facilities. (We can suppose that the legislature has good reason to expect that these intentions about the contribution of the statute will be fulfilled, given the way in which the relevant courts interpret legislation.)

The reason for this combination of intentions is that the law-makers want, as much as possible, to gain favour with anti-abortion voters without alienating pro-choice voters. They have made a calculation that anti-abortion voters care a lot about symbols and that the anti-abortion communication will therefore play well to them even if it is not legally effective, and that the

---

[46] It might be said, in response to such cases, that the relevant intentions are imputed or constructed intentions, rather than actual ones. As outlined in section 1, however, the communication theory cannot appeal to imputed intentions. There are different possible ways of imputing intentions, which yield different contents. The crucial question is which content constitutes the statute's contribution. To answer this question, we will have to move away from philosophy of language to normative theory. See the discussion in my MS.

pro-choice voters are more pragmatic and will therefore not be too alienated by the communication of a message that does not change the law. Again, it runs strongly against lawyers' understanding that messages that the legislature deliberately chooses to convey in a way that it believes will prevent them from becoming legally effective must nonetheless become part of the law.[47]

At this point, the purpose of the examples is merely to raise doubts about the communication theory—to show that the legal impact of an action or an utterance need not be its communicative content. This finding undermines the suggestion that it is obvious, given basic facts about language, that a statute's contribution is its communicative content.

5. Different components and notions of communicative content

In this section, I argue that there are multiple candidates for a statute's contribution, and that the communication theory lacks the resources to support one candidate over others. One candidate we have already mentioned is the semantic content of the relevant text—roughly its literal meaning. Two other candidates for a statute's contribution are familiar to legal theorists.

First, there is what a member of the audience would reasonably take the semantic content of the text to be, given only the information that is widely available. Such a notion seems to be roughly what textualists typically have in mind when they talk about 'public meaning', 'publicly available meaning', and the like, though textualists' accounts of public meaning also have elements of what a reasonable member of the audience would take *communicative* content to be.[48] I will use the term *public meaning* because it is widely used in the legal literature.

Second, there is the content of the legislature's intentions *with respect to the legal impact of the enactment—legal intentions,* for short. I will use the content

---

[47] The example illustrates, among other things, that an utterance may communicate different contents to different audiences. This point raises additional difficulties for the communication theorists because they need an account of which content communicated by the statutory text is the relevant one. (See section 5 for related discussion.)

[48] See, eg Easterbrook (1988), Scalia (1997) at p 17 and Manning (2003) at pp 2457–65; (2006) at pp 75, 101. Solum's (2008) at pp 51–4, preferred candidate also seems to be, roughly, what a reasonable member of the audience would take semantic content to be. There are different ways in which semantic content may come apart from what it is reasonably taken to be. For example, on some views, context, sometimes including certain intentions of the speaker, plays a role in determining the referential content of some context-dependent expressions. The relevant aspects of context may reasonably be taken to be different from what they actually are. A similar point applies with respect to ambiguous expressions.

of legal intentions to illustrate a competitor to communicative content for a statute's contribution.

A legal intention is an intention, by enacting a given statute, in order to change the law in a particular way. For example, when a legislature (or individual legislator) votes for a statutory provision, it (or he or she) may have an intention to change the law in a particular direction, say to restrict diversity jurisdiction, to make punishments for white-collar crimes stricter, or to prohibit a particular toxin from being used in pipes carrying drinking water. Such intentions can be extremely general—to protect the public health, say—or much more specific—to require employees of restaurants to wash their hands. Legal intentions differ from communicative intentions in a basic way. The content of a legal intention is *to change the law in such and such way.* As the above examples illustrate, the content need not include any reference to linguistic expressions. By contrast, the content of a communicative intention is, to put it in a simplified form, *to communicate thus and so by uttering* 'S' (where 'S' is a linguistic expression).

Despite this fundamental difference in the nature of legal and communicative intentions, one might think that the difference does not matter much for present purposes. According to this line of thought, a legislator who has the legal intention (say) to provide a subsidy to farmers who grow soybeans will intend to use certain sentences to communicate precisely that farmers who grow soybeans will receive a subsidy. In general, for each legal intention, a legislator will have a communicative intention to use certain words to implement that legal intention. If this simple model were correct, legal intentions would not be a genuine competitor to communicative intentions because they would yield the same legal content.

In fact, though they are not always carefully distinguished, a legislature's legal intentions often would yield different legal content from its communicative intentions. It will help to have an illustration.

In *Saadeh v Farouki*,[49] the DC Circuit faced the question whether a suit between two aliens, one of whom is a permanent resident of a state, qualifies for diversity jurisdiction under 28 USC §1332. (Very roughly, diversity jurisdiction allows suits to be brought in federal court if the plaintiff and defendant are citizens of different states or of a state and a foreign nation.) In 1988, Congress had amended §1332 by adding that, for purposes of diversity jurisdiction, 'an alien admitted to the United States for permanent residence shall be deemed a citizen of the State in which such alien is domiciled'.[50] The legislative history

---

[49] 107 F3d 52 (DC Cir 1997). Many thanks to Stephen Yeazell for bringing this case to my attention.

[50] ibid at p 55.

was abundantly clear that the point of the statutory amendment was to reduce the scope of diversity jurisdiction by removing a loophole under which diversity jurisdiction encompassed a suit between a resident alien domiciled in a given state and a citizen of that state. This goal was in accord with the general congressional policy of restricting the scope of diversity jurisdiction and with congressional concern over the workload of the federal courts.[51]

The semantic content of the amendment, if it constitutes a legal rule, would, however, in addition to removing the loophole, *expand* diversity jurisdiction to cover a lawsuit between a permanent resident of a state and another foreign citizen who is not a permanent resident of that state. The DC Circuit interpreted the statute in accordance with the legislators' legal intention to restrict diversity jurisdiction, not in accordance with the semantic content of the amendment.[52]

For present purposes, *Saadeh* illustrates the way in which legislators' communicative intentions can diverge from their legal intentions. The legislators' legal intention, let us assume with the DC Circuit, was to remove the loophole mentioned above, not to expand diversity jurisdiction in any way. It is very likely that the legislators' communicative intention with respect to the crucial sentence (quoted above) was to stipulate that a resident alien counts for diversity purposes as a citizen of the state in which he resides—relevantly the same as the semantic content of the sentence. Members of Congress almost certainly did not anticipate the legal consequence of expanding diversity jurisdiction that this stipulation would have. If the problem had been anticipated, the statute would have been drafted differently. So, it is *not* that the members of Congress used the words 'shall be deemed a citizen of the state in which such alien is domiciled' intending to communicate something along the lines of *shall be deemed a citizen of the state in which he or she is domiciled when, and only when, the opposing party is not a foreign citizen*. Rather, they simply did not understand the legal consequences that their communicative intentions would have, were they to become law.[53]

As *Saadeh* illustrates, the content of communicative intentions and the content of legal intentions can come apart in the sense that those contents would have different consequences for the content of the law. I have already made the point that legislatures often have no communicative intentions with respect to the relevant statutory language. Even setting this point aside, communicative intentions and legal intentions can come apart because lawmakers can be

---

[51] ibid at pp 58–61.

[52] ibid at p 61.

[53] *Griffin v Oceanic Contractors* 458 US 564 (1982) provides another example of a case in which Congress's legal intentions and communicative intentions likely came apart.

wrong about which specific linguistic contents will achieve their legal intentions. Legislators frequently do not consider the statutory language with care. In addition, it is difficult to anticipate all the legal and practical consequences of specific rules.

As communicative intentions and legal intentions can come apart, legal intentions provide a competing candidate for statutes' contributions. My main concern is not to argue for one candidate over another, but it is worth mentioning two reasons that legal intentions cannot easily be dismissed by the communication theorists. First, the fact that legislatures are more likely to have relevant legal intentions than relevant communicative intentions might be thought to favor legal intentions over communicative intentions. Indeed, the view that a statute's contribution is its communicative content will have the peculiar consequence that statutory provisions often make no contribution to the content of the law.

Second, in arguing for communicative content over *semantic content*, the communication theorists often emphasize that semantic content is a means for conveying communicative content. But given the way in which communication theorists understand legislation, communicative content is a means for achieving legal intentions. Legislatures intend to use particular words to communicate particular contents in order to change the law in a desired way. Legislators are more likely to have thought carefully about their legal intentions than about their communicative intentions, and it can be difficult to know which linguistic contents will achieve particular legislative goals. Legislators will therefore often fail to have communicative intentions that are suitable means to achieving their legal intentions. To the extent that the ends-over-means argument favors communicative content over semantic content, it favours the content of legal intentions over communicative content.

The communication theorists have nothing to say about why communicative content is a better candidate for a statute's contribution than the content of legal intentions. This lack is unsurprising, for philosophy of language and linguistics do not address legal intentions. There are many problems with the position that a statute's contribution is constituted by the content of the legislature's legal intention, but identifying these problems requires appeal to the nature and purpose of law and legislation. I consider the kinds of arguments that could support one candidate over another in section 6.

Even if we grant for the sake of argument that communicative content is the right place to look for a statute's contribution, the communication theory encounters further obstacles. Pre-theoretically, we might well think that some aspects or components of communicative content should not have an impact on the content of the law—or, at least, that some components should be treated differently from others with respect to their potential to affect the content of the law.

For example, consider the familiar distinction between what is said and what is merely implied, implicated, or presupposed. There are many legal examples. For example, the Tenth Amendment states: 'The powers not delegated to the United States by the Constitution...are reserved to the States.' The amendment has often been argued to implicate or presuppose, though it does not say, that there are some powers reserved to the states. My abortion-funding example in section 3 illustrated another possible implicature—from 'if necessary to save the mother's life' to *only if necessary to save the mother's life*. One might well think that what is merely implicated or presupposed by a statute does not have the same bearing on the statute's contribution as what is said.[54]

The literature draws many further distinctions that plausibly have relevance to a statute's contribution. For example, implicatures that are partly conventional might have a better case to be part of a statute's contribution than implicatures that are purely pragmatic.[55]

In addition to the distinctions developed in the philosophy of language literature, there are distinctions that may seem especially relevant in the legal context, regardless of whether they are theoretically important in the study of language. The abortion-funding example illustrated a distinction between contents that the legislature intended *not* to affect the content of the law and contents with respect to which the legislature had no such intention. Perhaps the legislature's intention that a component of communicative content not form part of the content of the law makes a difference to the statute's contribution.

The abortion-funding case also illustrates a distinction between, on the one hand, implicated content that the legislature did not include in what it explicitly said simply because it chose the most natural means of expression and, on the other hand, implicated content that the legislature deliberately avoided including in what it explicitly said in order to avoid political responsibility. Again, one might think that implicated contents in the latter category have a different status with respect to the statute's contribution.

The communication theorists have not systematically addressed the issue of whether some components of communicative content do not form part of a statute's contribution. Some communication theorists want to exclude certain components, though they offer no theoretical justification for doing so.[56]

---

[54] See Marmor (2008) at pp 435–40; (2011); and Neale (2009) at p 56.

[55] See Marmor (2008) at pp 444–7.

[56] These communication theorists are the ones most influenced by the philosophy of language. See note 7. To my knowledge, theorists in the group not drawing on philosophy of language have not addressed the issue.

Soames, for example, wants to draw the line at cases in which the communicative content would yield 'transparently undesirable results in cases not previously contemplated'.[57] He offers no theoretical basis for responding to these unwanted consequences of the communication theory's basic thesis by excluding the contents in question from the content of the law (as opposed to, for example, considering them counterexamples to the communication theory). In his view, those components of communicative content that he wants to exclude are 'legally incorrect'.[58] He does not give much explication, but the idea seems to be that a component of a statute's communicative content is legally incorrect because it yields 'transparently undesirable results in cases not previously contemplated' or because it 'violates the clear intention driving the legislators in adopting it'.[59] Soames offers no account of why such a component is not part of the content of the law. Instead, he simply recasts his central thesis: what a statute contributes to the law is a soft-focus or fuzzy version of its communicative content.

In sum, it is plausible that different aspects or components of communicative content are differently situated with respect to whether they form part of a statute's contribution. Some communication theorists have recognized this point and seem to think that they can simply rely on common sense and ad hoc stipulation to specify which aspects of communicative content get to be part of the law. Given the basic structure of the communication theorists' position, however, is difficult to see how they can have a principled basis for treating different components of communicative content differently with respect to whether they form part of the content of the law. Their appeal to basic truths about linguistic communication is supposed to provide a blanket refutation of legal theorists who rely on legal practice, legal theoretical considerations, the goals of legal systems, political morality, and common sense to support competing positions about what constitutes the content of the law. Given the nature of this argument, there is no room for the communication theorists to rely on considerations not deriving from the study of language to modify the position that the content of the law is the communicative content of the legislative text. In fact, when the communication theorists suggest excluding various parts of communicative content from the content of the law, they seem to be implicitly relying on normative considerations, but without engaging with the large relevant literature that discusses the bearing of

---

[57] (2009b) at pp 417–18. For other examples, see Neale (2009) at p 56; Marmor (2008) at pp 435–48; (2011).

[58] Soames (2009b) at pp 415–16.

[59] ibid at 417–18.

normative considerations on the contribution of statutes to the content of the law.[60]

Could communication theorists retreat to the position that the content of the law is what is *said* or *stated* by the legislature—which, on some views, has an important pragmatic component and may not even include the semantic content of the words—as opposed to everything that is communicated? First, this move would not in all cases yield the results that the communication theorists prefer, let alone avoid all unpalatable consequences. The communication theorists seem to want to include some pragmatically communicated content beyond what is said and to exclude some content that they would count as part of what is said. [61]

More fundamentally, what would the argument for the position be? Why is the relevant content what is said rather than, for instance, the semantic content of the text, what would reasonably be taken to be said (even if not said), or the total communicative content of the legislative text? The appeal to the total communicative content of the legislative text at least is not ad hoc in light of the communication theorists' general claim that the full linguistic content of a text is what is communicated by its utterance (see p 225 above). Once the communication theorists retreat from the position that the content of the law is the communicative content of the relevant utterances, it is not clear what grounds they have for preferring one linguistic or mental content associated with the relevant utterance over others.

Moreover, given the current state of play in philosophy of language, it is reasonable to think that there are multiple legitimate notions of what is said (and of what is stated, and so on).[62] Which notion is most fruitful plausibly varies depending on the theoretical purposes of the inquiry. How could purely linguistic considerations determine which notion is the relevant one in the legislative context?

---

[60] eg Neale (2009) at p 56. Marmor (2011) explicitly accepts that the question of which components of communicative content are relevant to the content of the law is a normative one. (He also seems to be committed to the view that the communicative content of a statute is partially normatively *constituted*, though it is unclear how this view is consistent with the rest of Marmor's position.) Yet he takes several positions on which aspects of communicative content form part of a statute's contribution without offering any normative considerations in their favor or even suggesting that they rest on normative grounds: eg (2011) and (2008) at pp 444–5, 447.

[61] At some points, Soames uses broad language (eg 'the *linguistically based* content of the relevant legal texts—including everything asserted and conveyed therein', (2009b) at pp 403, 410, 422), and, at other points, narrower formulations (pp 16, 417). He tells me (in personal communication), however, that his view is that a statute's contribution is only what the legislature *says*. Notice, however, that the contents discussed above that Soames excludes from a statute's contribution can be part of what is said.

[62] For a small sample of a large literature, see Grice (1989) at pp 24–5, 87–8, 117–22; Bach (2001); Carston (1988); King and Stanley (2005); Recanati (1989); and Soames (2009b) at chs 10–11.

The communication theorists may bite the bullet and insist that the content of the law is the total communicative content of the authoritative legal texts. Just as there is more than one legitimate notion of what is said, however, there is more than one legitimate notion of the total communicative content of an utterance; again, different notions are plausibly more fruitful for different purposes.[63] Therefore, there are competing candidates for the communicative content that constitutes the content of the law, and some further principle is needed to support one candidate over others.

Early in this chapter, I contrasted the neo-Gricean notion with a family of objective notions of what is communicated. Neo-Gricean communicative content is what the speaker intended to communicate. On the neo-Gricean notion, therefore, Grice's Principle of Cooperation and the maxims of conversation, properly understood, are not constitutive of what is communicated, but are simply a means for inferring what the speaker intended. If the maxims are treated as constitutive of what is communicated, we get an objective notion of communicative content.

Specifically, let us consider a notion on which, for a particular content X to be part of the communicative content of an utterance is for it to be the case that, in order to be in compliance with the principles of communication that apply in the context (given what the speaker has uttered), the speaker would have to have intended to communicate X.[64] A speaker may in fact fail to have the relevant intention, for example because he is confused about the applicable principles. On such an account, what is communicated depends constitutively on what the norms require, rather than on what was actually intended. The intuitive idea behind this objective notion of communicative content is that the speaker is reasonably understood as intending to communicate what he would have had to have intended in order for his utterance to be in compliance with the maxims.

It will be helpful to have a concrete example in which different notions of communicative content have different consequences for the content of the law (assuming the content of the law is the total communicative content of the relevant authoritative text). The following example is loosely based on an actual case. A statute specifies that, with respect to certain tenancies in government-owned housing, 'a tenant may choose to (a) convert the existing tenancy to a 50-year lease; or (b) purchase the freehold' at a price based on a

---

[63] See, eg Davis (2003) at chs 4–5, Bach and Harnish (1979) at pp 15–16, Levinson (1983) at pp 15–16, Sperber and Wilson (1986), and Boudreau et al (2007). See also Saul (2002).

[64] The principles of communication applicable in the case of an ordinary conversation have been much discussed in the relevant literature. I address the question of the principles applicable in the legislative context in the next section and in my MS.

specified formula. A tenant realizes that choosing both options—converting to a 50-year lease and purchasing the freehold—would, because of the way in which the price formula is specified, produce a disproportionately large financial benefit to the tenant. In enacting the statute, the legislature had the intention to communicate that the choice was inclusive—that is, that a tenant may choose either option or both.

Suppose in addition that, given the context, in order to be in compliance with the applicable principles of statutory drafting and interpretation, the legislature would have had to have had the intention to communicate that the tenant may choose one option or the other but *not* both. Given its actual communicative intentions, the legislature violated the applicable principles by drafting the statute in the way that it did.

We could flesh out the facts of the example in various ways in order to provide grounding for this supposition. For example, it could be well established in the local jurisdiction's canons of statutory interpretation that legislative provisions of the form 'X may do A or B' permit one option or the other but not both. In order to specify that both options may be chosen, a statute must use language of the form 'X may do A or B, or both'. The legislature simply failed to observe this canon.

On the objective notion of communicative content, the legislature communicated that the tenant may not choose both options. On a neo-Gricean notion, the legislature communicated that a tenant may choose both options. Thus, the case turns on which notion is the correct one for legal purposes.

Our question is not which notion of communicative content is the legally relevant one, but what could favor one notion of communicative content over others. Let us assume for purposes of argument that the neo-Gricean notion is the more theoretically fruitful notion for many purposes in the study of linguistic communication. The assumption does not, without more, settle which notion is the relevant one for legal purposes. Without some deeper understanding of the underlying rationale or purpose that lies behind the appeal to the notion of communication in legal interpretation, it is hard to see how to adjudicate between different notions of communicative content (as candidates for a statute's contribution).

I want to emphasize that the problem is not specific to the neo-Gricean notion of communicative content. If the communication theorists were to opt for a more objective notion, for example, they would still lack the resources for defending the claim that a statute's contribution is the statute's communicative content. The problem is that considerations based exclusively in the study of language and communication do not afford the resources for defending the legal relevance of one notion of communicative content over others. To understand how legislation affects the content of the law, we need an understanding of the nature and purposes of legislation. The point, of course, is not that it is indeterminate what constitutes a statute's contribution, but rather that the communication theory lacks the resources to explain which candidate is the relevant one. (To the extent that there is indeterminacy, it does not derive from the considerations discussed here.) In the next section, I take up the question of how legislation is relevantly different from communication.

6. Legislation and communication

The communication theorists seem to think it is obvious that legislating is intimately tied to communicating—perhaps even that legislating is a fundamental kind of communicating. They might therefore reply to my arguments by questioning why the enactment of legislation is relevantly different from communicative uses of language such as commanding.[65]

I first want to clear away any thought that communication is required for legislation in Anglo-American legal systems as they in fact are. Even if such a thought were correct, it would not give the communication theorists what they need. It falls far short of the conclusion that a statute's contribution is constituted by what is communicated. But the point is mistaken, so the communication theorists' argument for their thesis about a statute's contribution cannot simply assume that legislation requires communication.

The claim that communication is necessary for successful legislation is ambiguous. We need to distinguish, on the one hand, the claim that the enactment of a statute does not make a contribution unless *that contribution* is communicated from, on the other, the claim that the enactment of a statute does not make a contribution unless *the fact that the statutory text was validly enacted* is communicated. Plainly, only the first claim is relevant to the communication theory—the communication theory would not get off the ground if the relevant communicative content were merely that a particular text had been enacted!

If I do something in public, others can derive information about what I was thinking or doing, but, if I had no intention to convey such information to others, my action is not usefully termed communicative. At a minimum, for an utterance to be communicative, it must be the case that the speaker makes the utterance with the intention of getting a hearer to recognize a content. (The paradigm of linguistic communication requires more.) And for a communication to be successful requires that the hearer understand or recognize

---

[65] Thanks to Scott Shapiro and Seana Shiffrin for encouraging me to discuss these issues at greater length.

what the speaker intends to communicate. On this standard understanding, there is no non-question-begging reason to think that the enactment of legislation does not make a contribution unless it communicates that contribution. First, it is crucial to distinguish a publicity condition from a requirement of communication. It is often said that there is a publicity condition on the enactment of legislation, but the term 'publicity' is misleading. As Raz points out,[66] the publicity condition can be met by secret legislation, 'All that is denied [by the publicity requirement] is that legislation can consist in a private mental act.' The publicity condition must not be confused with a requirement that a statute's contribution be recognized by anyone—still less that the legislature's actual intentions be recognized.

Second, as we have seen, legislatures need not intend to communicate anything by enacting a bill. A majority of the members of the legislature needs to vote for the bill, but neither the individual members nor the legislature needs to have any communicative intention in order to do this.[67] We could rely on a fiction—for example that the legislature intends what a single rational person who had uttered the legislation under stipulated conditions would have intended to communicate. But, in that case, we could not justify the fiction on the ground that enacting legislation is in fact communicating; rather, we would need an argument why it should be treated like actual communication. The communication theorists have not attempted a revisionary argument that legislation does not make a contribution unless the legislature has appropriate communicative intentions. (The communication theorists cannot rely on their conclusion about a statute's contribution here, as the question at issue is whether the argument for that conclusion relies on an unwarranted assumption that legislation is, or requires, communication.) I will argue below that important goals of law-making may be better served without such a requirement.

Third, on the standard understanding, a statute's contribution is made on the legislation's effective date, regardless of whether anyone has even read the legislation. Even if the legislature has an appropriate communicative intention, no recognition of that intention is required for the statute's contribution to be effective. (Even if recognition of the statute's *contribution* were required, communication of the *fact of the enactment* of the relevant statutory language would be sufficient for such recognition to occur.)

It is true that we ascertain what the law is, in important part, by reading legislation. But given that the enactment of legislation uncontroversially plays an important role in *making* the content of the law what it is, this truth about

---

[66] Raz (1996) at p 284, n 18.   [67] See, eg Kelsen (2006) at pp 33–4.

how we ascertain the content of the law does not support the claim that legislation requires communication. Compare: given the underlying facts, we can recognize that someone committed fraud or kidnapping without the perpetrator's or anyone else's communicating that he did so. So, in order to make the law publicly accessible (as opposed to in order to create law), a legislature can publish statutes with the intention to communicate the fact of their enactment. Then members of the audience—many of whom are more expert than legislators in working out statutes' contributions—can ascertain the content of the law.

I now turn to the reasons that communication is not a useful model for understanding legislation. In addition to the frequent absence of appropriate communicative intentions in the legislative context, there are many other differences between the prototypical personal communication context and the legislative context. The legislative context is impersonal: the members of the legislature and the overwhelming majority of the members of the audience do not know each other personally.[68] The legislative context is less cooperative than the typical communicative context—there is strategic behavior both within the legislature and between the legislature and the audience.[69] Such differences, however, do not necessarily take us outside the realm where the theory of linguistic communication may be directly relevant. The theory could perhaps be elaborated to handle these features of the legislative context, which, after all, are present to some degree in other communicative situations.

The most important reason that the communicative model is inapt is that many of the purposes of legislation may be better served if a statute's contribution is not constituted by what is communicated. Consider what goals we would try to promote if we were designing a legislative system. We would presumably want to design the system in such a way as to increase the likelihood of creating legal standards that would promote justice and welfare. We would also plausibly have more procedural goals, such as making the legal system morally legitimate (and the closely related goal of making legal obligations binding), ensuring that law-making is democratic and public, making the law publicly accessible, creating legal standards that will be complied with, and creating legal standards that do not conflict with the system's constitution. One might also think that a legislative system could have less noble goals, such as maintaining the status quo, advancing the interests of a particular group, promoting a particular ideology, or ensuring that legal standards reflect the distribution of power among interest groups. We will see that advancing such goals, whether of the more or less elevated sort, may not

---

[68] See Shapiro (2010), ch 3.   [69] See Marmor (2008, 2011).

depend on successful communication—on fulfilling the legislature's communicative intentions. Indeed, many of the goals are goals of the legislative system or the society, and need not be purposes of the legislature. Consequently, the achievement of these goals is independent of whether the legislature's intentions are fulfilled.

There is no parallel in the theory of linguistic communication. The study of linguistic communication is the study of the way in which speakers and hearers use language to exchange information. What makes an utterance communicative is the speaker's intention to communicate, and the communication is successful to the extent that intention is fulfilled. Of course many other purposes can be served *by* communication, and the theory of communication may have to take account of them. But the study of communication does not concern purposes that could be better served *without* communication or by creating norms whose contents are distinct from what is communicated.

The fundamental difference in the nature of the goals of legislation and communication—along with other differences between the legislative context and the typical context of communication—provides several kinds of reasons why the most fruitful notion in the study of communication may not be the most fruitful notion in the context of statutory drafting and interpretation.

First, because there are great obstacles to a legislature's having communicative intentions with respect to the statutes it passes, it would be advantageous if legislation could succeed in achieving its goals without requiring the legislature to have communicative intentions. We noted in section 3 that legislatures in large contemporary societies probably have no communicative intention with respect to typical statutory provisions. In addition to the sheer volume and technicality of legislation, the legislature typically does not choose its words in order to implement a communicative intention; rather, the words are the outcome of a complex process of negotiation and compromise. As a result, the language is often chosen not in order to implement anyone's communicative intention, but because, for example, it is unclear enough for a majority to accept. Another difficulty is presented by well-known paradoxes of collective preference (such as Arrow's Paradox). To require legislators representing constituents with diverse and conflicting interests to have a collective communicative intention would make it very difficult for them to enact legislation. Given the difficulties with communicative intentions, goals of lawmaking such as promoting justice and welfare provide a reason for having a legislative system that could create law without the legislature having a relevant communicative intention.

There are also reasons why, regardless of whether a communicative intention exists, it is better that the law not depend constitutively on what is in anyone's mind. For reasons of fairness, democracy, and effectiveness, it is important that the law be publicly accessible. Legislators must create law for people they will never meet and who are not even born when the legislation is passed. The usual means of ascertaining what is in others' minds are not available. We have already mentioned that the words of the legislation are not chosen to implement the legislators' communicative intentions. Background knowledge of the legislators' beliefs, goals, and other mental states that could be used to help infer their communicative intentions is not available to all members of the relevant audience. And it is not possible simply to ask the speaker for clarification, as it is in many communicative situations. Finally, so-called legislative history—the main evidence of the legislature's intentions, other than the text of the legislation, that it is permissible to consult—is notoriously manipulable and unreliable.

It is not just that the law must be accessible to people who lack evidence of the legislature's communicative intentions. There are reasons of democracy and rule of law why it should not be permissible to consult much ordinary evidence of the legislature's intentions. For example, it would give undue power to the members of the legislature to allow their later testimony—even testimony on which they unanimously agreed—to be evidence of what the law is.

The goals of law-making provide deeper reasons why it is better that the content of the law not depend constitutively on what is communicated. These goals may well be best served by a system in which a statute's contribution is different from what it communicates. One example is provided by canons of statutory interpretation. The canon that statutes are to be construed so as to avoid constitutional questions could promote the goal of making a statute's contribution consistent with the legal system's constitution. Similarly, many canons promote the goal of making a statute's contribution publicly accessible. The canons are sometimes regarded as evidentiary devices for ascertaining the legislature's intentions. But this is a controversial substantive claim. A competing understanding of the canons is as norms that are partially constitutive of statutory content. On this understanding, the reason legislation is treated as conforming to the canons, other things being equal, is that the canons specify how legislation properly contributes to the law, rather than what the legislature is likely to have intended as a matter of actual psychological fact.

To take another example, suppose a legal system has the goal of making it the case that its legal standards reflect interest-group power. This goal could be advanced by a model according to which a statute's contribution reflects the position of the group whose power was decisive in the statute's enactment—for example, as explicated by positive political theory.

A very different example is provided by Dworkin's theory of law, according to which, again, a statute's contribution consists of the principles that would best justify the enactment of the statute. Dworkin argues, very roughly, that if this account were true, the legal system would be more morally legitimate than it would be if other accounts of a statute's contribution were true. If so, then the goal of making the legal system morally legitimate would be promoted by a system in which a statute's contribution is not constituted by what the statute communicates. Of course, Dworkin's argument is controversial. The point is that, once we recognize the nature of the goals of law-making, we cannot assume that the model of personal communication is helpful. There is no reason to think that, in general, such goals as promoting justice, making statutes' contributions reflect the distribution of interest-group power responsible for their enactment, fostering the moral legitimacy of the legal system, or making law that is consistent with the constitution, will be most effectively advanced if a statute's contribution is what the statute communicates.

In light of this discussion, it cannot be assumed that situations in which a legislature enacts a statutory provision without an appropriate communicative intention are either abnormal or parasitic upon situations in which the legislature has an appropriate communicative intention. Rather, given the goals of legislation, such situations may simply be normal and primary cases of legislating. Therefore, it is unwarranted in theorizing about legislation—and authoritative legal texts more generally—to idealize to the normal or paradigm communicative situation. Any idealization must be appropriate to the nature and goals of law-making.

But do we not delegate law-making power to legislators so that they can make decisions for the society and then communicate to us what they have chosen? Is not the point of representative government therefore undermined if the law does not depend on what the representatives communicate?

First, as the discussion has indicated, there can be many purposes to a legislative system other than the aim of benefiting from the wisdom of the legislators. These purposes, to repeat, may be better served if the law does not depend on what the representatives communicate.

Second, it is simply a confusion to think that, if a statute's contribution does not depend *constitutively* on what the legislators intend, the legislators' intentions are made irrelevant. On any view, a statute's contribution will depend *causally* on the legislators' decisions and intentions. Even if the content of legislation is not *constituted* by what the legislators intend, if legislators can know how statutes contribute to the content of the law, they can work out how to enact a statute that will make the contribution to the law that they wish. (In fact, as long as the members of the legislature know how to affect the *direction* of the contribution that a statute would make, they can rationally use legislation to further their goals.) And there are important advantages in not having to ascertain what was in legislators' minds in order to figure out what law they created.

7. Conclusion

I have argued that, even if we accept its claims about linguistic communication and many of its basic assumptions, the communication theory does not give us a satisfactory account of how a statute contributes to the content of the law. What has led the communication theorists in the wrong direction? An important part of the explanation is surely a reliance on analogies to communication, especially personal communication.[70] I have argued that the goals of law-making make such analogies unhelpful, even misguided. It is not just that law-making has goals other than communication. More fundamentally, legislative systems have goals that are at odds with the nature of communication—in particular, goals that may well be better served if a statute's contribution is not constituted by the statute's communicative content. Legislation uses language to make law in the service of such goals. Its doing so neither requires communication nor is well understood on the model of communication.

Finally, it might be suggested that, even if legislation should not be understood on the model of communication, philosophy of language might be developed, in a way parallel to Gricean theory, to accommodate the enactment of legislation. Grice's principles are based on assuming a goal of efficient exchange of information, but perhaps an analogous theoretical structure could be worked out with parallel principles based on the goals of legislation. Philosophy of language certainly has much to say about uses of language that are not communicative, and no doubt there is much more to be said. The point that I want to make, however, is that if the goals of law-making include the kinds of moral goals discussed in the previous section—advancing justice, making law-making democratic, or fostering the legitimacy of the legal system—then which principles would be parallel to Grice's conversational maxims would depend on considerations of political morality, such as democracy, fairness, and welfare, as well as legal theory. Even if the goals of a legal system were less lofty—preserving the status quo, promoting a particular ideology, ensuring that the legal standards that are created will be enforced and complied with—the relevant principles would depend on normative and practical considerations. Consequently, a philosophy of language that works out such principles, and the theoretical framework in which they are embedded, would be a philosophy of language heavily implicated in normative theorizing and, in that way, very different from contemporary philosophy of language.[71]

---

[70] See Berman (2009) at pp 54–5 for a nice discussion of a related point.

[71] I do not mean to suggest that such a direction would be an appropriate one for philosophy of language to take; my point, rather, is to clarify the limited nature of the contribution that philosophy of language (as it currently is) can make to the question of what constitutes the contribution of statutes or other authoritative legal texts to the content of the law. For related discussion, see my MS. Thanks to Sam Cumming for encouraging me to address the issue raised in this paragraph.

Bibliography

Alexander, L. (1995) 'All or Nothing at All? The Intentions of Authorities and the Authority of Intentions', in A. Marmor (ed), *Law and Interpretation*. Oxford University Press.

Alexander, L., and Prakash, S. (2004) ' "Is That English You're Speaking?" Why Intention Free Interpretation is an Impossibility'. 41 *San Diego Law Review*, 967–95.

American Law Institute, *Restatement of the Law (Second)*, Contracts 2d.

Aristotle (1980) *The Nicomachean Ethics*, D. Ross (trans). Oxford University Press.

Austin, J.L. (1962) *How to Do Things with Words*. Harvard University Press.

Ayres, I., and Gertner, R. (1992) 'Strategic Contractual Inefficiency and the Optimal Choice of Legal Rules'. *Yale Law Journal*, 101.

Bach, K., (2001) 'You Don't Say?' 127 *Synthese*, 11–31.

—— (1994) 'Conversational Implicature'. 9 *Mind and Language*, 124–62.

Bach, K., and Harnish, R.M. (1992) 'How Performatives Really Work'. 15 *Linguistics and Philosophy*, 93–110.

—— (1982) *Linguistic Communication and Speech Acts*. MIT Press.

—— (1979) *Linguistic Communication and Speech Acts*. MIT Press.

Bentham, J. (1843) *The Works of Jeremy Bentham*, J. Bowring (ed). William Tait.

Berman, M. (2009) 'Originalism is Bunk'. 84 *New York University Law Review*, 1–96.

Boudreau, C., Lupia, A., McCubbins, M.D., and Rodriguez, D.B. (2007) 'What Statutes Mean: Interpretive Lessons from Positive Theories of Communication and Legislation'. 44 *San Diego Law Review*, 957–92.

Campos, P. (1996) 'A Text is Just a Text'. 19 *Harvard Journal of Law and Public Policy*, 327–33.

—— (1993) 'Three Mistakes about Interpretation'. 92 *Michigan Law Review*, 388–97.

Carston, R. (1988) 'Implicature, Expliciture, and Truth-Theoretic Semantics', in R. Kempson (ed), *Mental Representations: The Interface between Language and Reality*, 155–81. Cambridge University Press.

Coleman, J. (2001) *The Practice of Principle: In Defence of a Pragmatist Approach to Legal Theory*. Oxford University Press.

Corbin, A. (1952) *Corbin on Contracts*, One Volume Edition. West.

—— (1965) 'The Interpretation of Words and the Parol Evidence Rule'. *Cornell Law Quarterly* 50.

Dan-Cohen, M. (2002) *Harmful Thoughts: Essays on Law, Self, and Morality*. Princeton University Press.

Dancy, J. (2004) *Ethics Without Principles*. Oxford University Press.

—— (1983) 'Ethical Particularism and Morally Relevant Properties'. 92 *Mind*, 530–47.

Davidson, D. (2005) *Truth and Predication*. Harvard University Press.

——(1990) 'The Structure and Content of Truth'. 87 *Journal of Philosophy*, 279–328.

——(1973) 'Radical Interpretation'. 27 *Dialectica*, 313–28.

——(1967) 'Truth and Meaning'. 17 *Synthese*, 304–23.

Davis, W. (2007) 'How Normative is Implicature?' 39 *Journal of Pragmatics*, 1655–72.

——(2005) *Meaning, Expression, and Thought*. Cambridge University Press.

——(1998) *Implicature: Intention, Convention, and Principle in the Failure of Gricean Theory*. Cambridge University Press.

Devitt, M. (1981) *Designation*. Columbia University Press.

Donnelan, K. (1966) 'Reference and Definite Descriptions'. *The Philosophical Review*, 77.

Duff, R.A. (1996) *Criminal Attempts*. Oxford University Press.

Dworkin, R. (2002) 'Thirty Years On'. 115 *Harvard Law Review*, 1655–87.

——(1998) 'Comment', in Scalia, A. (1998), 115–28.

——(1996) *Freedom's Law: The Moral Reading of the American Constitution*. Harvard University Press.

——(1986) *Law's Empire*. Harvard University Press.

——(1985) 'The Forum of Principle', in *A Matter of Principle*. Harvard University Press.

——(1977) *Taking Rights Seriously*. Duckworth.

Easterbrook, F.H. (1988) 'The Role of Original Intent in Statutory Construction'. 11 *Harvard Journal of Law and Public Policy*, 59.

Endicott, T. (2005) 'The Value of Vagueness', in V.K. Bhatia, J. Engberg, M. Gotti, and D. Heller (eds), *Vagueness in Normative Texts*, 27–48. Peter Lang.

——(2001) 'Law is Necessarily Vague'. 7 *Legal Theory*, 377–83.

——(2000) *Vagueness in Law*. Oxford University Press.

Fara, D.G. (2000) 'Shifting Sands: An Interest-Relative Theory of Vagueness', in 28 *Philosophical Topics*, 48–81 (originally published under the name D. Graff).

Farnsworth, E.A. (2004) *Contracts*, 4th edn. Aspen.

Finnis, J. (1980) *Natural Law and Natural Rights*. Oxford University Press.

Fish, S. (2005) 'There is No Textualist Position'. 42 *San Diego Law Review*, 629–50.

Fletcher, G. (1986) 'Constructing a Theory of Impossible Attempts'. 53 *Criminal Justice Ethics*, 53–69.

Fogelin, R. (1987) *Wittgenstein*, 2nd edn. Routledge.

——(1976) *Wittgenstein*, 1st edn. Routledge.

Frege, G. (1948) 'Sense and Reference'. 57 *The Philosophical Review*, 209–30.

Fried, C. (1981) *Contract as Promise: A Theory of Contractual Obligation*. Harvard University Press.

Fuller, L. (1964) *The Morality of Law*. Yale University Press.

Gazdar, G. (1979) *Pragmatics: Implicature, Presupposition, and Logical Form*. Academic Press.

Geach, P. (1982) 'Wittgenstein's Operator "N"'. 41 *Analysis*, 168–171.

Gilmore, G. (1974) *The Death of Contract*. Ohio State University Press.

Graglia, L. (1992) ' "Interpreting" the Constitution: Posner on Bork'. 44 *Stanford Law Review*, 1019–50.

Greenawalt, K. (2005) 'A Pluralist Approach to Interpretation: Wills and Contracts'. 42 *San Diego Law Review*, 533.

Greenberg, M. (forthcoming 2011) 'Beyond the Standard Picture'. *Oxford Studies in the Philosophy of Law*, vol 2.

—— (2010) 'The Standard Picture and Its Discontents'. 1 *Oxford Studies in the Philosophy of Law*, vol 1.

—— (2006) 'Hartian Positivism and Normative Facts: How Facts Make Law II', in S. Hershovitz (ed), *Exploring Law's Empire: The Jurisprudence of Ronald Dworkin*, 265–90. Oxford University Press.

—— (2005) 'A New Map of Theories of Mental Content: Constitutive Accounts and Normative Theories'. 15 *Philosophical Issues*, 299–320.

—— (2004) 'How Facts Make Law'. 10 *Legal Theory*, 157–98.

—— 'The Communication Theory of Legal Interpretation and Objective Notions of Communicative Content' (16 December 2010). UCLA School of Law Research Paper No. 10-35. Available at SSRN: <http://ssrn.com/abstract=1726524>.

Greenberg, M., and Litman, H. (1998) 'The Meaning of Original Meaning'. 86 *The Georgetown Law Journal*, 570–619.

Grice, H.P. (1989) *Studies in the Way of Words*. Harvard University Press.

—— (1975) 'Logic and Conversation', in P. Cole and J.L. Morgan (eds), *Syntax and Semantics, 3: Speech Acts*, 41–58. Academic Press.

Hall, J. (1960) *General Principles of Criminal Law*, 2nd edn. Bobbs-Merrill.

Hart, H.L.A. (1994) *The Concept of Law*, 2nd edn, P. Bulloch and J. Raz (eds). Oxford University Press.

—— (1981) 'The House of Lords on Attempting the Impossible'. 1 *Oxford Journal of Legal Studies*, 149–66.

—— (1961) *The Concept of Law*. Clarendon Press.

—— (1958) 'Positivism and the Separation of Law and Morals'. 71 *Harvard Law Review*, 593–629.

Hart, H.M., and Sacks, A.M. (1994) *The Legal Process: Basic Problems in the Making and Application of Law*, W.N. Eskridge, Jr. and P.P. Frickey (eds). Foundation Press.

Hasnas, J. (2002) 'Once More Unto The Breach: The Inherent Liberalism of the Criminal Law and Liability for Attempting the Impossible'. 54 *Hastings Law Journal*, 1–77.

Holmes, Jr., O.W. (1898–9) 'Theory of Legal Interpretation'. 12 *Harvard Law Review*, 417.

—— (1881) *The Common Law*. Little, Brown.

Holton, R. (2010) 'The Exception Proves the Rule'. 18 *The Journal of Political Philosophy*, 369–88.

—— (2002) 'Principles and Particularisms'. *Proceedings of the Aristotelian Society*, Supplementary Volume 67, 191–209.

Horty, J. (2008) 'Reasons and Precedent'. Available at philpapers: <http://philpapers. org/s/John%20Horty>

—— (2007a) 'Reasons as Defaults'. 7 *Philosophers' Imprint*, 3.

—— (2007b) 'Defaults with Priorities'. 36 *Journal of Philosophical Logic*, 367–413.

—— (2001) 'Nonmonotonic Logic', in L. Goble (ed), *The Blackwell Guide to Philosophical Logic*, 336–61. Blackwell Publishers Ltd.

Hurd, H. (1990) 'Sovereignty in Silence'. 99 *Yale Law Journal*, 945–1028.

Johnson, S. (1785) *A Dictionary of the English Language*. J.F. and C. Rivington.

Karttunen, L., and Peters, S. (1979) 'Conventional Implicature', in C.K. Oh and D.A. Dineen (eds), *Syntax and Semantics 11, Presupposition*, 1–56. Academic Press.

Kay, R.S. (1989) 'Original Intentions, Standard Meanings, and the Legal Character of the Constitution'. 6 *Constitutional Commentary*, 39–50.

—— (1988) 'Adherence to the Original Intentions in Constitutional Adjudication: Three Objections and Responses'. 82 *Northwestern University Law Review*, 226–92.

Keedy, E. (1954) 'Criminal Attempts at Common Law'. 102 *University of Pennsylvania Law Review*, 464–89.

Kelsen, H. (2006) *General Theory of Law and State*. Transaction Publishers.

Knapp, S., and Michaels, W. (2005) 'Not a Matter of Interpretation'. 42 *San Diego Law Review*, 651–68.

—— (1983) 'A Reply to Our Critics'. 9 *Critical Inquiry*, 790–800.

—— (1982) 'Against Theory'. 8 *Critical Inquiry*, 723–42.

Kripke, S.A. (2009) 'Presupposition and Anaphora: Remarks on the Formulation of the Projection Problem'. 40 *Linguistic Inquiry*, 367–86.

—— (1977) 'Speaker's Reference and Semantic Reference'. 2 *Midwest Studies in Philosophy*, 255–76.

Leslie, S. (2008) 'Generics: Cognition and Acquisition'. 117 *Philosophical Review*, 1–47.

Levinson, S. (1983) *Pragmatics*. Cambridge University Press.

Lewis, D. (1983) 'Scorekeeping in a Language Game', in D. Lewis, *Philosophical Papers*, vol 1, 233–49. Oxford University Press.

Manning, J. (2006) 'What Divides Textualists from Purposivists?' 106 *Columbia Law Review*, 70–111.

—— (2003) 'The Absurdity Doctrine'. 116 *Harvard Law Review*, 2387–486.

Marmor, A. (2009) *Social Conventions: From Language to Law*. Princeton University Press.

—— (2008) 'The Pragmatics of Legal Language'. 21 *Ratio Juris*, 423–52.

—— (2005) *Interpretation and Legal Theory*, revised 2nd edn. Hart Publishing.

McCubbins, M.D., and Rodriguez, D.B. (2005) 'Canonical Construction and Statutory Revisionism: The Strange Case of the Appropriations Canon'. 14 *Journal of Contemporary Legal Issues*, 699.

McKean, E. (ed) (2005) *The New Oxford American Dictionary*, 2nd edn. Oxford University Press.

Miller, G.P. (1990) 'Pragmatics and the Maxims of Interpretation'. 5 *Wisconsin Law Review*, 1179–227.

Moore, M. (1981) 'The Semantics of Judging'. 54 *Southern California Law Review*, 151–294.

Neale, S. (2009) 'The Intentionalism of Textualism', <http://lawold.usc.edu/academics/centers/ clp/papers/documents/Neale.pdf>.

——(2007) 'On Location', in M. O'Rourke and C. Washington (eds), *Situating Semantics: Essays in the Philosophy of John Perry*, 251–393. MIT Press.

——(1992) 'Paul Grice and the Philosophy of Language'. 15 *Linguistics and Philosophy*, 509–59.

Oddie, G. (2007) 'Truthlikeness'. *Stanford Encyclopedia of Philosophy*, <http://plato.stanford.edu/entries/truthlikeness>.

Ornstein, N.J., Mann, T.E., and Malbin, M.J. (2008) *Vital Statistics on Congress 2008*. Brookings Institution Press.

Posner, R. (1993) *The Problems of Jurisprudence*. Harvard University Press.

Rakove, J.N. (1996) *Original Meanings: Politics and Ideas in the Making of the Constitution*. Alfred A. Knopf.

Raz, J. (2004) *Incorporation by Law*. 10 Legal Theory, 1–17.

——(1999) *Practical Reasons and Norms*, new edn. Oxford University Press.

——(1996) 'Intention in Interpretation', in R.P. George (ed), *The Autonomy of Law: Essays on Legal Positivism*, 249–86, Oxford University Press.

——(1994) *Ethics in the Public Domain: Essays in the Morality of Law and Politics*, revised edn. Oxford University Press.

——(1986) *The Morality of Freedom*. Clarendon Press.

——(1979) *The Authority of Law: Essays on Law and Morality*. Oxford University Press.

Recanati, F. (1991) 'The Pragmatics of What is Said', in S. Davis (ed), *Pragmatics: A Reader*, 97–120. Oxford University Press.

Reiter, R. (1980) 'A Logic for Default Reasoning'. 13 *Artificial Intelligence*, 81–132.

Ring, K.A. (ed) (2004) *Scalia Dissents: Writings of the Supreme Court's Wittiest, Most Outspoken Justice*. Regerny Publishing.

Rodriguez, D.B., and Weingast, B.R. (2003) 'The Positive Political Theory of Legislative History: New Perspectives on the 1964 Civil Rights Act and Its Interpretation'. 151 *University of Pennsylvania Law Review*.

Rosen, G. (2010) 'Metaphysical Dependence: Reduction and Grounding', in B. Hale and A. Hoffman (eds), *Modality*. Oxford University Press.

Saul, J. (2002) 'Speaker Meaning, What is Said, and What is Implicated'. 36 *Noûs*, 228–48.

——(2001) Review of *Implicature: Intention, Convention, and Principle in the Failure of Gricean Theory*, by Wayne A. Davis. 35 *Noûs*, 630–41.

Scalia, A. (1997) *A Matter of Interpretation: Federal Courts and the Law*, A. Gutmann (ed). Princeton University Press.

Scanlon, T. (1999) *What We Owe to Each Other*. Harvard University Press.

Schroeder, M. (2004) 'The Scope of Instrumental Reason', 18 *Philosophical Perspectives*, 337–64.

Searle, J.R. (1989) 'How Performatives Work'. 12 *Linguistics and Philosophy*, 535.

——(1979) *Expression and Meaning: Studies in the Theory of Speech Acts*. Cambridge University Press.

——(1976) 'A Classification of Illocutionary Acts'. 5 *Language in Society*, 1–23.

——(1969) *Speech Acts*. Cambridge University Press.

Shapiro, Scott (2011) *Legality*. Harvard University Press.

Shapiro, Stewart (2006) *Vagueness in Context*. Clarendon Press.

——(2001) 'On Hart's Way Out', in J. Coleman (ed), *Hart's Postscript: Essays on the Postscript to* The Concept of Law, 169–82. Oxford University Press.

Shiffrin, S.V. (2008) 'Promising, Intimate Relationships, and Conventionalism'. 117 *The Philosophical Review*, 481–524.

Simpson, A.W.B. (1989) 'Contracts for Cotton to Arrive: The Case of the Two Ships *Peerless*'. 11 *Cardozo Law Review*, 287.

Simson, J., and Weiner, E. (eds) (1989) *The Oxford English Dictionary*. Oxford University Press.

Sinclair, M.B.W. (1985) 'Law and Language: The Role of Pragmatics in Statutory Interpretation'. 46 *University of Pittsburgh Law Review*, 373–420.

Skilton, R.H. (1937) 'The Requisite Act in Criminal Attempt'. 3 *University of Pittsburgh Law Review*, 308–19.

Smith, J.C. (1957) 'Two Problems in Criminal Attempts'. 70 *Harvard Law Review*, 422–48.

Soames, S. (2010a) *Philosophy of Language*. Princeton University Press.

——(2010b) 'The Possibility of Partial Definition', in R. Dietz and S. Moruzzi (eds), *Cuts and Clouds: Essays on the Nature of Vagueness*. Oxford University Press; reprinted in Soames (2009c).

——(2009a) 'Interpreting Legal Texts: What Is, and What Is Not Special about the Law', in Soames (2009b), 403–23.

——(2009b) *Philosophical Essays*, vol 1. Princeton University Press.

——(2009c) *Philosophical Essays*, vol 2. Princeton University Press.

——(2008a) 'Truth and Meaning in Perspective'. 32 *Midwest Studies in Philosophy*, 1–19; reprinted in Soames (2009b).

——(2008b) 'The Gap between Meaning and Assertion: Why What We Literally Say Often Differs from What Our Words Literally Mean', in Soames (2009b), 278–97. Princeton University Press.

——(2008c) 'Why Incomplete Definite Descriptions Do Not Defeat Russell's Theory of Descriptions', in Soames (2009b), 377–400. Princeton University Press.

——(2003a) *Philosophical Analysis in the Twentieth Century*, vol 2. Princeton University Press.

—— (2003b) 'Higher-Order Vagueness for Partially Defined Predicates', in J.C. Beall (ed), *Liars and Heaps: New Essays on Paradox*. Clarendon Press; reprinted in Soames (2009a).

—— (1999) *Understanding Truth*. Oxford University Press.

—— (1989) 'Presupposition', D. Gabbay and F. Guenthner (eds), *Handbook of Philosophical Logic*, vol IV, 553–616. Reidel; reprinted in Soames (2009b).

—— (1983) 'Generality, Truth Functions, and Expressive Capacity in the *Tractatus*'. 92 *Philosophical Review*, 573–89.

Solum, L. (2008) 'Semantic Originalism' (22 November 2008). Illinois Public Law Research Paper No. 07–24. Available at SSRN: <http://papers.ssrn.com/abstract=1120244>.

Sperber, D., and Wilson, D. (1986) *Relevance: Communication and Cognition*. Oxford: Blackwell.

Szabo, Z.G. (ed) (2005) *Semantics versus Pragmatics*. Oxford University Press.

Stalnaker, R. (1994) 'What is a Nonmonotonic Consequence Relation?'. 21 *Fundamenta Informaticae*, 7–21.

Stannard, J.E. (1987) 'Making Up for the Missing Element—A Sideways Look at Attempts'. 7 *Legal Studies*, 199.

Strahorn, J.S. (1930) 'The Effect of Impossibility on Criminal Attempts'. 78 *University of Pennsylvania Law Review*, 962–98.

Strawson, P.F. (1971) 'Intention and Convention in Speech Acts', in *Logico-Linguistic Papers*, 170. London-Methuen.

—— (1964) 'Intention and Convention in Speech Acts'. 73 *The Philosophical Review*, 163.

Waldron, J. (2010a) 'Dignity, Rank, and Rights', in *The Tanner Lectures on Human Values*, vol 29, S. Young (ed). University of Utah Press.

—— (2010b) *Torture, Terror, and Trade-Offs: Philosophy for the White House*. Oxford University Press.

—— (2008) 'Cruel, Inhuman, and Degrading Treatment: The Words Themselves' (5 October 2008). NYU School of Law, Public Law Research Paper No. 08-36. Available at SSRN: <http://ssrn.com/abstract=1278604>.

—— (2005) 'Torture and Positive Law: Jurisprudence for the White House'. 105 *Columbia Law Review*, 1681.

—— (1999) *Law and Disagreement*. Oxford University Press.

—— (1995) 'Legislators' Intentions and Unintentional Legislation', in A. Marmor (ed), *Law and Interpretation*. Oxford University Press.

—— (1994) 'Vagueness in Law and Language: Some Philosophical Perspectives'. 82 *California Law Review*, 509.

—— (1992) 'The Irrelevance of Moral Objectivity', in R. George (ed), *Natural Law Theory: Contemporary Essays*, 158–87. Clarendon Press.

Weber, M. (1970) 'Politics as a Vocation', in H.H. Gerth and C.W. Mills (eds), *From Max Weber: Essays in Sociology*, 77. Routledge & Kegan Paul.

Webster, N. (1828) *American Dictionary of the English Language*.

Wigmore, J.H. (1923) *Evidence in Trials in Common Law*, 2nd edn.

Williams, G. (1961) *Criminal Law: The General Part*, 2nd edn. Stevens & Sons.
——(1991) 'Intents in the Alternative'. 50 *Cambridge Law Journal*, 120–30.
Williamson, T. (1994) *Vagueness*. Routledge.
Williston, S. (1920) *The Law of Contracts*. Baker, Voorhis.
Wittgenstein, L. (1922) *Tractatus Logico-Philosophicus*, trans C.K. Ogden. Routledge.
Yaffe, G. (2004) 'Conditional Intent and Mens Rea'. 10 *Legal Theory*, 273–310.
——(2010) *Attempts*. Oxford University Press.

Legal Citations

Chevron USA Inc v Natural Resources Defense Council Inc 467 US 837 (1984).

Chisom v Roemer 501 US 380, 404 (Scalia J. dissenting).

Citizens United v Federal Election Commission 130 S Ct 876 (2010).

Entores Ltd v Miles Far East Corp [1955] 2 QB 327, Denning L.J.

Frigaliment Importing Co v BNS International Sales Corp 190 F Supp 116 (SDNY 1960).

Garfinkel v Morristown Obstetrics & Gynecology Associates, PA 773 A 2d 665, 672 (NJ 2001).

Griffin v Oceanic Contractors 458 US 564 (1982).

Griswold v Connecticut 381 US 479 (1965).

Harmelin v Michigan 501 US 957 (1991).

Holy Trinity Church v United States 143 US 457 (1892).

Hotchkiss v National City Bank 200 Fed 287, 293 (1911)).

In re the Estate of Ira Collins Soper 196 Minn 60; 264 NW 427 (1935).

Mabo v Queensland (No 2) [1992] HCA 23; (1992) 175 CLR 1 (3 June 1992).

National Association for Advancement of Colored People v Button 371 US 415 (1963).

Nix v Hedden 149 US 304 (1893).

Pacific Gas & Electric Co v Thomas Drayage and Rigging Co 442 P2d 641 (Cal 1968).

People v Dlugash 41 NY2d 725 (1977).

People v Jaffe 185 NY 497, 78 NE 169 (1906).

Raffles v Wichelhaus (1864) 159 Eng Rep 375, Ct of Exchq.

Random House, Inc v Rosetta Books LLC 150 F Supp 2d 613 (SDNY 2001).

Roe v Wade 410 US 113 (1973).

Saadeh v Farouki 107 F3d 52 (DC Cir 1997).

Smith v United States 508 US 223 (1993).

State v Schaeffer 96 Ohio St 215, 117 NE 220 (1917).

TVA v Hill 437 US 153 (1978).

United States v Crow 164 F3d 229 (5th Cir 1999).

Index